New Geographies 12
Commons

Edited by
Mojdeh Mahdavi and
Liang Wang

New Geographies 12
Commons

Editors
Mojdeh Mahdavi and Liang Wang

Editorial Board
Michael Chieffalo, Mariano Gomez-Luque,
Jeffrey Nesbit, Julia Smachylo, Guy Trangoš

Former Editors
Daniel Daou, Gareth Doherty, Ali Fard, Rania Ghosn,
Ghazal Jafari, El Hadi Jazairy, Daniel Ibañez,
Nikos Katsikis, Taraneh Meshkani, Pablo Pérez Ramos,
Antonio Petrov, Stephen Ramos, Neyran Turan

Advisory Board
Eve Blau, Gareth Doherty, Antoine Picon,
Charles Waldheim, Sarah M. Whiting

Academic Advisor
Eve Blau

Production Advisor
Meghan Ryan Sandberg

Copyeditor
Elizabeth Kugler

Proofreader
Tamar Kupiec
and Elizabeth Kugler

Graphic Designer
Sean Yendrys

New Geographies is a journal of design, agency, and territory founded, edited, and produced by doctor of design candidates at the Harvard University Graduate School of Design. *New Geographies* presents the geographic as a design paradigm that links physical, representational, and political attributes of space and articulates a synthetic scalar practice. Through critical essays and projects, the journal seeks to position design's agency amid concerns about infrastructure, technology, ecology, and globalization.

New Geographies 12: Commons has been made possible with support from the Graham Foundation for Advanced Studies in the Fine Arts and Harvard Graduate School of Design.

All attempts have been made to trace and acknowledge the sources of images. Regarding any omissions or errors, please contact:

New Geographies Lab
Harvard University Graduate School of Design
48 Quincy Street
Cambridge, MA 02138

Distribution
Harvard University Press
www.hup.harvard.edu

Printed in Estonia by Printon.
ISBN: 9781934510810

www.gsd.harvard.edu/publications

Harvard University
Graduate School of Design

New Geographies 12: Commons would not have been possible without the generous support of various individuals, departments, and institutions. We thank the Harvard GSD Publications Department for their assistance in the publication processes. In addition, we would like to acknowledge the excellent work by copyeditor Elizabeth Kugler and graphic designer Sean Yendrys. As *New Geographies 12* went through major institutional changes and the global crisis of the COVID-19 pandemic, we thank our colleagues on the editorial board whose support was fundamental to the continuation of our work. We acknowledge and thank our academic advisor and faculty who serve on the advisory board for their keen and productive feedback. Finally, this project would not be possible without the support of the Graham Foundation, for which we are immensely grateful.

Introduction

Mojdeh Mahdavi and Liang Wang

Today, the concept of "the commons" sweeps the political imaginaries of both the Far Left and Far Right across the globe. It is the basis for polarized and often avaricious geopolitics and, at the same time, mobilized to form radical social movements that constitute an alternative to capitalism. The same tension lies at the emergence of "we the people." Egalitarianism is stimulated at the community level in an effort to empower hitherto marginalized social groups, without any explicit reference to power and authority, exploitation and domination. At the individual level, we sense things are moving in directions we do not control,[1] subordinating almost every form of life and knowledge to the market's logic[2] and trapping us in the net of seemingly unrelated ecological, social, and economic crises.

These crises converge at their deep roots, revealing the dynamic material and immaterial interdependency between individuals and the capitalist system that enacts the core of commons' discourse. The concept of the commons involves a community of interest, "the commoners," who constitute and reconstitute their shared resources, or "commons," and strive to protect, expand, and govern them through "commoning" practices.[3] Technological advances have engendered new modes of collective resource production and sharing, giving birth to new material and immaterial commons. These new commons,[4] from the ocean floor to extraterrestrial space, and from the language and culture to the World Wide Web, have increased the power of the multitude.[5] Commoning practices have been mobilized as a critical instrument to inquire into the commonwealth of human and nonhuman communities and to serve as frameworks for the creation of alternative solutions to the crisis of the Capitalocene.[6]

However, the emergence and maturation of commons have gone hand in hand with their exploitation and commodification by the state as it seeks to cover its incompetence in welfare delivery[7] and by the private sector as it explores new avenues of profit-making. Commoning brings visibility to hitherto unknown collective values, social relations, and ways of life, making them transparent to mainstream political ideologies and vulnerable to exploitative practices. That's why neoliberalism gives a pivotal role to neo-communitarianism and uses it as a model to address its crisis and further sustain it.[8] Here, commoning is instrumentalized as a political fix—for which Midnight Notes Collective coined the phrase "new enclosures."[9] The entanglement between the production of shared resources and their enclosure and commodification by the socioeconomic forces of capitalism points to the necessity of distinguishing the capitalist and

1
M. De Angelis, introduction to Omnia Sunt Communia: On the Commons and the Transformation to Postcapitalism, In Common (London: Zed Books, 2017).
2
Silvia Federici, Feminism and the Politics of the Commons, 2011.
3
See "Commons as Systems" in M. De Angelis, introduction to Omnia Sunt Communia, 29–75.
4
We consider the emergence of new commons as a recurring event in the historical process. As such, our use of the term "new commons" is different from Charlotte Hess's concept of "new commons." See Charlotte Hess and Elinor Ostrom, Understanding Knowledge as a Commons: From Theory to Practice (Cambridge, MA: MIT Press, 2007).
5
Michael Hardt and Antonio Negri, Multitude (East Rutherford, NJ: Penguin Publishing Group, 2005).
6
J. W. Moore, "The Capitalocene, Part I: On the Nature and Origins of Our Ecological Crisis" (Fernand Braudel Center, Binghamton University, 2014).
7
Bob Jessop, "Liberalism, Neoliberalism, and Urban Governance: A State-Theoretical Perspective," Antipode 34, no. 3 (2002): 451–472.
8
This is yet another area where cities or city-regions acquire significance in the neoliberal project, since they are major sites of civic initiative as well as of the accumulating economic and social tensions associated with neoliberal projects. (Jessop)

9
David Harvey argues that the common is not something that exists only in history, but something similar to the urban commons that is "continuously being produced." He further points out that "the problem is that it is just as continuously being enclosed and appropriated by capital in its commodified and monetary form." See D. Harvey, "The Future of the Commons," *Radical History Review* 2011, no. 109 (2010): 101–107.

10
George Caffentzis and Silvia Federici, "Commons against and beyond Capitalism," *Community Development Journal* 49, no. suppl 1 (January 1, 2014): 92–105, https://doi.org/10.1093/cdj/bsu006.

11
See Amy J. Elias and Christian Moraru, introduction to *The Planetary Turn: Relationality and Geoaesthetics in the Twenty-First Century* (Evanston, IL: Northwestern University Press, 2015).

anti-capitalist value production system in the produced commons. Another aspect of this entanglement lies in the dynamic between the emancipation and manipulation of communities through the practices of commoning. Participatory self-organization can either empower or puppetize the commoners. Rising from within the capitalist system, the anti-capitalist commons question, deconstruct, and alter the monetary logic, reweaving the social fabric that was threatened by previous phases of commodification.

In addition to this external tension, the commoning process bears an intrinsic strain. Commoning entails an act of selection and boundary-making; hence it embraces enclosure as an ontological element. Commoning-enclosure forms a dialectical process whose modality of value production defines whether it is a capitalist or anti-capitalist common. As commons are social and relational constructions formed by and around a community of commoners, the revolutionary power of the collective rests in constant negotiation, reconstruction, and redefinition of those boundaries. Commoning is thus as much a condition as it is a process. Commons are fragile achievements that lie between a riotlike sequence of transient events, such as social and political movements, and processes of commodification. If the anti-capitalist commons is to exist as a site of alterity, transformation, and emancipation,[10] it will only be through the constant resistance and struggle against the dominant system.

New Geographies 12 aspires to open a conversation to delineate the historical and theoretical knowledge that shapes the idea of commons today. In particular, it deciphers both the external and intrinsic tensions central to the commoning-enclosure dialectic. It mobilizes the concept of the commons (singular) as a politico-spatial framework to interrogate and politicize various forms of contemporary commons (plural). It grounds the processes and conditions of commons that are in constant flux as the production of space is reconceptualized and restructured to address the requirements of (re)production in late capitalism. Expanding the discourse of commons into a planetary territory, *New Geographies 12* encompasses the intimate and subjective scale of the human body and the more-than-human yet omnipresent living environment and earth. It transcends the subjective world of humans—its perceived boundaries and territories—and recalibrates the terrestrial scale of things to a cosmological framework of the Capitalocene.[11] The commons in this volume is foregrounded as a sociopolitical project—one that embraces various modes of commoning practice and knowledge production across the globe—to chart an epistemological heterogeneity that is fundamental for an alternative framework for the production of space.

Since 1833, when the political economist William Foster Lloyd first reflected on the "dilemma" between a common and its commoners,[12] "the commons," as both a discursive and conceptual framework, has evolved to capture the dialectical processes of the enclosure of the commons, shedding light on new relationships between elements that were historically obscure. Situating the commons within the broader sociopolitical dynamics, scholars in the fields of political and social sciences, political economy, feminist studies, ecology, and human geography have further delineated the concept's epistemological and practical boundaries.

Drawing upon the work of these scholars, this issue is organized around three major sets of concerns and presumptions. The first and most fundamental is the relationship between human collectives and natural resources, as described by William Foster Lloyd, whose work arguably prefigured assumptions that manifested themselves in the debates on capitalist modes of production in the following centuries.[13] The superior efficiency of private ownership, one of these assumptions further developed by Garrett Hardin in his 1968 essay "The Tragedy of the Commons,"[14] signified the demise of the commons as a collective framework for the production of the common good and the primacy of capitalism—its institutional devices and mechanism of capital accumulation. However, as David Harvey elucidated, the logic of capitalistic development and the threats to labor and land—two primary common property resources that essentially constitute all forms of production— have confused private and collective ownership and created a new *"tragedy"* of the commons.[15] Such confusion subordinates the political nature of the commons to the scaffolding of capitalist private ownership. It confines the possibility of collective commons to an oscillating position between the state and the market.

A second presumption entails a fixity in the scalar conceptualization of the commons. In her groundbreaking studies, Elinor Ostrom demonstrated that, by implementing an individualized, citizen-centered approach and a regulatory scheme based on collaboration, people could often devise and implement creative ways to manage common property for collective benefit.[16] Even though the implied scale in these commons was local or regional, together they illustrated "rich mixtures of public and private instrumentalities."[17] Proposing a new political philosophy of "multitude" and "commonwealth," Michael Hardt and Antonio Negri[18] questioned conventional conceptual categorizations such as "the people" and "the state" and challenged the dichotomy of "public" and "private" that reinforced

12
W. F. Lloyd, *Two Lectures on the Checks to Population: Delivered before the University of Oxford, in Michaelmas Term 1832* (England: J. H. Parker; J. G. and F. Rivington, 1833, 1965).
13
David Harvey argues that the thinking on the commons often embodies "a far too narrow set of presumptions, and polarized between private-property solutions or authoritarian state intervention." See Harvey, "The Future of the Commons."
14
Garrett Hardin, "The Tragedy of the Commons," 1968.
15
See Harvey, "The Future of the Commons."
16
See Elinor Ostrom, *Governing the Commons: The Evolution of Institutions for Collective Action*, Political Economy of Institutions and Decisions (Cambridge: Cambridge University Press, 1990).
17
See Elinor Ostrom, "A Framework for Analysis of Self-Organizing and Self-Governing CPRs," *Governing the Commons* (Cambridge: Cambridge University Press, 2015).

18

See Michael Hardt and
Antonio Negri, *Empire*
(Cambridge, MA: Harvard
University Press, 2000);
Hardt and Negri, *Multitude*;
Michael Hardt and Antonio
Negri. *Commonwealth*
(Cambridge, MA:
Belknap Press of Harvard
University Press, 2009).

19

Reinhold Martin argues
that, for Hardt and Negri,
the categorization of
"public" and "private"
is simply "two different
means to the same end:
the reproduction of
capital." He also asserts
that the reconceptualization
from "public" and "private"
to "multitude" and
"commonwealth" is not "a
postindustrial upgrade of
the modern state"; rather,
it encompasses both the
"natural environment"
and the "products of
social interaction." See
Reinhold Martin, "Public
and Common(s)," *Places*
(Cambridge, MA), 2013:
2013-01-24 (2013).

20

Neil Brenner, Peter
Marcuse, and Margit
Mayer, *Cities for People,
Not for Profit: Critical
Urban Theory and the
Right to the City* (London:
Routledge, 2012).

21

Henri Lefebvre, "Le droit
à la ville," *L'Homme et la
société* 6, no. 1 (1967):
29–35. doi:10.3406/
homso.1967.1063.

22

See Henri Lefebvre,
The Production of Space,
Democracy and Urban
Landscapes (Oxford, UK;
Cambridge, MA: Blackwell,
1991).

23

See Stavros Stavrides,
*Common Space: The City
as Commons*, In Common
(London: Zed Books,
2016).

nation-states' capital reproduction.[19] They encouraged us to think beyond the state's intrinsic scale and its institutional structure for everyday practices, pointing out the multi-scalar nature of the commons and the "multitudes" of the planet and the nonhuman community all as part of commoning practices.

The third concern engages with the production of urban space, with an increasing emphasis on exchange-value over use-value.[20] The spatial value here is unceasingly measured in commodified, utilitarian, and monetary forms, rather than by its potential for enhancing the city's social and cultural meanings through new encounters and experiences. Operating against urbanists' "right to the city,"[21] which thrives on the collective action of reclaiming the city,[22] the capitalist mode of spatial production detaches the urban space from its meanings and memories. Thus, urban commons are a highly contested political project and a spatial and cultural one. Focusing on spatial configurations that facilitate the social reproduction of capitalism, more recent strands of scholarship have mobilized the concept of urban commons as a way of rethinking the production of space. As the commoning process continuously involves the substance of urban space—be it physical or virtual, material or cultural—the concept of commons has actively contributed to reshaping spatial imaginations such as urban islands, archipelagoes, and thresholds.[23] As affirmed by Paolo Virno, these imaginations epitomize the idea of "potentiality" that instrumentalizes an infinite range and scale of possibilities and alternatives.[24]

III

New Geographies 12 loosely organizes the contributions into four categories, creating a constellation of pathways to navigate its theoretical and practical terrains. Adopting an inter-scalar approach, the essays presented here challenge taxonomies such as "public and private," "local and global," and "state and market," and engage with various elucidations of commons within and across the categories. They aspire to restore the wholesomeness of commons and its inclusion where heterogenous existences constantly negotiate boundaries and form fluid spaces.

The first set of articles demarcates the commons' conceptual significance as both a material and immaterial resource. **Ivonne Santoyo-Orozco** describes how the techno-managerial approach of green capitalism is prioritized over the nature of Indigenous cosmologies of Mexican common lands, or *ejidos*, putting the commons at risk of becoming a "green enclosure" and turning the *ejidatarios* from commoners into technocrats of the forest. **Rosetta Elkin** grapples with the conundrum of the climate crisis by introducing aliveness and "natural contract" as the denominators for understanding the future's commons, which connects terrestrial humans and other life-forms. **Marina Otero Verzier** dissects the nature of advanced technological ways of (re)production and discusses how automation moves the boundaries of exploitation further from the Cartesian separation of human and nonhuman, one that has historically justified the exploitation of working (human and animal) bodies. **Fanny Lopez** captures the processes of enclosure engendered by recent technological advances and exemplified in old telecommunication centers, which have been privatized by the state and engulfed in the digital infrastructures by the market's enclosing forces.

In between the first and the second categories is a visual essay by **Amy Balkin** that portrays the rarely seen seabed community and the merging deep-sea mining industry, provoking us to contend with the question of an other-than-human commons.

The second series of texts focuses on the production of spaces, processes, and institutions of the commons. Grasping the temporal aspect of the concept, the contributions probe the institutional expression of the struggle for "the commons" that does not fall back into a depoliticized governance. **Niklas Plaetzer** uses the *giletsjaunisation* (yellow-vesting) of French politics, through a radical novelty arising from within the cracks of supposedly stable institutions, to discuss the formation of counterinstitutions of commons which combines the permanence of common space with a dissonance that becomes generative for actors from plural standpoints. **Taraneh Meshkani** argues that sociopolitical movements' ephemerality constitutes the formation of temporary commons through which a new culture of everyday life can be nurtured. **Stavros Stavrides** introduces housing as the vehicle for urban commoning and examines its role in confronting the status quo of the political system and market dominance, constructing popular power, and shaping the diversity of urban life. **Stefan Gruber** takes this argument further, demonstrating how constant agonistic encounters yield the possibility of public-commons partnerships as an institutional framework for transformative politics through ongoing processes of claiming and reclaiming. **Yan Zhang** applies the social-ecological systems (SES) framework to examine the possibility of enduring a human cooperation governance that could prevent the social dilemma. **William Conroy** concludes this category by questioning the politics of contemporary production of "wasteland" through a Marxian value lens, revealing how state-driven initiatives of commoning work as a "common fix" and produce a "capitalist common."

24
Virno compared the notion of the "common" and the "singular" to that of "potentiality" and "actuality," and he defined "potentiality" as the "infinite possibilities not yet determined into finite things," whereas "actuality" was the "determination of what is potential in the form of finite things and events." See Paolo Virno, *A Grammar of the Multitude*, Semiotext(e) Foreign Agents Series (Cambridge, MA; London: Semiotext (e), 2004). See also Pier Vittorio Aureli, "The Common and the Production of Architecture: Early Hypotheses" in *Common Ground: A Critical Reader*, ed. David Chipperfield, Kieran Long, and Shumi Bose (Venice, 2012).

The second interlude of this journal features **Rachel Cobb**'s photographic documentation of the space created by the COVID-19 pandemic, in which she captures the ephemeral, emotional, and poignant moments between people and their spaces.

Essays in the third category seek to understand the negotiation of boundaries around the commons, based on commoners' similarities and needs and the problematique of such categorizations. **Alan Wiig** depicts the transformation of London's Royal Albert Dock into a business enclave, one that is an urban void shaped by the Chinese-British net of financialized capital and the absence of commoners to claim their city. **David Bollier** advocates for the commons as living social systems and for commoning as a shift from a world of separation to a world of mutuality, where relationality derives from within the communities. **Neeraj Bhatia** illustrates, through the analysis and a design proposal for the San Francisco Southeast Waterfront, how collective action can create communities of interest among urban dwellers and empower them with the right to the city in resisting the capitalist forces of commodification. **Paolo Cardullo** makes a case for commoning the "network of networks" through ownership of Internet infrastructure and public data by the citizen, engendering alternative ecologies for the development of the Internet of People (IoP) rather than the Internet of Things (IoT).

A conversation with **Massimo De Angelis** offers an essential passage leading toward the final category of this journal, reflecting some of his insights into the relational core between the commons and commoning as well as the revelation of recent political occurrences.

Finally, the last group explores how design knowledge can generate a common framework in overcoming the homogenizing forces of capitalism and informing new modes of space and knowledge production where everyone is a "commoner." **Katherine Melcher** invites us to rethink the delineation of public space as a space of "in-being-with" to celebrate the singularity and plurality of commoners. Through the example of R-Urban, **Doina Petrescu** and **Constantin Petcou** argue that designers should perform the act of "blending" in the process of commoning, as well as defending and sustaining the commons in the process of designing and building. Under the same rubric, **Nadia Bertolino** discusses how the role of architects in the process of commoning leads to a self-reflective way of practice that draws on a critical understanding of specific contexts and situations, their uncertainty, and their unique potential. **Paola Viganò** investigates how design can help to shape and sustain a "biopolitical project" based on the understanding of "life as a common." The journal concludes with **Peggy Deamer**'s critical reflections on architectural pedagogy and the challenges of effectively training an "architectural citizen"; she proposes the notion of an "architectural common" that empowers design disciplines at large for a new mode of knowledge production.

IV

Initiated in late 2019, this issue of *New Geographies* has been unpredictably impacted, in its inception, development, and production, by the calamitous effects of the global pandemic in parallel with the Black Lives Matter movements across the world, the unpeaceful transition of power within one of the most prominent Western democracies, the furious wildfires, and the massive ice melt in the Arctic. In the aftermath of these events, whose sociopolitical and ecological consequences have yet to fully unfold, it has become clear that the very parameters defining the concept of life in common are being modified by the convoluted events of our time: the isolation of the self in domestic spaces, the shrinkage of the social relations and interactions into the minuscule dimension of smart devices, the further penetration of codes and algorithms into hidden corners of our lives, and the new investments of biogenetic capitalism in the genetic code of almost all living matter. As the varied contours that constitute the terrain of commons come into focus, we believe that its ideal is neither fixed nor achieved. Commons, perhaps more than ever, epitomizes an evolving epistemology that transcends the fixed, inherited schemas of the past. Commons are at stake, and commoning necessitates collective efforts in recalibration, questioning, and decategorizing the current commons and reconstructing the conceptual boundaries so that we, the commoners, can thrive in our collective endeavors and imaginations.

Green Enclosures:
Common Lands in the Climate Debate,
the Case of the Mexican *Ejido*

Ivonne Santoyo-Orozco

For a long time, architectural production has addressed the climate crisis mainly through technical and technological means—optimizing, improving, and adapting our ways of life toward a supposedly more "sustainable" future. Yet it is becoming clear that our planetary emergency cannot be addressed only through technocratic means. Green technologies alone will not change the institutionalized habits of a carbon-intensive society. The challenge is not to adjust, nudge, or incentivize but to radically reimagine and empower collective sociopolitical orders through which to inhabit the planet otherwise. This is an issue that asks all of us engaged in architectural discourse to recognize that, for far too long, we have collectively contributed to a spatial imaginary of the I, the you, and the yours, and that the only way we will ever be able to meaningfully address the climate crisis will be by constructing new collective spatial imaginaries of the world around the we, the us, and the ours. For me, if architecture is to be involved in confronting the climate crisis it is because it will involve reimagining the multiple ways in which to live a political life in common.

Leaving disciplinary boundaries behind, we might begin by situating the question of the commons in broader terms. As Silvia Federici understands it, the commons is a "principle of socio-political organization, it is not a set of things, but rather a principle that changes the way we think of how society is organized."[1] And yet, as a political principle and under conditions of advanced capitalism, the commons today is also a site of negotiation and struggle between the collective forces predetermined by the status quo of capital and the social relations it engenders, and the possibility to imagine alternative collective models of cooperation, resistance, and socialization that reconceive how we live together. As Pierre Dardot and Christian Larval have succinctly stated, today "the common has to pass through capitalism."[2] With this seemingly simple acknowledgment, I will argue that today many commons are entangled in a double tension: on the one hand, they hold the capacity to act as sites of alternative collective futures; on the other hand, they are ever more vulnerable to appropriation by neoliberal narratives of development in their attempt to privatize and partition the planet.

Mexican common lands, formally known as *ejidos*, are a crucial spatio-political device for grounding this argument. The *ejido* is a communal form of land tenure in Mexico with a complex history that goes back to colonial times. Throughout this long history, the *ejido* has been a site both of resistance and of control, of emancipation and of struggle. Analyzed as a whole, the *ejido* presents a complex picture that might allow us to resituate the commons today. While it would be impossible to cover its entire history in this brief piece, I will highlight a few key historical moments to question

1
Graciela Montaged and Silvia Federici, "Women Reclaim the Commons: A Conversation with Silvia Federici," *NACLA Report on the Americas* 51, no. 3 (March 2019): 256–261, https://doi.org/10.1080/10714839.2019.1650505.
2
Pierre Dardot and Christian Laval, *Common: On Revolution in the 21st Century*, trans. Matthew MacLellan (London: Bloomsbury Academic, 2019), xi.

the contemporary status of the *ejido*. I will pay specific attention to resituating historically the relation between *ejidos* and contemporary practices of sustainable development. In doing this, I will argue that, under the guise of this form of development and despite its good intentions, there is a risk of inscribing *ejidatarios* (Mexican commoners) in new forms of subjugation reminiscent of its colonial history. Far from romanticizing the commons as an emancipatory spatial and legal instrument, I will outline the history of the *ejido* in order to invite us to question the relation between land, collective forms of life, and dominant capitalist forms of production.

Ejido between Resistance and Subjugation

Nowadays, *ejido* is the most common form of social property in the country, dedicated primarily to agricultural production in rural and peri-urban locations.[3] It currently occupies approximately 52 percent of the Mexican territory.[4] Yet, as opposed to the geometrical rationality of other forms of modern territorial spatial organization, *ejidos* create a pointillist pattern, spreading irregularly throughout the Mexican territory. The boundaries and scale of *ejidos* are not defined by an overall order, a grid, a consistent geometric alignment, or a master document. Instead, *ejidos* are the product of decades of legal and territorial negotiations as well as violent uprisings. By this nature, in the popular imagination the *ejido* stands as an "instrument of peasant and indigenous representation."[5]

Ejidos *and Agrarian Communities officially registered in the National Agrarian Registry* (RAN), Mexico, 2019. Courtesy of the author. Sources: *Sistema de Información Geoespacial del Catastro Rural Mexico*, https://www.gob.mx/ran

3
Ejido is officially registered as a rural property in the Mexican Rural Cadastre known as the National Agrarian Registry (Registro Agrario Nacional, RAN), yet over the last four decades the urban footprint of many major Mexican cities has blurred the distinction between the *ejido* and the city.

4
Cámara de Diputados and Centro de Estudios para el Desarrollo Rural Sustentable y la Soberanía Alimentaria, *Boletín de Comunicación Social* 0175 (2015), http://www5.diputados.gob.mx/index.php/esl/Comunicacion/Boletines/2015/Octubre/10/0175-En-Mexico-52-por-ciento-de-la-superficie-es-ejidal-y-comunal-de-1992-a-2014-aumento-en-2-mil-has.

5
Gustavo Gordillo, "Campo: El Ejido De La Revolución," sec. Opinión, *La Jornada*, July 13, 2019, https://www.jornada.com.mx/2019/07/13/opinion/019a1eco.

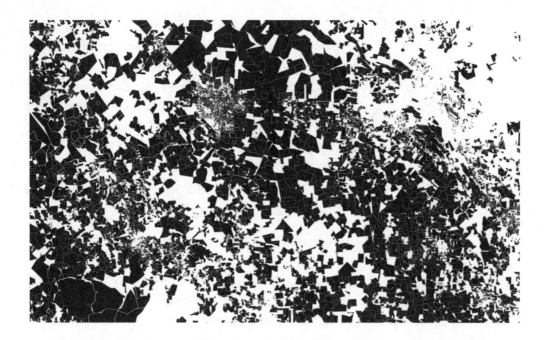

This understanding of the *ejido* celebrates a symbolic moment during the early 20th century, when many landless and Indigenous communities joined the Mexican Revolution to radically transform land distribution practices.[6] After many attempts and programs that attempted to formalize the land question, the *ejido* was institutionalized in the Mexican Constitution of 1917, and as such, it is partly consider a revolutionary victory.[7] As it was written into law then in Article 27, the *ejido* was defined as a communal form of land tenure with usufructuary rights, granting landless peasants the possibility to use and cultivate a common land but not to sell or to lease it. To guarantee the rightful use of the land, a complex agrarian juridical framework accompanied its legitimation, opening up a space for both autonomy and control. In other words, it is the same legal framework that at once allows commoners to develop their own forms of social organization and, at any given moment, makes them subject to state intervention—making the *ejido* a very flexible spatial category to govern the countryside. While the *ejido* gradually enabled the distribution of land rights in Mexico, it also institutionalized a framework by which Indigenous communities were able to be inscribed within modern forms of national governance and its accompanying trajectory of modern development. As historian Emilio Kourí suggests, "The *ejido* is a site of antagonism and contradictions where political local autonomy exists against its absence."[8] Today, the *ejido* is still widely popular, considered "the main institutional innovation of the Mexican Revolution."[9] In the context of the 20th century, it offered the possibility for collective

6
The struggle for land and liberty, *Tierra y Libertad*, is more clearly captured in the southern section of the Revolutionary cause led by Emiliano Zapata. For more on this issue, see Enrique Krauze, *Emiliano Zapata: El Amor a La Tierra*, book 3 of *Biografía del Poder* (Mexico City: Fondo de Cultura Económica, 1987).
7
Crucial here is the clandestine newspaper *Regeneración*, as well as the Programa del Partido Liberal y Manifesto a la Nación, of 1906.
8
Emilio Kourí, "La invención del ejido," *Nexos*, January 1, 2015, https://www.nexos.com.mx/?p=23778.
9
Gordillo, "Campo: El Ejido De La Revolución," 2019.

The Cause of the Mexican Revolution, 1913.
In *Regeneración*, No. 136, April 12, 1913.
Archivo Electrónico Ricardo Flores Magón.

Tina Modotti, *Manifestación del Primero de Mayo*
[May Day Demontration], 1926. Fototeca Nacional
SINAFO INAH. Mexico City. Archivo Instituto
Nacional de Antropología e Historia, México.

10
Massimiliano Tomba,
"1994: Zapatistas and the
Dispossessed of History,"
in *Insurgent Universality:
An Alternative Legacy
of Modernity* (New York:
Oxford University Press,
2019), 5. Thanks to my
friend and colleague Olga
Touloumi for bringing this
reference to my attention.

11
Felipe II, Ordenanzas
de Descubrimiento, Nueva
Población y Pacificación
de las Indias. July 13,
1573, Segovia. Archivo
General de Indias de
Sevilla. The English
translation can be found
in Zelia Nuttall, "Royal
Ordinances concerning
the Laying Out of
New Towns," *Hispanic
American Historical
Review* 4, no. 4 (1921):
743–753.

12
Nuttall, "Royal
Ordinances," 752.

forms of life to exist within a modern state framework, countering the tendency of protecting private property. Yet to fully understand the "innovative" character of this type of common lands, we might have to look elsewhere in history.

> Colonial violence not only dispossesses colonized populations of land, water, and future but it also destroys memory.[10]

While in Mexico we tend to associate the *ejido* with the revolutionary struggles of the 20th century, it originates as an instrument of colonial appropriation. It was in the 16th century, amid much violence and dispossession, that what was then known as *exido* was first introduced. *Exidos* were more clearly described in the Royal Ordinances of 1573, issued by Don Felipe II, King of Castille, in a document that specified how to lay out new towns and, correspondingly, how to organize the life of Indigenous peoples in relation to that space.[11] This decree was distributed to colonial officials and had at its core the purpose of alleviating the massive violence and dispossession brought about by colonization. In a brief passage, we read then that *exidos*, or common lands, were to be created for the purpose of enjoyment and for the pasture of animals outside new towns for the "Indians or naturals"—as Indigenous peoples were commonly called.[12] By this nature, the introduction of the *exido*

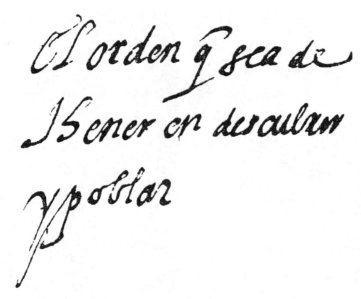

El orden que se ha de tener en descubrir y poblar [The order to hold in discovery and settling], 1573. In Felipe II, Ordenanzas de Descubrimiento, Nueva Población y Pacificación de las Indias. July 13 1573, Segovia. Archivo General de Indias de Sevilla. Detail.

must be read as a moral gesture and an attempt to change the politics of colonial domination. It was meant to—we might say—"offset" the horrible misery of enslavement and dispossession experienced by Indigenous peoples under Spanish rule. It is in this moment of moral recognition of the horrors of domination in colonial times that the *exido* is introduced.

　　While the mention was brief, *exidos* remained a crucial component of new colonial settlements, as outlined in *The Law of the Indies*.[13] There, we read another stipulation from 1618 that states, "The sites where new towns will be settled should have the comfort of water, mountains, cultivation lands . . . and an *exido*, a league in length, where Indians could have their cattle without mixing with Spaniards."[14] As presented here, *exido* serves not only as a means of reconciliation but also as a territorial device to separate rulers from the ruled. By its nature, the *exido* was not only incapable of addressing the violent dispossession of lands, it also reinforced the production of otherness while transforming customs and practices that previously constituted a life in common and cosmological connections to the land. The *exido* was just another spatial mechanism of colonial subjugation—a token attempt to trade a limited area of land for the remaking and othering of subjects. It implied the inscription of Indigenous peoples within a regime of property while continuing the massive expropriation of their lands. Camouflaged as a benevolent concession, the colonial *exido* was nothing

13
"De Las Reducciones y Pueblos De Indios. Tomo Segundo. Libro Sesto. Titulo Tercero. Ley VIII." In *Recopilación De Leyes De Los Reinos De Las Indias: Mandada Imprimir y Publicar Por La Magestad Católica Del Rey Don Carlos II*, 5th ed. (Madrid: Boix, 1841), 2:229.
14
Ibid., my translation.

but a spatial device not dissimilar to other 16th-century *enclosures*—a violent mechanism that abolished collective use of the land as previously known. As Indigenous interpreter Gaspar Antonio Chi put it in 1582:

> In olden times all lands were communal and there were no property marks, except between provinces, for which reason hunger was rare as they planted in different places, so that if the weather was bad in one place, it was good in another. Since the Spaniards have arrived in this country, this good custom is being lost, as well as the other good customs which the natives had, because in this land there are more vices to-day than fifty years ago.[15]

While the term "enclosure" is commonly understood in the context of 16th-century England to describe the process of appropriation of common lands by English lords, enclosure is also a mark of the emergence of violent capitalist extraction.[16] This is precisely what was at stake in the *exido*. Disguised as a space of enjoyment, the *exido*, just like any other capitalist enclosure, redefines the relation between land, wealth, and subjectivities. It dispossessed commoners of their land while imposing not only new economic and power relations but also racialized distinctions.

In practice, the *exido* did not become a generalized space, yet it established a precedent by which we can resituate the colonial traces of modern *ejidos*. Today's *ejidos* continue to act as spatial concessions—a compromise of land against control, where resistance and subjugation exist in the same space. While we saw this already with the institutionalization of common lands in 1917, and we have seen it throughout other moments in the history of the Mexican *ejido*, a few instances are worth recalling. It was not until decades after its legitimation that the *ejido* began to move from decree to a reality transforming the Mexican territory. Only in the late 1930s did the administration of then president Lázaro Cárdenas mobilize an agrarian reform that encouraged the massive distribution of *ejidos*. It was then that, in the eyes of the government, the *ejido* moved from a symbolic reminder of a revolutionary struggle to become the standard unit of Mexican agricultural production.[17] At that time, *ejidos* became deeply entangled with the agendas of the national economy.[18] Under these terms, it became clear that, for the government, the *ejido* was not to be celebrated as a space that enabled alternative forms of life or a society that valued subsistence-farming practices but, rather, as a possible means to extend economic calculations into the countryside.

15
Gaspar Antonio Chi, cited in Frans Blom, "Gaspar Antonio Chi, Interpreter," *American Anthropologist* 30, no. 2 (April–June 1928): 250–262.

16
For more on enclosures, see Karl Marx, "Part Eight: So-Called Primitive Accumulation," in *Capital: A Critique of Political Economy*, trans. Ben Fowkes (London: Penguin Books in association with New Left Review, 1990), 1:877–904. For a contemporary reading of the concept, see Michael Perelman, Midnight Notes Collective, Silvia Federici, Massimo De Angelis, and Werner Bonefeld, "Enclosures, the Mirror Image of Alternatives," *Commoner* 2 (0AD), https://thecommoner.org/back-issues/issue-02-september-2001/.

17
For more about the debate over the productivity of *ejidos*, see Salomon Eckstein, *El Ejido Colectivo En México* (Mexico City: Fondo de Cultura Económica, Sección de Obras de Economía, 1978).

18
On the role of Lázaro Cárdenas and his vision for the *ejido*, see Adolfo Gilly, *El Cardenismo, Una Utopía Mexicana* (Mexico City: Ediciones Era, 2001).

Tina Modotti, *Communidades Agrarias en Chinconcuac* [Agrarian Communities in Chinconcuac], *Estado de México*, 1927. Fototeca Nacional SINAFO INAH. Mexico City. Archivo Instituto Nacional de Antropología e Historia, México.

Yet the alignment of Mexican common lands with the agendas of national development were never as intertwined as they became during the early 1990s, when a sweeping agrarian reform radically altered the tenure system of the *ejido*. Typical of the neoliberal interventions of that time, and reminiscent of Margaret Thatcher's right-to-buy policies, this reform granted, for the first time, full ownership rights to all *ejidatarios*. As a result, today's *ejidatarios* are allowed to sell, lease, mortgage, or even subdivide their lands. This is how many Mexican common lands are becoming privatized, as simultaneously *ejidatarios* are implicitly encouraged to abandon subsistence-farming practices and social forms of collective life. From now on, in the eyes of the state, the World Bank, and other global organizations encouraging the modernization of the country-side, the task of the *ejido* is to enter into even more "productive" market relations.[19] Left to the whims of the market, the reform has enabled the commodification of the *ejido*. Commoners have been encouraged, incentivized, and even coerced to join the capitalist imperative to develop, to produce, to compete. In other words, to privatize the commons. The reform undermined any political substance of an autonomous collective life possible within its boundaries. Not surprisingly, the Zapatista uprising in Chiapas took place shortly after this reform in 1994. Zapatistas took arms to remind the state and the global network of developmental institutions that the commons required political and economic autonomy if they were to reimagine life in common. In the hands of Zapatistas, the commons are a site of emancipation, where collective life is indeed a political

19
Already in 1975, the World Bank had concerns about the low economic productivity of the Mexican *ejido*. See World Bank, "Land Reform. Sector Policy Paper," Annex 2 (May 1975): 71–72. Relatedly, in a report of 1966 by the International Bank for Reconstruction and Development, *ejidatarios* were described as follows: "The farmers of this group do not represent a picture of stagnation only but, as a whole, they do not tell a success story either." See International Bank for Reconstruction and Development, "Current Economic Position and Prospects of Mexico," Vol. 4, Annex VII, Agriculture. Western Hemisphere Department, October 26, 1966, 42.

20
It is not surprising to remember that among the issues that sparked the Zapatista uprising in Chiapas in 1993–1994 was this *ejido* reform, as they feared the dissolution of Indigenous collective practices, the undermining of subsistence farming, and alternative relations to the land. For an account of the uprising, see Sub Comandante Marcos, *Our Word Is Our Weapon: Selected Writings* (New York: Seven Stories Press, 2002).

21
See, for example, the recent land struggle between the *ejidatorios* of Ejido Santa María Malacatepec in Puebla, Mexico, and the real estate developer Grupo Proyecta. For a broader discussion of how neoliberal practices of real estate housing developers affect *ejidos*, see Ivonne Santoyo-Orozco, "From the Right to Housing to the Right to Credit," in Tatiana Bilbao, *A House Is Not a House*, ed. Isabelle Kirkham-Lewitt (New York: Transcripts on Housing, Columbia Books on Architecture and the City, 2018), 114–135.

22
Emissions Reduction Program Document (Mexico: Forest Carbon Partnership Facility, November 2017), 41, https://doi.org/https://www.forestcarbonpartnership.org/system/files/documents/__ENGLISH_6november_2017_Mx.pdf.

23
Ibid.

24
Ibid., 83.

force. Yet, under the conditions set out by the reform of the 1990s, emancipation was achievable only through direct resistance to the state.[20] Zapatistas have reminded the world that, for as long as common lands continue to be inscribed within a dominant capitalist form of production, they will continue to exist between the forces of appropriation and those of resistance.

And indeed, despite much resistance, many *ejidatarios* have taken the incentive to develop their lands. Following the reform, many *ejido*s located in peri-urban areas were sought after as cheap land to be bought up by ravenous real estate developers, who took advantage of the capacity to buy *ejidos* and use them as sites of unregulated urban development.[21] Soon thereafter, developers turned a space of collective organization into vast housing tracts à la Levittown, reinforcing instead an ideology of private property. This commodification of common lands has been a consistent story of *ejidos* since the reform of the 1990s.

Green Enclosures

A new form of land and power relations in the *ejidos* arose in the late 2000s in the context of climate change and the various mechanisms that have been developed by global institutions of green capitalism. This was part of a new tendency taking place globally by which many rural commons in the global south have been celebrated and simultaneously heavily incentivized to enter into climate-related projects. Communal lands in Mexico are no exception. Increasingly, *ejidos* have been identified as sites to test projects of capitalist "sustainable" development.

Crucial here has been the role of the *ejido* in carbon-offsetting programs, especially the one initiated by the World Bank in 2007, known as FCPF (Forest Carbon Partnership Facility) through its initiative REDD+ (Reduction of Emissions from Deforestation and Forest Degradation). This program aims to reduce global carbon emissions by identifying forest degradation and by setting in motion forest-management strategies. In this context, it is not surprising to see *ejidos* celebrated in many of their reports for holding 45 percent of the Mexican forest cover.[22] Chiapas was among the first Mexican states to confront the implications of REDD+. Chiapas was crucial to the FCPF not only for having "the largest surface area with deforestation and forest degradation" in the country between 1993 and 2012,[23] but also because its *ejidos* hold 74 percent of the total forest in the state.[24] Once again, while praising common lands for their environmental footprint, the same documents identify commoners as lacking organizational capacities to manage their own forests.[25] Typical of developmental strategies, and based on standardized metrics, the *ejido* forests are now categorized as sites of improvement.[26]

Ejidos, Agrarian Communities and Forest Cover in Mexico, 2019. Courtesy of the author. Sources: Sistema de Información Geoespacial del Catastro Rural Mexico, https://www.gob.mx/ran and *Global Forest Watch*, https://www.globalforestwatch.org

This became clearer with a REDD+ partnership launched in 2010 between Chiapas, California in the US, and Acre in Brazil. The aim of their partnership was to "link California's cap and trade compliance system with reduced deforestation efforts in Acre and Chiapas through the use of carbon offsets."[27] In brief, the program celebrated the possibility of mitigating the pollution created in California by caring for forests in the global south. But, of course, this "offset" is not so simple. While today many *ejidos* participate voluntarily in the program, at the beginning its mobilization brought confusion, violence, land disputes, and many protests. Consultation strategies have been heavily criticized, and the benefits to *ejidos* have remained unclear.[28]

As opposed to the neoliberal reform of the 1990s, projects like the REDD+ California, Chiapas, Acre acknowledge Indigenous land rights and, at least on paper, show disgust for practices of land grabbing. The program presented itself through purely technical means, identifying deficiencies in both *ejidos* with forests and in *ejidatarios* themselves. But, once again, in the history of *ejido*, what appears as a benevolent concession turns common lands into profit and makes commoners wage-laborers. We begin to see the traces of a new enclosure emerging: *Ejidos* with forest degradation were declared in need of technical

25 Leandro Carlos Fernández, Peter Saile, Andreas Dahl Jorgensen, and Lucio Andrés Santos Acuña. Rep. *Resolutions on Readiness Preparation Plan. Mexico Review* (Mexico City: Forest Carbon Partnership Facility Participants Committee, 2010), 46, https://www.forestcarbonpartnership.org/system/files/documents/4c_Mexico_RPP_PC_working_group_review_for_gabon.pdf.

26 For a wonderful sustained reflection on the relation between developmentalism and improvement, see Tania M. Li, *The Will to Improve: Governmentality, Development, and the Practice of Politics* (Durham, NC: Duke University Press, 2007).

27 Daniel Nepstad, Derik Broekhoff, Ludovino Lopes, Michelle Passero, Peter Riggs, Rosa M. Vidal, Steve Schwartzman, Toby Janson-Smith, Tony Brunello, and William Boyd, "California, Acre and Chiapas. Partnering to Reduce Emissions from Tropical Deforestation," ed. Evan Johnson (REDD Offset Working Group, 2013).

28 For the debate around the adoption of REDD+ and the process of decision making as it affects *ejidos*, see Tim Trench, Ane Larson, Antoine Libert Amico and Ashwin Ravikumar, "Análisis De La Gobernanza Multinivel En México. Lecciones Para REDD+ De Un Estudio Sobre Cambio De Uso Del Suelo y Distribución De Beneficios En Chiapas y Yucatán," *Center for International Forestry Research*, 2018, https://doi.org/10.17528/cifor/006798.

Anonymous, *Protest against 'Cumbre Verde'*, San Cristobal de las Casas, Chiapas México, September 2012. In REDDeldia, http://reddeldia.blogspot.com/p/fotos-y-videos-encuentro.html

improvement, turning forest into data, trees into tons of CO_2 sequestration, and *ejidos* into future markets on the stock exchange.

In this picture, nature is no longer lived according to Indigenous cosmologies but valued for its capacity to serve as a unit of measure in the emerging metrics of green capitalism. Insofar as the West needs evidence of their guilt in offsetting, forests are becoming monitored and surveilled, and today the life of many *ejidatarios* is now centered around the gathering of data, turning commoners into technocrats of the forest. In return for their "service," commoners are paid in what are commonly referred to as PES, or Payments for Environmental Services, a payment that transforms their livelihoods in the name of climate mitigation. This is nothing but a wage that encloses them in new relations to the land and new relations to capital. This is, again, another signal that the *ejido* is at risk of becoming a new enclosure—a "green enclosure." While *ejidatarios* are subjectivized, capitalism is again seen as the only solution to the climate crisis.

Insofar as REDD+ encloses *ejidatarios* under new legal, institutional, and labor relations, it dictates and commands how *ejidatorios* must live, appropriating their lives, labor, and livelihoods—this is precisely the "green enclosure." It is a new form of expropriation that commodifies common lands and appropriates their labor as ecological bailouts for the West. We must ask, what does it mean to impose a job on someone else's livelihood? What does it mean to commercialize

Carlos Herrera, *Forest Engineer Sara Camacho explaining forest carbon measurements*, 2015. In Felicia Line, "Linking Community Forest Monitoring Up With Jurisdictional REDD+," *Ecosystem Marketplace*, September 30, 2015. https://www.ecosystemmarketplace.com/articles/linking-community-forest-monitoring-up-with-jurisdictional-redd/

Anonymous, *Distribution of PES* (Payment for Environmental Services) in *Ejido* Amador Hernandez, Reserva de Biosfera Montes Azules, Selva Lacandona, Chiapas, Mexico, 2013. In *Environmental Justice Atlas*, https://ejatlas.org/conflict/redd-pilot-lacandon-jungle-chiapas-mexico

their forests, their oxygen, their work? Five centuries apart and yet we see that this appropriation of the commons through the benevolence mechanism of improvement is no different from the disrupter of social cohesion of Indigenous forms of life that accompanied the colonial *exido*. This is just another form of appropriation of common lands, labor, and forms of life. As an anonymous Zapatista woman tell us: "They think that what we want is a wage. They cannot understand that what we want is freedom."[29] This attempt to address the climate crisis not only breaks the collective fabric of *ejidos*, it also individualizes forms of life beyond the *ejido*. The climate crisis is seen as the concern of responsible and conscious individuals and not as a collective existential question tied to systematic concerns.

This inclusion of *ejidos* in "sustainable" practices of development is simultaneously a strategy to include them in the Western capitalist metrics and its accompanying hierarchy of values. Just as in the colonial *exido*, it continues to separate those who rule—or pollute—from those who are ruled or mitigate. And, with this, the *ejido* shifts from its collective political potential for social organization to nothing more than a site of capitalist "improvement." As Zapatistas remind us, we must remember that, under this system of capitalist values, if the commons is to exist as a site of alterity and of emancipation, it will only be on the terms of resistance and struggle against the dominant system.

29
Anonymous, Zapatista woman, "No Habrá Encuentro De Mujeres En Territorio Zapatista," *LATFEM*, February 11, 2019, http://latfem.org/no-habra-encuentro-mujeres-territorio-zapatista/.

ARTE :SANTIAGO ARMENGOD | DISEÑO: MELANIE CERVANTES

Santiago Armengod, Melanie Cervantes. *No REDD*, 2012.

The Living Environment
Or, Designers Are Stuck in the Holocene

Rosetta S. Elkin

The sheer scale, diversity and volume of life on Earth surpasses the imagination. Take a square metre of European or North American forest and slice off the top 15 centimetres of soil, and you will find, among numerous other life forms, as many as 6 million tiny worms—nematodes—perhaps 200 different species. It is possible that there are as many as 10,000 species of bacterium in a single gram of soil, yet only 3,000 have so far been identified and named by microbiologists. Conservative estimates put the number of different species on Earth at 14 million; no one knows for sure and some have claimed that there are at least 30 million. Of these, only a few per cent—2 million at most—have been studied, identified, named. Indeed, almost all biological research has been based on a few hundred different life forms, at most.
—Steven P. R. Rose[1]

1
Steven P. R. Rose,
Lifelines: Biology beyond Determinism (London: Oxford University Press, 1998), 2.

The earth is undergoing what is agreed to be an interval of accelerated biological change. More than ever, this "change" is guided by anthropogenic drivers that compound our human responsibility within the diversity of life that *still* surpasses the imagination. In our time, change is often correlated to climate, rather than positioned as a social engagement between human life and *other life-forms*. At present, design projects feel awkward and ill suited to the "change" challenges of the 21st century precisely because we continue to insist on "built environment" tactics, rather than cooperate with "living environment" practices. While the past is overwhelmingly difficult to overcome, recognition of the disparity between building and living helps explain why designers are irrevocably entrenched in repetitious eco-arguments and redundant bio-arrangements. It also explains why we no longer know how to share the planet with the magnitudes of earthly organisms that transmute, adapt, and migrate in response to accelerated change.

It is my hope that the position of design can expand to encompass the *living* environment, in order to shape an inclusive appreciation of *processes*—rather than *products*—of the environment. If built-environment theory produces planetary urbanization, overwhelms global carbon concentrations, and creates the great social inequalities of the Holocene, then perhaps design in the Anthropocene can consider humankind's role within the richness of 14–30 million other species. Consequently, I am suggesting that professional practices that claim solutions to "change" dynamics would benefit from paying closer attention to the implications of their ideas within an environment that is very much alive.

The pressing question of how to include aliveness in design is a question of commons. Commons as a politics does not need to be redefined or suffer a modifier. Rather, the commons of the 21st century must be able to ask how land is distinguished by its past in order to advance without recurring injustices. It can also ask how land can be shared more equitably in the future. A closer consideration of the *living* environment invites us to exchange antiquated professional standards for a future crafted by inclusive and shared practices. It is time to recognize that although designers enjoy the benefits of Anthropocene theory, the profession is stuck in the Holocene.

The Commonalities

What a world to inhabit, where the assembly of millions of different organisms is embraced by the term "living." For instance, the smallest breathing alga is no more than 0.8 micrometers, while the world's smallest flowering plant, duckweed (*Wolffia*), reaches 300 micrometers when fully grown. A micrometer is a unit of study that describes one millionth of a meter, a prompt to interpret, explain, and predict biological processes that dwell below the surface. On the other hand, the African bush elephant (*Loxodonta africana*) is the heaviest living terrestrial animal, yet only half the weight of the largest redwood trees (*Sequoia sempervirens*).[2] Consider that within the continuity of human knowledge production, both *Wolffia* and *Sequoia* are considered plant species despite their incredible variety that *surpasses the imagination*. Still, duckweed is not part of a designer's specification sheet because it self-propagates and cannot be patterned across a masterplan. At the same time, it would be pointless to approach planting *Sequoia* without paying attention to how gradually it grows and develops, requiring timescales far outside a typical scope. In such a community, the living world flourishes without design.

In fact, design is so far from being part of a commons that it is hard to imagine a future where practices are correlated with confident and constructive outcomes. Perhaps a designer might imagine herself positioned between social engagement and ecological change, between terrestrial human life and *other life-forms*. This would evoke commonalities, features, and characteristics held in common. Can humans share behavior with other life-forms? If so, the environment has never looked so alive. It pulses with the *Wolffia* and the *Sequoia* equally. It overwhelms us with herds of salamanders and vast domains of clonal roots. It trusts in soil as an organism rather than a cubic equation. Even the

2
For a succinct overview of Darwinian evolution, see Stephen Jay Gould, "Evolutionary Theory, Evolutionary Stories," in *Dinosaur in a Haystack: Reflections in Natural History* (New York: Harmony Books, 1995), 325–414.

term "living" does little to encompass the magnitude of earthly organisms that we work with as the ground erodes, shakes, slides, dries, and floods underfoot.

The decision to include the *living* environment is one that every designer must make on her own. But once she has committed, it helps shed light on the misguided pursuits of professional projects and the particularly chilling new focus on design solutions for a changing climate. The solution mandate assumes that the past can give us textbook precedents from which to shape the future. To paraphrase William Cronon, perhaps we are getting back to the wrong nature.[3] Of note is the designer's reliance on outcomes that do not acknowledge entanglement |among other life-forms, let alone the particular disparity between plant and human life.[4] Labeling a relationship ecological without recognizing the value of other living species is not only a cop-out, it is a relic of Holocene thinking.

The tendency toward problem-solution assertions influences design discourse in two ways: (1) through the acceptance of geoengineering, a conceit for high-tech manipulation of the earth's atmosphere, and (2) in the reappearance of environmentalism and its confidence in conservation policy. One tactic explicitly uses past technological advances to advocate for increased predictability and human jurisdiction. The other relies on a fragile version of nature that needs to be protected from other humans. In both cases, the repercussions of short-term, singular solutions protects *here* in order to exploit *there*. The immediacy of the encounter neglects the slower paces of living, verified by the *6 million tiny worms, 200 different plants, 10,000 species of bacterium and millions of yet unnamed species in the top 15 centimeters of soil.* The professional authority of problem-solution assertions also confronts the complex of Indigenous diversity, the loss of practical skills and oral history, not to mention the exclusion of knowledge that is garnered only through personal, land-based practices. We are inheriting a present shaped by inconsistencies and inequalities of all kinds—a present inadequately positioned to inform the future.

Problem-Solution Assertions

In 1990 Michel Serres bravely articulated the sine qua non between fragile nature and social humans, situating the conflict in our astonishing reliance on human lifetimes: "We are proposing only short-term answers or solutions, because we live with immediate reckonings, upon which

3
William Cronon, "The Trouble with Wilderness; Or, Getting Back to the Wrong Nature," *Environmental History* 1, no. 1 (1996): 7–28.

4
The word "entanglement" is more acceptable since its use by Donna Haraway to refer to the complex interrelation between species. See, for instance, Donna Jeanne Haraway, *The Companion Species Manifesto: Dogs, People, and Significant Otherness* (Chicago: Prickly Paradigm Press, 2003), 8.

most of our power depends."[5] In this short sentence Serres reveals that exchanges of power are hinged not only on "solutions" but on the temporal conflict between human-time thinking (short) and the time of nature (long). Time defines the solution. It offers a rational frame built of human assertion. It normalizes to advance. Yet time tends to work against design intentions, as nature lags behind budgets, failing to keep pace with an ever-impatient cultural context. But time also breaks down the elusive experience of belonging and alienation because nature can be quick, fierce, and vengeful. Consider the single-day records of COVID-19 infections, the six-minute duration of the Tohoku earthquake and tsunami, or the fact that Louisiana loses one football field's worth of land every hour and a half. How might time, the base of this weighty conflict, empower designers to slow their practices rather than speed up the profession?

Serres asks us to consider a "natural contract" that begins with a temporal distinction apart from human privilege. This has more relevance than ever as we respond to a temporally faster, more assertive, and less predictable planet. Whether we can sign a contract with the natural world is overly reductive, according to his thesis. Instead, what is at stake is our own insistence on immediate techno-solutions implicit in the project of geoengineering and carbon-offsetting calculations as solar panels blanket the land and aerosols are eagerly introduced into the stratosphere. Solution tactics pile up precisely because they hold together human contracts.

In the opening pages of the essay, Serres sets up his thesis by drawing our attention to a Goya painting depicting a human duel. Our attention to the battle is rendered as a human struggle. Serres points the reader toward what we *don't notice*, what evades our attention—the marsh into which the struggle is sinking.[6] He goes on to say: "Aren't we forgetting the world of things themselves, the sand, the water, the mud and the reeds of the marsh?" The centuries of small beginnings and transformations produce a messy and concealed context for the battle. Consider the *6 million tiny worms, 200 different plants and 10,000 species of bacterium* living in proximity to the battle. Consider the unapologetic exclusion of Indigenous livelihoods expelled prior to the battle. Consider the layers of thriving dormancy that will transform the marsh in the future. Serres suggests that human struggle diverts our attention from our struggle to live with the earth. If we have not been paying close enough attention, it is because the same temporally normalized, human-centered struggles continue to divert us from the living environment.

5
Michel Serres, *The Natural Contract*, trans. Elizabeth MacArthur and William Paulson (Ann Arbor: University of Michigan Press, 1995), 30. Originally published in French as *Le Contrat Naturel* (Paris: Editions François Bourin, 1990).

6
Serres, *The Natural Contract*, 1.

Singular, short-term solutions appear perverse when the living environment is considered for how it holds us together. In this way, "best practices" emerge as remnant products of the Holocene, clever approaches that serve only to validate the keen designer rushing to identify a problem in order to source ever-increasing specialists. A problem, once identified, begs a solution. And solutions contour the profession. Design is historicized across this linear trajectory of administrative prowess, as project leaders allocate services in order to validate their own shortcomings. With evidence all around us, each singularly maladapted solution is achieved with guidance from the engineering sciences, as details trace redundant techniques. Projects prompt solutions, which create more problems as the cycle is professionalized away from the living environment. The prompt by Serres vividly expresses this temporal friction between human calculation and the dynamic earth:

> To become effective, the solution to a long-term, far-reaching problem must at least match the problem in scope. Those who used to live out in the weather's rain and wind, whose habitual acts brought forth long-lasting cultures out of local experiences—peasants and sailors—have had no say for a long time now, if they ever had it. It is we who have the say: administrators, journalists and scientists, all men of the short term and of highly focused specialization.[7]

7
Serres, The Natural Contract, 32.

The misalignment between short-term political power and long-lasting cultural bias is another temporal struggle that Serres formulates as he follows his argument with an appeal to replace humans as "experts" at the center with humans as a species on the periphery. Consigning the gradual adaptation of biophysical life to the center embraces the time of the earthly world, though I would argue for less spatial hierarchy, a world without centers or peripheries. How can we respond without hierarchy when the questions posed *leave out* most of the living environment? Are humans the *most* living species? If misalignment is the incorrect position of something in relation to something else, then the argument is that human experts (in this case, designers) are at present inadequately aligned with the time of the earth.

The misalignment grows with professionalization. This is why Serres's *Natural Contract* resurfaces as a warning. In his description, "nature" emerges from the 19th century as an object to dominate and in the 20th century as an object to *possess*.[8] Thus professionalization works to objectify, rather than share commonalities. The perverse sense

8
Serres, The Natural Contract, 32–34.

of comfort that accompanies qualifications without experience and elite education without familiarity serves only to engender distance from land-based practices. Consider the present state of plant life: an object currency that trades in Photoshop silhouettes, AutoCAD blocks, carbon units, pots by the gallon, and the indices of commercial trade. Plant-as-object or environment-as-commodity endures only to proliferate solutions for a few privileged professionals.

Can design embrace *practices* rather than sustain *professionalization*? The practice lineage brings hope to the future of design, as it engages repetition of effort and firsthand experience, evoking belief, method, and skill. After all, we are practitioners. Practices are actively turned toward knowledge as something that grows and connects through common care for the living environment.

1. Engineering Earth

Geoengineering is one of the most perverse manifestations of how the complicated ties and relations made in the human world—namely, between constructing a scientific truth, generating a resource, and misleading public understanding—are physically manifest in the land-scape. Two of the most widely voiced techniques of geoengineering are Solar Radiation Management (SRM) and Greenhouse Gas Removal (GGR).[9] Invariably, both techniques are tendered by intergovernmental panels, advised by climate scientists, and constrained by existing technologies. The growing attention is well documented by the knowledge economy: the rise of journal articles, academic papers, and scientific publications.[10] Underlying questions about research governance aside, the intellectual experiment is naturalized into the design fields because it trades in solution tactics.

Science is mixed up with politics in ways that are too often overlooked by designers eager for capital gain. The tension in the design professions is fashioned by a constructed reality that relies on science to make sense of things *out there*, as it were. The temporal misalignments raise alarming questions as evidence is appropriated in the rush for solutions:

> Since the nineteenth century, the sciences have been mobilized, have become "fast" sciences, with researchers regarding whatever concerns that do not directly contribute to "the advancement of knowledge" as a sinful waste of time. Now, within the knowledge

[9]
http://www.geoengineering.ox.ac.uk/www.geoengineering.ox.ac.uk/what-is-geoengineering/what-is-geoengineering/.

[10]
See, for instance, P. Oldham, B. Szerszynski, J. Stilgoe, C. Brown, B. Eacott, and A. Yuille, "Mapping the Landscape of Climate Engineering," *Philosophical Transactions: Mathematical, Physical and Engineering Sciences* 372, no. 2031 (2014): 1–20.

economy, fast sciences are perceived as not fast enough; they are making patents and launching fabulous promises of technological revolutions that are attractive for investors but do not need reliable knowledge. The apotheosis of this paradigm is geo-engineering, the mobilization of technology against the Earth.[11]

11
Interview with Isabelle Stengers in Etienne Turpin, *Architecture in the Anthropocene: Encounters among Design, Deep Time, Science and Philosophy* (n.p.: Open Humanities Press, 2013), 179.

Geoengineering is a clever means to extend the paradigm of human dominance over the living environment; it rehearses the same pattern of controlling or profiting from the outcomes by mobilizing technology against the earth. Physical, material, and biotic phenomena are framed as problems and are tackled by "solutions." For instance, one of the core tactics of GGR is afforestation, the deliberate planting of trees in otherwise treeless environments. While afforestation has a long history, it is obscured by the plant-as-object inheritance. Planting trees is framed as a do-good mechanism, without questioning who is planting the tree, or where. Species selection is certainly too mundane for impatient development campaigns. Endless research is enforced, as corporate testing and control continue to inform decision making because planting trees is offered as a solution. Can planting trees realistically lessen large-scale deforestation, extreme urbanization, megadrought, or global ice melt? Positioning afforestation in the 21st century as a viable means to remove carbon dioxide or other greenhouse gases from the atmosphere counts only as an industrialized gain, obscuring the spectrum of ecological losses.

The landscape of afforestation is made rigid, predictable, and static. It categorically disregards the extant environment and proposes a substitute biome. Woody trees reduce fibrous perennial forbs and grasses. Dryland is not vacant or deserted because it is arid. It is alive with millions of unnamed species and billions of dormant seeds in unknown relationships that surpass the human imagination. This is not to say that we should not organize planting projects, plant trees, advance conservation, or plant in drylands. It is the means and methods of our plans that require our attentive notice. What I am interested in is a practice that is less reliant upon speed, scalability, and unit-based valuation, instead paying close attention to the landscape as an organism—the living landscape.

The conflict of tree planting is found in the thickness of extant drylands, those dormant layers of earth that *surpass the imagination.* Correspondingly, the temporal durability of seeds exemplifies not only the inability to name, identify, or exploit, but also the failure of analysis in relation to the duration of biological existence. Of interest is an experiment conducted by Dr. William Beal over 120 years ago.[12] The experiment involved burying glass jars with tall-prairie-grass seeds in order to test dormancy in the prairies. Beal's own words best explain the simple experiment:

> I selected fifty freshly grown seeds from each of twenty-three different kinds of plants. Twenty such lots were prepared with the view of testing them at different times in the future. Each lot or set of seeds was well mixed in moderately moist sand, just as it was taken three feet below the surface, where the land had never been plowed. The seeds of each set were well mixed with the sand and placed in a pint bottle, the bottle being filled and left uncorked, and placed with the mouth slanting downwards so that the water could not accumulate about the seeds. These bottles were buried on a sandy knoll in a row running east and west and placed fifteen paces northwest from the west end of the big stone set by the class of 1873. A boulder stone, barely even with the surface soil, was set at each end of the row of bottles, which were buried about 20 inches below the surface of the ground.[13]

Beal worked with the temporal scales inherent to the living environment in order to inform the future. His work has lasting impact because it was contingent on the time of seeds, not the time of his career. The experiment continues to yield successful germination rates to this day, confirming not only that grassland seeds are viable for a future that extends past the 120 years of his experiment, but that our applied practices demand timescales aligned with prolonged coexistence and a consortium of other species. Emergent seeds might certainly be ancient grassland species, but many other species are more likely to emerge as well, including plants that are better adapted to the present and to the torn, depleted ground we have designed. Human determination for immediate reckoning cannot serve as a substitute to the century-old prairie formation that Beal so carefully estimated. To cultivate and redevelop the superficial layers of the planet works against the intelligence of physical dormancy found in deeper soil horizons that host seeds, roots and rhizomes, mycorrhizal agents, moisture thresholds, and bacterial exchange. There is no problem statement to assign the experiment. It can neither be scaled up nor sped up, and it resists any commercial gain statistics that could distort his practice as a solution.

12
H. T. Darlington, "Dr. W. J. Beal's Seed-Viability Experiment," *American Journal of Botany* 9, no. 5 (1922): 266–269; Frank W. Telewski and Jan A. D. Zeevaart, "The 120☐Yr. Period for Dr. Beal's Seed Viability Experiment," *American Journal of Botany* 89, no. 8 (2002): 1285–1288.

13
Darlington, "Dr. W. J. Beal's Seed-Viability Experiment," 266.

2. Conserving the Holocene

14
According to Jason Moore. See Jason W. Moore, ed., *Anthropocene or Capitalocene? Nature, History, and the Crisis of Capitalism* (Oakland, CA: PM Press, 2016). See also Erle Ellis et al., "Involve Social Scientists in Defining the Anthropocene," *Nature* 540, no. 7632 (2016): 192–193.

15
Large gaps in human footprints can be found in several key biomes, including equatorial (central Africa), subtropical (central Australia, Sahara), temperate (Himalayas), and Palearctic (Russia and Canada) latitudes. See Tim Caro et al., "Conservation in the Anthropocene," *Conservation Biology* 26, no. 1 (2012): 185–188.

16
See, for instance, Jason W. Moore's end of cheap nature, Tsing's loss of refugia, and the irreversible catastrophes studied by Andreas Malm. The Anthropocene even boasts its own website and dedicated academic journal and popular reader. For instance: http://www.anthropocene.info, https://www.journals.elsevier.com/anthropocene, and Erle C. Ellis, *Anthropocene: A Very Short Introduction* (Oxford: Oxford University Press, 2018).

In the Anthropocene, we are not only pioneers, creators, heroes, inventors, designers, and developers—now we are also a force. As a result, theory abounds over solution and resolution, posing questions scholars cannot answer.[14] In order to propose *something*, proponents often suggest conservation because it appears to be a means to balance the equation. At stake is how these so-called solutions sneak into the designer's playbook. Arguments are contingent on the few areas of the biosphere that are still deemed "intact" and can be placed on life support to maintain public confidence.[15] Such claims are debated but are worth considering for how a monolithic view of nature proliferates, setting into motion the terms of environmentalism that focus on immediate outcomes under the assumption that previous states can inform future conditions. The continued reliance on this ideology ignores the influence of humans and our compound effect over time. Thus the Anthropocene grants us self-designated creator status, replete with solutions. It is time to take down the singular genius of humanity as the inventor of planetary evolution and invite other significant forces into an earthly narrative.

Why do advocates of the Anthropocene so often rely on conservation? Threatened areas, endangered species acts, and red lists are appeased by principles that insinuate how protection by humans can disentangle our predicament, despite the fact that human affairs more broadly have brought about the concern. The fragile version of nature reappears by calling upon heavily degraded landscapes, ocean acidification, greenhouse emissions, and other decline statistics.[16] Equating fragility with nature is the point of departure for traditional environmental thought, including Aldo Leopold's *Sand County Almanac* (1966), Rachel Carson's *Silent Spring* (1963), and Al Gore's *Earth in the Balance* (1993).[17] Accordingly, assertions are usually followed by expressions such as "there is very little nature left," seemingly due to the crisis of an ever-expanding base of fossil fuel consumption and the ensuing population explosion that pairs with destructive technology. This statement "there is very little nature left" profoundly limits the terms of the Anthropocene because it is predicated on the inclusion of humankind in the earthly world—part of, not outside, nature.

Anthropocene conservation tactics continue to make judgment calls about which *assemblages* are legitimate and which are not.[18] In much the same way, expecting preservation to keep out the mess or restoration to clean up the mess is unreasonable because it prioritizes some species over others. Thus any act of conservation is also an act of destruction. The possibility of adapting or evolving conservation to reflect the times requires a broader appreciation of inclusion, beyond the polygon outlines of policy.

Maintaining islands of Holocene parcels can actually create an atmosphere in which people see nature as the enemy. Proponents of the Anthropocene—rather than debating a precise date of the decline—might transform the opportunity of a new epoch in which religious, nostalgic, or corrupt ideas of nature can be replaced by terms that are more equitable to the vast array of species that humans depend upon to survive. The ambition requires redefining conservation because it cannot be reduced to National Park boundaries, wildlife preserves, or the restrictions of human-free restoration projects. Witness the number of alien, or "invasive," species that overwhelm universalized databases and fund the emergent field of invasion biology.[19] European wasps are now pollinating New Zealand, Asian raspberry thickets are establishing roots in the Hawaiian Islands, and an imported blight feasts on American chestnut trees—these are all active, extant examples that diametrically oppose current interpretations that life-forms are withdrawing. Thriving examples abound whereby a great aliveness is coherent, if only it were not labeled as a foreign or invasive agent. Moreover, such species richness provides a wealth of ecosystem variation, catalyzed by human activities. Having entered into the relationship of changing ecosystems, we have to accept responsibility for the outcomes.[20] I suggest assent to the variations that mingle species and reduce hierarchy, especially those in the first layers of the soil and the atmosphere.

The novel climate is forcing us to find other ways to integrate with other living organisms, asking the same of the theorists that aim to pose questions and structure relevant interpretations. Rather than establish a critique based on rejecting conservation or fearing change, I am suggesting that conservation in the Anthropocene can evolve and adapt precisely because we know that local actions create global feedbacks for all species, even those as yet unknown and unnamed.

Design—from ecological planning to landscape architecture—falters when it trusts in a conservation that distances us from the living environment. Our lands necessitate an ongoing exchange of information and collaboration in order to develop common evolutionary relationships. For instance, consider that 80 percent of the food derived from plants comes from only 17 flowering plant families.[21] Further, we get half our calories from just three flowering crops: rice, maize, and wheat. Here, the constriction of flowering plant species cannot be

17
Aldo Leopold, *A Sand County Almanac, with Other Essays on Conservation from Round River* (New York: Oxford University Press, 1966); Rachel Carson, *Silent Spring* (London: Hamish Hamilton, 1963); Al Gore, *Earth in the Balance: Ecology and the Human Spirit* (New York: Plume, 1993).

18
I use the term "assemblage" to connote multispecies relations. See Anna Lowenhaupt Tsing, *The Mushroom at the End of the World: On the Possibility of Life in Capitalist Ruins* (Princeton: Princeton University Press, 2015), 61.

19
For example, European wasps, *Vespula vulgaris;* raspberry, *Rubus ellipticus;* chestnut blight, *Cryphonectria parasitica.* See also Global Invasive Database, http://www.iucngisd.org/gisd/?st=100ss.

20
This line of reasoning is effectively argued in Robert H. Hilderbrand, Adam C. Watts, and April M. Randle, "The Myths of Restoration Ecology," *Ecology and Society* 10, no. 1 (2005).

21
FAO, *International Treaty on Plant Genetic Resources for Food and Agriculture* (Rome: FAO, 2009), http://www.fao.org/3/a-i0510e.pdf; Holly Vincent et al., "A Prioritized Crop Wild Relative Inventory to Help Underpin Global Food Security," *Biological Conservation* 167 (November 2013): 265–275.

stubbornly reinvented because our processes of selection have been so effective across time. As one of many potential examples, consider the long-standing relationship between humans and flowering plants. The association is our longest, most durable earthly relationship. If the collaboration between human and plant life was acknowledged, could the limits of selective conservation be reached in order to value our coevolution?

The unprecedented mixing between humans and plants is paired with an unprecedented intensification in species composition that can rework the boundaries of conservation. Consider how climate-controlled seed banks are funded and resistant crosses are fabricated to avoid a collapse in human food systems. Yet edible plants abound outside industrial burdens and toxic chemistry—those plants that are robust to our selective tendencies. Instead, we exclude select plants, using the conceits of conservation, as unpleasant language and offensive simplifications proliferate: consider an "invasive" plant such as the edible Japanese knotweed (*Fallopia japonica*), which spreads despite costly eradication strategies instead of being consumed for its spinachy leaves. The term "unproductive" often limits crops such as teff *(Eragrostis tef)* and finger millet (*Eleusine coracana*), which hold social and regional significance in Africa but cannot keep pace with the global marketplace. As a result, wheat is a cash crop in Ethiopia, and knotweed is sprayed with glyphosate across Georgia, for instance. Selective cultivation between human and flowering plant life has forever altered the definition of nature. Nature is no longer "out there" or "in here," it is a coproduction. This is not a problem: it is an opportunity to expand our practices.

The Future of the Ground

The history of life on earth is a history of organisms over time, from development through conception and death—the mingling of life so diverse that it includes minute duckweed, indeterminate algae, weighty blue whales, extinct mammals, giant redwoods, and the political theorists of the Anthropocene. Every relationship in between is an inseparable part of what we become in the future. These exchange cosmologies of the earthly planet have received less attention than the disaggregated individual organisms that humans dissect. If amalgamations abound, they do so in both theoretical and physical space, as professional autonomy is as outdated as the terms of singular solutions.

An appreciation of the living environment extends the domain of earthly influence from a superficial coating to a universe of survival and decision making. Living can be redefined through the mingling of millions of unknown species, motivated by the inputs and outputs of the atmosphere. Whether as a dormant seed or a germinated cotyledon, plant life is most agile in its early life stages. The life stages of flowering plants are necessarily embedded in the ground because the plants that support us are overwhelmingly terrestrial. Plant life is located out of sight, in the actions made by the smallest roots and rhizomes that structure the habitable earth and actively persist in the shallow horizons of the soil. Could scholarship share *the first 15 centimeters of soil* in order to participate fully in our earth's vitality? How does that attention alter our design practices? Attention paid to the living over the built environment might even produce entirely novel images of the climate, shifting our gaze from the atmosphere to the ground under our feet.

Cartesian Enclosures

Marina Otero Verzier

The relationships between human and nonhuman bodies, as well as their classification, have been an ongoing site of inquiry for disciplines ranging from philosophy, geography, and animal studies to science and technology, media studies, and radical social sciences. Whereas human/nonhuman ethics are at the center of contemporary conversations on issues of inequality and the climate emergency, the discipline of architecture has been only timidly thinking beyond the centrality of the human subject. Primarily developed around normative constructions of the "human"—and in particular the notion of Man as a universal, rational subject—architectural practices are nevertheless entangled in non-anthropocentric struggles.[1]

Architecture has a role in how encounters and assemblages between animals, humans, plants, and machinic and inanimate beings are structured in time and space, yet generally orchestrated to serve the comfort and privilege of some humans. It also supports systems where the distinction between machines and living organisms has been purposely blurred, and one such system, I would argue, is automated capitalist production.

As a form of production, automation results not only in commodities but in the biopolitical production and reproduction of forms of life in common through technology. In so doing, automation poses a conundrum for architecture: it allows the discipline to venture beyond its Cartesian postulates and operate with minimal or reduced human intervention, prompting its critical reinvention; simultaneously, it further intensifies the enclosure and exploitation of larger territories and their laboring bodies, thus participating in the extraction of what is common.

While problematic, these architectures also serve as a lens to today's challenges and responsibilities, and a testing ground for transcending the Cartesian divide through radical notions of ethics emerging from queer, decolonial, and Indigenous studies. Thinking beyond the Cartesian and the human demands the dismantling of the borders that currently define, protect, and exploit the common world and the common interest. The boundaries on compassion. The compartmentalization and instrumentalization of relations. Such a dismantling supports ecological regeneration. It resists extractivist dynamics. It dismisses architecture centered around the white humanist masculinist subject who sees the world as his own possession.

1
Some of these ideas have emerged from conversations held with the editorial team of the forthcoming reader *More-Than-Human*, a project focusing on the entanglements, frictions, and cooperations between animals, humans, plants, technology, and inanimate beings. The book is edited by Andrés Jaque, Marina Otero Verzier, and Lucia Pietroiusti, together with associate editor Lisa Mazza. *More-Than-Human* is a collaboration between Het Nieuwe Instituut, Manifesta Foundation, and the General Ecology Project at the Serpentine Galleries.

The Metaphor of the Machine

The work of philosopher and historian of science Georges Canguillhem offers an avenue for examining the biological philosophy of technology as a precursor to debates on automation. In "Machine and Organism," Canguillhem reflects on the interdependency between early machines and humans and animals. Indispensable to propel and run early machines, living organisms became part of the mechanical and technical models they were entangled with.[2] The metaphor of the machine, therefore, resulted in a common trope and reference in the study of organisms, Canguillhem argues.

Parallels between animal movements and automatic mechanical movements, "between the organs of animal movement and "oreana," or parts of war machines, already appear in Aristotle's writings.[3] For Aristotle, the principle of all movement was the soul, an argument that justified the demarcation of beings and machines, and which eventually led him to categorize the slave as an animated machine.

The divide between soul and body permeated the work of philosophers in the eras to come. In the second half of the 16th century, and following Aristotle, the Spanish doctor Gomez Pereira suggested that animals were wholly machines without sensitive souls.[4] With his theory of the animal-machine, Descartes also referred to machines as models to explain the functioning of organisms—an idea that was greatly influenced by the technical creations of the early 17th century, such as clocks, water mills, church organs, as well as spring-operated and hydraulic automata. For Descartes, as Canguillhem explains, "the refusal to attribute a soul—that is, reason—to animals" was a means "to justify man's using it to serve his own purposes."[5] The animal is, for Descartes, what the slave was for Aristotle.

As the imperative of rationalization and theory of the animal-machine of Cartesiansim emerged as a driving force in the mechanical age and during the formation of Western capitalism, the metaphors comparing living organisms and mechanical and technical models serve to validate, even today, the exploitation of animals and certain humans—raced, gendered, classed—whose bodies have historically been rendered as laboring machines for the benefit of privileged humans' ends. A justification that supported the discrimination of entities, bodies, and identities under a seemingly rational and neutral system of categorization.

"Human society takes from the oppression of animals its structures and treatment of people," argues the writer, feminist, and animal

2
See Georges Canguillhem, "Machine and Organism," trans. Mark Cohen and Randall Cherry, in *Incorporations*, ed. Jonathan Crary and Sanford Kwinter (New York: Zone Books, 1992), 44–69.
3
Ibid., 48.

4
Ibid.

5
Ibid., 52.

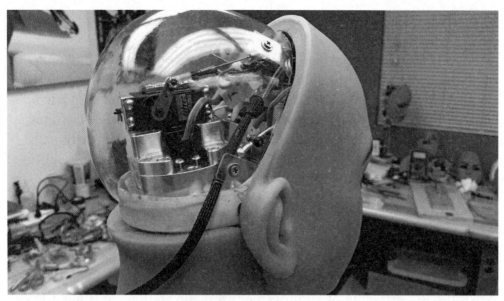

Head of a Realbotix sex robot, 2017. Photo: Realbotix.

rights advocate Carol J. Adams.[6] In Adams's view, the concept and category of the animal, and the way in which it has justified humans' treatment of animals as "animals," have also legitimized the treatment of humans as "animals." "Violence against people and against animals is interdependent. Caring about both is required," Adam insists.[7]

At the core of the question is the concept of "other" and "otherness," which inevitably demands a normative one —or ones— against whom the other is measured, categorized, and valued.[8] Speciesism is precisely the hierarchy constructed to organize the other in relation to the human. And as Adams explains, it has been a tool of colonialism and xenophobic violence. "European colonizers," she points out, "evaluated indigenous peoples according to their relationship with animals and the land."[9] Categorization channeled the impulse to conquer lands for extraction, subjecting populations to violence and slavery for that purpose.

It was nevertheless in the 19th and 20th centuries that these types of classifications of beings, demarcations of species, and theories of racism gained scientific legitimacy, through studies in medicine, psychiatry, and anthropology, among other disciplines.[10] Studies provided the basis for differential conditions between humans and animals, which in turn solidified a notion of humanness in contrast with those that are not included in the category of human. And yet the definition of "the other"—in this case, animals—was precisely what allowed humans to self-identify and vindicate themselves as human. These clusters— forms of enclosure and self-enclosure that put the limit at the threshold

6
Carol J. Adams, "The War on Compassion," in *The Animal Catalyst: Towards Ahuman Theory*, ed. Patricia MacCormack (London: Bloomsbury, 2014), 21.
7
Ibid., 15, 25.
8
Ibid., 21.
9
Ibid.
10
Ibid., 18.

11
Ibid., 16.

12
Jacques Derrida, "The Animal That Therefore I Am (More to Follow)," in *Critical Inquiry* 28, no. 2 (winter 2002): 394.

of the human/animal—are, as Adam claims, boundaries on compassion and care guided by a false idea of scarcity.[11]

In the last two centuries, the forces behind the differential treatment of the living animal have been continuously fueled by the development of zoological, ethological, biological, and genetic forms of knowledge. According to Jacques Derrida, "genetic experimentation, the industrialization of what can be called the production for consumption of animal meat, artificial insemination on a massive scale, more and more audacious manipulations of the genome, the reduction of the animal not only to production and overactive reproduction (hormones, genetic crossbreeding, cloning, and so on) of meat for consumption but also of all sorts of other end products" are carried out "in the service of a certain being and the so-called human well-being of man."[12] Contemporary automated technologies could be added to Derrida's list as one of these developments behind the exploitation and violence against animals and other living beings.

Dairy Farm De Klaverhof, Moerdijk. Photo by Johannes Schwartz.

Marina Otero Verzier

Dairy Farm De Klaverhof, Moerdijk. Photo by Johannes Schwartz.

Relentless Workers, Captive Bodies

The architectures of automated production are redefining notions of human and nonhuman, as well as their labor ethics, under the spell of Cartesian logics. Occupying and enclosing large parts of the territory in countries such as the United States, China, or the Netherlands, these enclosures control and maximize the productivity of the ground and the bodies that labor in it, their uptime increasingly stretched through automated technologies.

While machines mirror human dreams of relentlessness, human and nonhuman bodies are urged to adopt the pace of automation for the sake of efficacy and productivity. Inside automated spaces such as farms and greenhouses, data, technology, and energy fuel the maximization of the land for year-round crops. Unrestricted by exterior conditions and seasons, these architectures work 24/7 through climate control, artificial lighting, water and nutrient distribution systems, and the pushing of bodies to their maximum uptime.[13] Commercially produced insects are deployed to pollinate fruits and vegetables and to control populations of other insects and living organisms. Cows and plants are handled by robots, their morphological traits, movements, and behaviors quantified and transformed into data and biometrics. In these highly technological and industrialized spaces, animals and plants are rendered less as living beings and more as objects deployed in the service of human needs.[14] These

13
See Automated Landscapes, a long-term research project exploring the implications of automation in the built environment, launched in 2017 by Het Nieuwe Instituut and directed by its research department. The department, led by Marina Otero Verzier, includes Ludo Groen, Anastasia Kubrak, Marten Kuijpers, Klaas Kuitenbrouwer, Setareh Noorani, and Katía Truijen, in close collaboration with various external collaborators, such as Merve Bedir of the Shenzhen-based Aformal Academy, Víctor Muñoz Sanz from the Faculty of Architecture and the Built Environment at the Delft University of Technology, and Grace Abou Jaoude.

14
Adams, "The War on Compassion," 19.

enclosures also enhance forms of subjection, extraction, and exploitation of certain humans are also enhanced. The low-wage human workforce, particularly with raced and gendered bodies, is monitored in real time, evaluated and managed by performance systems. Machines are dreamt in flesh, while bodies are technologized and managed by machines.

Greenhouse Ter Laak Orchids, Wateringen. Photo: Johannes Schwartz

LED lighting inside a greenhouse, Koppert Cress. Photo: Jan van Berkel.

If precision-based automated production came with the promise of a society liberated from the bondage of labor, while allegedly reducing energy, water consumption, and the use of chemical products, it has done so while being supportive of neoliberal regimes and dependent on the exploitation and invisibility of working bodies—human and non-human—treated in this case as automated machines. These production spaces expose how the persistent presence of unequal and extractive structures is manifested in Cartesian forms of enclosure, some of them enacted by architectural practice.

Architecture, as a biopolitical and normalizing technique, participates in the construction of distinctions and categories, or the lack thereof. In coordination with other social and institutional techniques, architecture produces a differential social space and is too often put at the service of the containment and exclusion of bodies, facilitating or preventing their encounter and their free movement. The structural conditions implemented in the contemporary spaces of automated labor are not an exception but another historical episode of how unfolding violence is unleashed upon certain bodies in support of growing production and capital accumulation.

I am referring here to the systematic structures that have previously served to enslave and, under unrelenting pressure, exhaust bodies. The conditions of containment and exploitation unleashed by the Door(s) of No Return, the hold of the slave ship, the plantations, and other spatial and conceptual boundaries are still reproduced and articulated in contemporary architectures and the multiple afterlives of slavery. In these spaces, those regarded as "the other" become sources of energy for the ambitions and enterprises of particular human groups. After all, the category of the human was never applied to the whole of humanity.

As Achille Mbembe argues in *A Critique of Black Reason*, the notion of race "made it possible to represent non-European human groups as trapped in a lesser form of being. They were the impoverished reflection of the ideal man, separated from him by an insurmountable temporal divide, a difference nearly impossible to overcome."[15] Mbembe identifies the enclosure not only in the categorization and race, or the spaces where Black bodies have been confined or blocked from entering, but in a constructed form of belated temporality. As he puts it, Black bodies are "locked into a belatedness in becoming human enough in relation to the ideal (white) humanist subject, the spatializing of time along a vertical line is used as a mechanism to deny juridical rights."[16] To produce Blackness, Mbembe asserts, is to produce a body of extraction, an exploitable object from which to obtain maximum profit.

15
Achille Mbembe, *A Critique of Black Reason* (Durham, NC: Duke University Press, 2017), 17.

16
Kathryn Yusoff, *A Billion Black Anthropocenes or None* (Minnesota: University of Minnesota Press, 2018), 77.

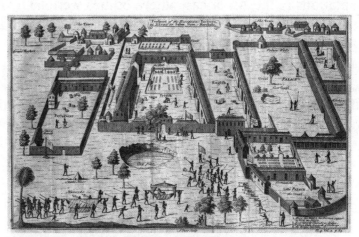

'Prospect of the European Factorys, at Xavier or Sabee, from Marchais'. Artist/engraver/cartographer: N. Parr, from Marchais. Provenance: "A New General Collection of Voyages and Travels"; Printed for Thomas Astley, Published by His Majesty's Authority, London. Type: Antique copperplate map. Date taken: 1746. Location: Benin. Source: Antiqua Print Gallery / Alamy Stock Photo

Slavery and the possibility of Black bodies becoming property served to redistribute energy and accumulate profits in particular geographies that largely benefited from the exploitation of human and nonhuman bodies, profits that constituted the base for the economic growth of, for instance, Western Europe and the Americas.[17] And it was precisely in

17
Ibid.,15.

the transatlantic slave trade where the categories of human, nonhuman, and inhuman morphed and crystalized in different constructions of space and time, and persistent and systemic forms of property ownership and misappropriation. Prompted by growing mineral extraction in the New World, in particular gold and silver, which later served to boost European markets, the transatlantic slave trade supported European world building. As Kathryn Yusoff argues in *A Billion Black Anthropocenes or None*, it was a world dependent on the subjugation and de facto categorization of the enslaved, the land, and ecologies as inhuman property. "The property lines of empire," Yusoff insists, "instigated and marked Blackness as both a consequence of labor requirements and a possibility of capital accumulation through geologic extraction."[18]

Yet as the demand for labor in the plantation economy of the Americas grew, the selling of slaves turned into a more lucrative enterprise than the trade of gold, Saidiya Hartman points out. Having until then stored trade goods such as porcelain, cloth, and copper, edifices such as Elmina Castle—controlled by the Dutch and located in present-day Ghana—filled their storage rooms with captive bodies.[19] These were gateways between Africa, the ports and trade centers of Europe, and the plantations in the Americas, where bodies were later transported in the holds of slave ships to satisfy the European demand for human labor on New World plantations.

Plantations, like mines, were sites where enslaved human bodies were rendered inhuman, not by their entanglement with mineral commodities, but by being subjected to the inexorable work comparable only to that of an automated machine. As captive laboring bodies,

The Door of No Return, Gorée Island, Senegal, 2004.
Photo: Robin Elaine. Source: Flickr.

18
Ibid., 68.

19
Saidiya Hartman, *Lose Your Mother: A Journey along the Atlantic Slave Route* (New York: Farrar, Straus and Giroux, 2007), 52.

their life expectancy became an intrinsic part of these sites' production model. As such, Christina Sharpe notes, weather monitoring was a major part of the plantation management, as necessary for the growth and cultivation of crops as for the performance of the enslaved. The enslaved, Sharpe points out, were forced to labor relentlessly "in the rain, in the sun, in damp and in dry, cutting cane, laying dung, hoeing, and weeding," with deadly effects.[20]

Plantations and factories were therefore a testing ground for forms of enclosure, dispossession, appropriation, and accumulation, as well as economies and systems of labor and production that were soon exported from the New World and the colonies to the continent. The so-called tragedy of the commons, and the systematic fencing and privatization of common land formerly held in the open-field system, which served to mediate toward a full capitalist economy, is generally presented as one of its results. Similarly, in the ethos that gives shape to the labor systems inside automated greenhouses and factories, one can't avoid recognizing the Cartesian logic and mechanical conceptions of living organisms—a logic that for centuries has based the increase in production on the relentless labor of the other.

Pandemic Lockdowns

It seems inevitable to refer to the current situation and how the ongoing entanglement of humans and nonhumans dramatically alters spatial conditions, collapsing previous conversations in a common yet unseen scenario. As this essay is being written, the COVID-19 pandemic prompts millions of humans to radically reorganize their forms of living, producing, consuming, and relating to others: practicing social distancing, self-isolating, quarantining, working remotely, shifting education to virtual spaces. Governments are taking unprecedented measures to prevent or slow down the contagion of populations, including implementing lockdowns and paralyzing a large number of manufacturing and economic activities.

Bound to their domestic spaces, workers nevertheless continue to perform their jobs, assisted by digital technologies and infrastructures. In confinement, those who can carry out their tasks remotely have to keep up productivity and attentiveness even as they are drawn into an unprecedented production, circulation, and consumption of data.[21] Simultaneously, their immaterial labor increases exponentially—caring for others, maintaining the social fabric and forms of cohesion,

20
Christina Sharpe, *In the Wake: On Blackness and Being* (Durham, NC: Duke University Press, 2016), 112.

21
In the first weeks of the government-imposed self-isolation for populations in Europe and the United States, Microsoft teams reported a growth from 32 million daily active users to 44 million, who in turn generated over 900 million meetings and calling minutes per day. Facebook confirmed that traffic for video calling and messaging exploded. In Italy, quarantined youngsters playing PC games increased traffic over Telecom Italia SpA by 90 percent compared with the previous month. Downloads of Netflix's app jumped 66 percent. In Spain, they rose 35 percent. In other parts of Europe, traffic to WebEx, a Cisco video conferencing service, soared by as much as 80 percent.

educating children, assisting elderly—with no compensation or support under the premise of the need for empathy and solidarity.

Having effectively moved the office space to the domestic environment, workers are even more vulnerable to systemic forms of exploitation, discrimination, and inequality among populations and territories. The enforcement of self-isolation has evidenced how the house, long an object of real estate speculation and form of investment, is a basic right of which, unfortunately, many are dispossessed. The last global crisis had remarkably imposed some of the most draconian conditions on the housing systems and its inhabitants. Whether foreclosure or forced enclosure, or both, the politics of house are deployed with violence against its inhabitants.

The current mode of digital production in self-confinement and isolation also renders visible the uneven distribution of digital infrastructures and internet access, as well as the ongoing privatization of public life. The shift to digital labor and online social cultural, and economic activities presupposes that everybody has access to a reliable internet connection, data plans, digital devices, and machines. Not only for working but also for supporting basic contact with loved ones and public life while in confinement. In addition, the growth of current data production means increased surveillance, data mining, profits for certain companies, such as Facebook, Amazon, and Zoom, as well as a large environmental footprint, as data storage depends on high consumption of often-non-renewable energy. Certainly, the pandemic brought the world closer to some of the dreams—and nightmares—designed in Silicon Valley.

As humans isolate their breath, cover their mouths, eyes, hands, or entire bodies when in contact with others, are quarantined in interior spaces, their bodies framed by the grids of video communication companies, other forms of enclosure continue to proliferate. Cities and countries are experiencing lockdowns, governments impose travel bans and the closing of borders. The pandemic has accelerated dramatically the walling of states, a phenomenon that has been normalized in the last decade through rising nationalism and xenophobia, as well as the proliferation of support for the nation-state as a geographically confined site of belonging.

Movement, nevertheless, is not an evenly distributed right. Nor is breathing. While the movements and actions of a large number of human bodies is restricted, the rich have access to other conditions of containment and circulation involving lesser risk of contagion, while other communities—nurses, doctors, security forces—are mobilized to work. As David Harvey notes, "The workforce that is expected to take care of the mounting numbers of the sick is typically highly gendered,

22
David Harvey, "Anti-Capitalist Politics in the Time of COVID-19," *Jacobin magazine*, March 20, 2020, https://jacobinmag.com/2020/03/david-harvey-coronavirus-political-economy-disruptions.

23
Jeffery C. Mays and Andy Newman, "Virus Is Twice as Deadly for Black and Latino People Than Whites in N.Y.C.," *New York Times*, April 8, 2020, https://www.nytimes.com/2020/04/08/nyregion/coronavirus-race-deaths.html.

24
"Hospitalization Rates and Characteristics of Patients Hospitalized with Laboratory-Confirmed Coronavirus Disease 2019 — COVID-NET, 14 States, March 1–30, 2020," Centers for Disease Control and Prevention, https://www.cdc.gov/mmwr/volumes/69/wr/mm6915e3.htm?s_cid=mm6915e3_w.

25
Katie Mettler, "States Imprison Black People at Five Times the Rate of Whites—A Sign of a Narrowing yet Still-Wide Gap," *Washington Post*, December 4, 2019, https://www.washingtonpost.com/crime-law/2019/12/04/states-imprison-black-people-five-times-rate-whites-sign-narrowing-yet-still-wide-gap/.

26
Harriet Grant, "Vulnerable Prisoners 'Exploited' to Make Coronavirus Masks and Hand Gel," *Guardian*, March 12, 2020, https://www.theguardian.com/global-development/2020/mar/12/vulnerable-prisoners-exploited-to-make-coronavirus-masks-and-hand-gel.

racialized, and ethnicized in most parts of the world."[22] These workers are exposed to a double risk, Harvey insists, either contracting the virus through their jobs or being laid off. So are workers in the delivery sectors, whose labor allows the practicing of social distancing by the rest of the population. Similarly, age has become a category through which to assess the worthiness of healthcare treatments during the pandemic. Some bodies are deemed disposable by neoliberal governments and their social calculus by which they wrongly ask us to choose between the economy and death.

The present situation manifests a structural condition.[23] A recent report by the United States' Centers for Disease Control and Prevention revealed the disproportionate impact of the COVID-19 pandemic on African American communities.[24] Racial and ethnic disparities show how the afterlives of slavery continue to haunt minorities in the systems of incarceration.[25] As the pandemic makes inmates among the populations most vulnerable to COVID-19 infections, prison labor has proved to be one of the solutions used to face supply shortages during the pandemic in places such as the US and Hong Kong. Mass incarceration, which in countries such as the US involves Black people at five times the rate of whites, is exploited as a cheap solution to produce hand sanitizer and face masks.[26] Under the Cartesian logic of the animal-machine, enclosing structures based on the punitive, relentless work of "the other" continue to maintain the system.

If minorities are too often considered as machines, robots and artificial intelligence emerge as an alternative to deliver supplies, interact with sick patients, disinfect rooms, or control populations. Even before the crisis, supply chains were reliant on an important number of artificial-intelligent and automated systems, a trend that is likely to accelerate. The consecutive attempts to build a machine that can act and think like a human being are concurrent with the lack of diversity and intersectional thinking in the tech industry, as well as the data sets used by the coders, which inevitably manifest in AI, software, and algorithms with racial and gender bias. Social inequalities are magnified by the daily workings of algorithms that, using obscure scoring systems, assess millions of individuals and their reliability. The machine makes the human as the human makes the machine.

In confinement, entangled with viruses, gradually replaced by robots and AI, people's lives are differently valued, and the notion of what is human seems more than ever in flux. Rather than resorting to the forces of nostalgia and a long-criticized humanism, more important is perhaps to reimagine what being human might mean.

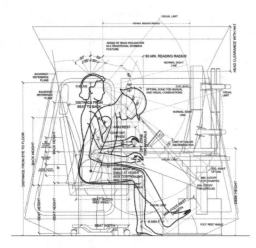

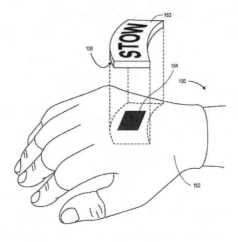

Anthropometric data. Crane cabin operator vs remote control operator. Drawing: Het Nieuwe Instituut, 2017.

Wearable RFID devices with manually activated RFID tags. Amazon Industries, Inc. Source: European Patent Office (EPO)

Becomings to Come

As humans retreated in self-isolation, the news on pollution levels reaching historic lows and wildlife bouncing back in cities made the unthinkable thinkable. Patricia MacCormack's words reverberated then more than ever: "Can the end of the human without replacement be a creative, jubilant affirmation of life?" she asks.[27]

In the *Ahuman Manifesto*, MacCormack advocates for the cessation of the reproduction of human life. According to her, the end of the human is not a denial of futurity nor its discontinuation: rather, human disappearance brings the possibility of a future that has not been thought of in advance by the human, a future not forged on human referents and not made according to the human.[28] "Ahuman ethics," MacCormack claims, celebrates "the death of the human—as subjectivity and ultimately as extinct" and unleashes forms of creativity opening spaces never before accessed.[29] Having invented the concept of species and, with that, the countless categories that validated the exploitation and denial of life to others, humans must now, MacCormack argues, "be the species to change the becomings to come."[30] "If all lives are of equal value, and some lives perpetrate more resource consumption or cause the liberty of other lives to be compromised, then is their value to be found in their absence rather than in their preservation?"[31] MacCormack ultimately demands that humans ethically address the purpose of our continuation on Earth.[32]

The possibility of an ahuman world unleashes, above all, alternative futures and forms of existence for nonexploitative, common,

27
Patricia MacCormack, "After Life," in *The Animal Catalyst: Towards Ahuman Theory*, ed. Patricia MacCormack (London: Bloomsbury, 2014), 180.

28
Ibid., 179.

29
Ibid., 183.

30
Ibid., 179.

31
Ibid., 57.
32
Ibid., 187.

and radically equal worlds. The prerogative of mind over matter, which rendered the human as separated from the rest of nature, propelled human dreams of landscape domination and the depletion of resources, with vast implications for the environment. Cartesian science, in its objectivation of identity and categorization, also had social consequences on those marginalized based on their ethnicity, gender, race. Today we see how these categories, as well as the primacy of man, are increasingly contested, even without having yet embraced the extinction of the human. The dualisms of Cartesian science, which led to the compartmentalization and instrumentalization of relations and to embracing rationality of economic efficacy instead of ethical and ecological awareness, are outdated. So is the dominant paradigm of Cartesian space that privileges materiality, functionality, and abstraction. A paradigm in which architecture has its foundations.

A non-Cartesian architecture for the becoming-other demands different imaginaries, epistemologies, and spatial relations. What would it mean for architecture to put an end to the anthropocentrism that has dominated its theories and practices? Conventional notions of space and architecture could give way to unknown dimensions of reality and perception brought about by the decentering of the human from architectural practice. Spatial and philosophical enclosures could perhaps be turned around and challenge the inevitability of the unequal relations that they

APM automated terminals in Rotterdam. Photo: Het Nieuwe Instituut, 2017.

Remote control room, office terminal of APM terminal, Rotterdam. Photo: Nelleke de Vries.

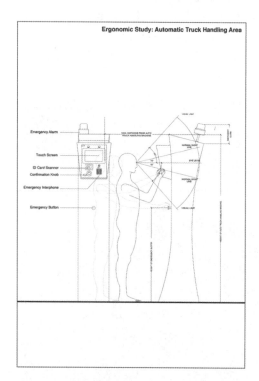

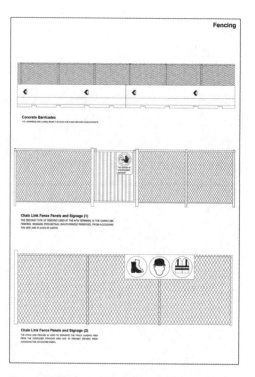

Ergonomic study. Automatic truck management area, APM terminal, Rotterdam. In the unmanned control point, truck drivers must show an identification card, write several codes, and use biometric data to continue their route. Drawing: Het Nieuwe Instituut, 2017.

Fence, APM terminal, Rotterdam. An array of concrete barriers, metallic fences, and CCTV surround the terminal to prevent unauthorized access. Drawing: Het Nieuwe Instituut, 2017.

Dockers' strike in Rotterdam to protect jobs. Image by International Transport Workers' Federation, January 7, 2016.

33
Anna Lowenhaupt Tsing,
*The Mushroom at the
End of the World: On
the Possibility of Life in
Capitalist Ruins* (Princeton,
NJ: Princeton University
Press, 2015), 267.

set forth. Unpredictable environments, structures, and relations could emerge in the interaction and melting of matter, technology, and beings. From the profound revision of received ideas about the threshold of humanity—as well as notions of comfort, care, empathy, property, and progress that account for humans and nonhumans—new forms of social life and life-in-common could emerge. "Sometimes common entanglements emerge not from human plans but despite them," Anna Tsing proposes while talking about the possibility of life in capitalist ruins. "It is not even the undoing of plans, but rather the unaccounted for in their doing that offers possibilities for elusive moments of living in common."[33]

By acknowledging humanity's ruins and the collapse of the dreams of industrial progress, a spatial imaginary for non-Cartesian architecture emerges. Far from being a unifying seamless space, it could be one outlined by the encounter of singularities (humans and nonhumans) in the common.

Data Centre AMS8 Interxion, Haarlemmermeer. Photo by Johannes Schwartz.

Coda

As a locked-down humanity produces more data than ever before, the enclosures that served for their control and storage are being rethought. While the rigid rectangular geometries of data centers continue to proliferate across the territory, experiments on the entanglement of data and organisms are resulting in architectures difficult to describe under dual categories and ethics.[34] Artificially encoded binary data is being stored within synthesized strands of DNA and the DNA of plants and seeds. The host organism not only preserves its ability to germinate, but as it grows and multiplies so does the encoded information, now contained in every cell, potentially archiving billions of gigabytes of data for millennia.[35] Yet as plant cells routinely repair their DNA, errors could alter the code over time, leaving room for unexpected developments.

If data is a human expression, plant-based digital data storage shakes Cartesian enclosures and categories. When a living forest could become the largest human repository on Earth, and even rewrite its history, architecture has no choice but to rethink its own postulates.

34
Further research on data centers is conducted in collaboration with Het Nieuwe Instituut and the Royal College of Art in London, within the framework of the architectural design studio "ADS8: Data Matter: Digital Networks, Data Centers & Posthuman Institutions," led by Marina Otero Verzier, Ippolito Pestellini Laparelli, and Kamil Dalkir.
35
Sean O'Neill, "I Plant Memories in Seeds," *New Scientist* 229, no. 3056 (January 16, 2016): 27.

Helena Francis, A cyborg future for the data archive. Cyborg plant—Liliaceae (April/2020).
Courtesy of the author.

The Ghosts of Parisian Telecommunications: The Obsolescence of the Large Telephone Exchanges

Fanny Lopez

1
"Le plus grand central d'Europe," *Postes et Télécommunications, mensuel d'information du ministère des postes et des télécommunications* 184 (1971): 11–12. Archive BHTP, Cote PC363.

On the southern side of the tree-lined lanes of the Tuileries gardens, near the Louvre, an underground access leads to what was once the largest telephone exchange in Europe.[1] The chipped fresco of the corridor cadences the descent into the depths of an infrastructural complex of 8,000 m². This maze of technical rooms and passages is almost totally empty today. In the large copper-wire connection room, only a few sections still flash. An infrastructural ruin from the golden age of telecommunications, the Tuileries exchange is, through the history of its construction, its location, and its size, the most emblematic of a series of large exchanges built by the Ministry of the Post, Telegraph and Telephone (PTT) in the mid-1970s. The ghost of the analogue telephone, this immense switching station housed equipment connecting the network lines with the subscribers. This forest of invisible networks dug enormous black holes in the urban space. To fill telephony demands and relieve the lines' saturation problems, exchanges were built everywhere in France—and elsewhere—in every neighborhood, sometimes underground as at the Tuileries, sometimes in dedicated or transformed buildings like the former air raid shelter on the boulevard Kellermann. There was also new construction, as at the emblematic Murat exchange at the porte d'Auteuil.

Telephone exchanges can look like office buildings, apartment houses, or suburban homes; certain facades are hidden, others listed as historic monuments. Every architectural style is represented, and

Access corridor to the telephone exchange Tuilerie, 2019, photo Fanny Lopez.

there is a great variety of construction systems, reflecting the different building periods from the late 19th century to today. There are over 40 exchanges in Paris itself and more than 200 in Île-de-France.[2] Of all the sites, only 20 percent are still functioning; the remaining 80 percent are either empty and sold or awaiting a second life. Real-estate transactions for these infrastructures are carried out with the greatest discretion. The mecca of connection, these building-infrastructures in the center of Paris remain strategic sites, prized for their land and their exceptional technical and spatial dimensions. Their history, however, is barely known.

This real-estate heritage has undergone a profound transformation over the last 20 years. The centralized technical objects of the telecoms are disappearing, prey to shifts in what constituted their value. In a similar vein, the liberalization of the telecom market and the development of digital technologies from 1990 to 2000 brought about profound political and technical changes that precipitated the transformation and abandonment of this large public-service infrastructure. This article proposes to analyze from a spatial angle the socio-technical reconfigurations generated by these mutations.

Housing the Telephone: Ever Larger Exchanges

The visibility and spatiality of the post office buildings in which the first telephone exchanges were inserted changed. From the late 19th to the early 20th centuries, their architectural expression gradually diminished.[3] In the late 1960s and early 1970s, the network became denser, the large-scale technical surfaces multiplied, and the invisibility of these public works became a fundamental urban issue. Telecommunications profoundly transformed the city. As the telephone network was urban at first,[4] density was an economic imperative on which profitability depended.[5] The first users were professionals (brokers, bankers, merchants). In Paris, it was in the business district on the avenue de l'Opéra that the first exchange was installed in 1880.

The nationalization of the telecom industry took place from the late 19th to early 20th centuries. The telecommunications buildings were the flagship public infrastructures of the Ministry of the PTT, which became France Télécom in 1988, then became an Independent Public-Law Operator under this denomination on January 1, 1991. Its real estate holdings were enormous, with sites throughout the country. As historian Guy Lambert explained:

2
Surveys and interviews were conducted by the author of this article in 2018 and 2019.

3
Guy Lambert, "Les PTT dans leurs murs: les ressorts privés d'une architecture publique," in Postes et télécommunications entre public et privé, jusqu'en 1990, proceedings of the FNARH colloquium, held in Paris on May 12–13, 2011, Les cahiers de la FNARH 120 (2011): 31–34.

4
Paul Claval, La logique des villes (Paris: Litec, 1981).

5
Catherine Bertho, Télégraphes et téléphones (Paris: Livre de Poche, 1981); Yves Stourdzee, "Généalogie des télécommunications française," in Alain Giraud, Jean Claude Missica, Dominique Wolton, Les réseaux pensants (Paris: CENT-ENST, MaNSSON, 1978).

At the PTT, the growing need for specific buildings like the telegraph and telephone exchanges (but also the sorting centers) would determine a public commission that gave rise to a continuous flow of construction, supervised by the postal administration, which very often undertook the project management. Previously, public telecom services had been based in private buildings, aristocratic mansions or former bourgeois residences, as was common [for the postal service] before the French Revolution and well into the 19th century. In the early 20th century, a corps of specialized architects responsible for PTT buildings emerged.[6]

6
Lambert, "Les PTT dans leurs murs."

Musée d'Orsay and Jardin des Tuileries from the Grande Roue de Paris, 2013, creative common, photo Martin Robson.

The large exchanges of the 1920s and 1930s were manifesto architecture. This is the case of the Littré building[7] by Jules-Alexandre Godefroy and works by François Le Cœur such as the Archives exchange—otherwise called "the telephone brain of France"![8]—and the Bergère exchange. Built in reinforced concrete and covered with hollow clay tiles, Bergère presents a monumental facade pierced by large glazed expanses; the play of pillars between the three slightly curved bays presents powerful verticals; a cornice crowns the building. The purpose of the spaces is distinctly expressed on the facade: glazed for the offices on the rue Bergère and windowless for the technical zones on the rue du Faubourg Poissonnière (three superimposed 600 m2 rooms).

7
The technical volumes were consolidated and the rest of the premises sold by Orange. Today it is the fashion and luxury house Balenciaga that occupies the premises.
8
This international switching station is still the largest exchange in France.

Rooms of the telephone exchange Tuilerie, 2019. Photo Fanny Lopez.

Initially manual, the transmission and switching equipment gradually became automatic in the 1910s, then electronic and computerized. Over time, the personnel were increasingly replaced by machines and technology, and management staff by maintenance crews. This influenced the typology of the exchanges, which required less office space. In the 1930s, the average size of the rooms was 300 m^2 for switching installations with, often, the possibility of creating a second room on a raised level (which corresponded

9
Louis Gueylard and
Hubert Fritz, "Où loger
le téléphone parisien,"
*Revue Française des
Télécommunications* 14
(January 1975), 16.
Archive BHTP, Cote TC543.

10
Gabriel Dupuy, "Un
téléphone pour la ville,
l'enjeu urbain des centraux
téléphoniques," *Metropolis*
52/53 (1982): 28–34.

11
Rémy Prud'homme,
"Le rôle des
télécommunications
dans l'aménagement du
territoire," *Metropolis*
52/53 (1982): 22–24.

12
Cécile Diguet and Fanny
Lopez, "L'impact spatial
et énergétique des data
centers sur les territoires,"
ADEME Report, February
2019, 141.

13
Gueylard and Fritz,
"Où loger le téléphone
parisien," 19.

to 10,000 subscribers, or twice that after adding a level). In 1965 a decision was made to enlarge the exchanges, increasing their minimum area to 1,200 m^2 and thereby adding 40,000 subscriber lines.[9] In the 1970s, the area of the rooms reached 3,500 m^2 for 100,000 subscribers. The increase in requests for connection and the constant rise in traffic exhausted the capacity of the existing exchanges. The financial investment for building new exchanges with more standardized interiors was included in the fifth and sixth plans of the Ministry of the PTT, starting in 1965.

In his article "Un téléphone pour la ville" (A telephone for the city), Gabriel Dupuy stressed the urban issue of the telephone exchanges and their fundamental role in the city's organization and functioning.[10] An instrument of contact and security between citizens, this "mass medium" supported the urban system in its "communicative essence," but in addition, it played a leading economic role. The relationship between the development of the urban space and the development of the telecoms was generally grasped in terms of regional effects, notably with regard to the distance of one's commute and its effects on mobility. Everything happened as if the telecoms by magic provided solutions to development problems by abolishing distances and inducing a spatial decentralization of activities. But for this magic to be effective, the massive infrastructures had to be made invisible. After the characteristic grandeur of early-20th-century buildings like Littré and Bergère in Paris, or the ones at 32 Avenue of the Americas and 111 8th Avenue in New York, came much more ordinary buildings for a program that was henceforth common. The growth of the telecoms and the development of their infrastructures were connected to urban growth, the financial concentration of companies with the creation of conglomerates in the 1960s to 1980s, and the development of service jobs that were difficult to relocate. As Rémy Prud'homme asserted in his article "Le rôle des télécommunications dans l'aménagement du territore" (The role of the telecoms in regional development): "The development of the networks seems to favor a growth in all forms of centralization."[11] The giantism and concentration of telephone exchanges in the center of Paris are a testment to this centralization, which can be compared today with Big Tech's massive data centers.[12]

In the 1970s, this centralization took the form of a large-scale national project to improve the quality of public service of the telecoms (the Delta LP) and an intensification of land acquisitions. In 1974 ground was broken at some 50 construction sites in Paris and the nearby suburbs.[13]

The Last Large Public Infrastructure of the Telecoms

Building in Paris is an arduous task because vacant land, or even land already built up, is as expensive as it is rare. Given the difficulties of constructing a large building on the surface in many parts of the city, the creation of underground exchanges sometimes proved to be an advantageous solution.

The decision to construct large urban exchanges on publicly owned land in the city of Paris and other urban areas was made in 1970. These were the projects: Tuilerie, Murat, Cévennes, Beaujon, Montsouris, Joffre. In this group, we will more specifically discuss four emblematic exchanges for their built features and the transformation issues they present: two totally buried telephone exchanges (Tuilerie and Beaujon), a building with an architecture manifesto on a stadium (Murat), and the transformation of a former air-raid shelter and a former SNECMA aircraft engine factory (Montsouris). For all these enormous sites, very specific constraints called for all the cutting-edge techniques of civil engineering.

The Tuilerie exchange, otherwise called "the hyper exchange," was built starting in 1971 under the Tuileries garden, at the intersection of the north-south and east-west telephone circuits. It was the first of the large underground exchanges built to lighten the load on telephone lines. At capacity, it could serve nearly a quarter of the subscribers in Paris at the period.

The work was handled by Marc Saltet, head architect of Bâtiments Civils et Palais Nationaux, responsible for the Louvre and

Construction of the Paris Beaujon telephone center in 1978. Collection Claude Rizzo Vignaud.

Tuileries area. Very rapidly, rumors about the construction site "created a general outcry: the gardens were going to be turned upside down, the trees uprooted, the lanes dug up. It was a serious attack on the integrity of Paris squares, a questioning of green spaces."[14] But the head architect reassured Parisians: not a single tree would be removed! Le Nôtre's garden would be exactly the same after the installation. After construction was finished, tourists and strollers could "relax in the shade of their favorite trees, without realizing for a single second that they have the largest telephone exchange in Europe under their feet."[15]

Telephone exchange Murat, exterior view, 2019. Photo Fanny Lopez.

Telephone exchange Murat, empty offices in the 2nd basement, 2019. Photo Fanny Lopez.

14
"Le plus grand central d'Europe."
15
"Le plus grand central d'Europe."

In fact, only two discreet entrances in the park and the air vents built into the stone balustrade could awaken the suspicions of an informed eye. The infrastructure, however, goes down to a depth of 17 meters below the level of the terrace. Contained in a double-reinforced-concrete envelope (a thick and airtight wall and a more traditional envelope), the main building covers an area of 81 by 74.5 m. The total area of 17,900 m² includes basements on two levels of 7,000 m² each.[16]

16
"Où en est le centre Tuilerie?," *Télécom de Paris, Bulletin d'information et de coordination des télécommunications de Paris* 10 (November–December 1971), Archive BHTP, Cote TC503.

The Murat telephone exchange, almost empty technical room, 2019.
Photo Fanny Lopez

The telephone exchange, empty space in the 3rd basement, 2019,
Photo Fanny Lopez

The arrival of optical fiber (which will be used in all connections by 2040) and other digital, technical transformations have made the exchange largely obsolete. It has been gradually emptied, starting in the early 2000s, and the only thing that remains today is some copper equipment and technical remnants that cannot be downsized or eliminated (distributing frame, transmission equipment, line concentrator).

Another large underground exchange, Joffre, was proposed in the 7th arrondissement under the Champs-de-Mars, at its southeastern end, opposite the École Militaire. The 10,000 m2 space, divided into three levels, was never built: in the end, the project proved to be too costly and complex. In 1974, however, construction began at two sites that were just as spectacular: Beaujon and Murat.

The Beaujon underground telephone exchange, at 206–210, rue du Faubourg Saint-Honoré, occupies a large part of the former Beaujon hospital. Over 200,000 m3 of earth were removed to build the four buried floors (25,000 m²) to which an elevation (15,000 m²) was added. The hospital's two lateral wings were demolished, but the central building was kept to house the Paris Prefecture of Police. The Beaujon exchange is still in use.

At the porte d'Auteuil, in the 16th arrondissement, the situation is quite different. The Murat exchange is now almost completely empty. In its place, the Council of Paris authorized a new project, on

The telephone exchange Montsouris, 1982. Collection Claude Rizzo-Vignaud

17
"Les grandes opérations du service des bâtiments," *Télécom de Paris, Bulletin d'information et de coordination des télécommunications de Paris Ile de France*, no. 2 (1974): 5–8, Archive BHTP, Cote TC503.

the condition that work include the reconstruction of the municipal stadium and the addition of a new athletic track, a basketball court, and a volleyball court. Pierre Vivien, architect of Bâtiments Civils et Palais Nationaux, proposed in a Brutalist retro-futurism style a raised building in a circular form. The footprint was reduced to avoid impacting the stadium's sports installations.[17] This was the visible part of the iceberg. A 150 m² central core on the ground floor provided access to the upper floor—700 m² mostly occupied by offices and the company restaurant—and to the basement, consisting of three levels of about 3,000 m², each housing technical areas, including automatic switch rooms to provide service for 180,000 subscribers. After 20 years of operation, this building met a fate similar to that of many other exchanges: miniaturization, the arrival of digital technology, ADSL, and then optical fiber strongly modified its original program. It became a data center in 1999 before the executive management of Orange, in an effort to consolidate the company's facilities, almost totally emptied it. Its transformation into a museum was considered—the historical telecommunications collection could have been presented in it—but the project never went forward. A small section of the exchange is now partially occupied by the RATP (metropolitan transit network) and offers mobile connections for users, the rest remaining empty.

Unlike the Murat exchange, the Montsouris exchange project involved the reuse and reconfiguration of a former air-raid shelter, partially built on the site of the former SNECMA plant on the boulevard

Kellermann. The exchange offered 12,800 m^2 of usable area and 700 m2 in an annex building. Though part of the building was sold, it is still one of the largest IT systems in Europe today, with about 15 people working in maintenance. It is also Orange's third-largest data center in use, with three floors of 1,000 m^2 each for storage and almost four times as much for the technical spaces. The data center is 60 percent filled; its occupancy has been continuously increasing since 2004, and the arrival of connected objects on the market requiring data treatment near their source favors the proliferation of urban data centers. As for electrical power, the building consumes 4 MW on average and 5 MW in the summer. For cooling, 80 m^3 permanently circulate in a closed circuit.

The history of these infrastructures allows us to understand the evolution and trajectory of telecommunications. In the late 1980s and early 1990s, with the expansion of computer science, new services emerged: faxes, teletex, videotext, then the all-digital technology, which further turned the technical systems of traditional telephony upside down and contributed to a miniaturization of components and a reconfiguration of buildings. Technical facilities became hybrid with the arrival of servers, further increasing energy consumption. In the 2000s, the privatization of the sector and the arrival of new digital and optical fiber operators (with, in 2008, the mobile/internet convergence: SFR, Orange, Bouygues, then Free) modified the market and radically reconfigured the businesses, as well as the real-estate heritage of the historic operator. Starting in 1997, the state, which was its sole shareholder, gradually opened the capital of France Télécom to private investors. In 2000, the French operator bought the British brand Orange. The state continued to divest itself of the capital and in 2004 dropped below the bar of 50 percent, making France Télécom a private company. In 2013 the historic operator dropped its former name and became Orange.

The NExT plan (Nouvelle Expérience des Télécommunications) was launched in 2006 with a triple objective: to drastically reduce payroll costs (elimination of 22,000 jobs), consolidate products and services, and lastly bring together all the group's company names under a single brand. The violence of its management methods—which pushed many civil servants to resign, others to commit suicide— resulted in legal action (certain directors and executives are on trial today for moral harassment).

The company's social and spatial reconfigurations were rapid and radical. Emptied of personnel and equipment, the underground telephone exchanges have gradually become obsolete, their slow decomposition marking a national public heritage that in a decade has shifted to the hands of supranational private groups.

Obsolete Fortresses:
Liberalization, Digitization, Privatization

Over the last 10 years, Orange has been compressing its technical operations in reduced spaces on its most strategic sites, with access reserved for the company. The rest of the sites are being sold to investors, notably Nexity, as juicy real-estate opportunities. Need we point out that Stéphane Richard, the current CEO of Orange, was the cofounder of Nexity?

Out of the 41 telephone exchanges in Paris itself, 21 are empty, either sold or on the market. About 15 interviews permitted us to better understand the real-estate fate of a few historic sites: the Brune and Marcadet exchanges were transformed into apartment houses, those of Invalides and Segur into luxury hotels, Élysées and Passy were sold to large private companies. The public service buildings of the telecoms have therefore become or are becoming once again private buildings, hotels, or bourgeois residences.

Digital technology has also turned the world and the telecom infrastructures upside down. Orange announced the end of traditional landline telephones by 2030. The Public Switched Telephone Network (PSTN) will gradually be cut, starting in 2023. All landline users will have to opt for access to internet via a box. Though the territorial footprint of the telecom technical system coincided with the appearance of the major infrastructures of the 20th century, such as those of transport or energy, they are more difficult to grasp because their technical and architectural materiality is less visible. And digital technology has further accentuated this phenomenon by the distancing made possible by optical fiber. In the first exchanges, there was nothing but network equipment, then little by little computer equipment was embedded.[18] In the late 1990s, new buildings dedicated to computing and data storage multiplied. The telecommunications center emerged only to be replaced by the data center. Geographer Bruno Moriset has traced the emergence of a very specific real-estate market that played a fundamental role in the renovation and revitalization of a certain number of urban districts via the conversion of industrial sites, food warehouses, or logistics platforms in large cities like Chicago, New York, and London.[19]

18
In the beginning, the data center was used only for personnel management and accounting—this was the first step. For the second step, people used data centers to store the technical files of the subscribers, the management of all the infrastructures, etc. Next, data centers were used to create service platforms.

19
Bruno Moriset, "Les forteresses de l'économie numérique. Des immeubles intelligents aux hôtels de télécommunications," *Géocarrefour* 78/4 (2003, put online August 21, 2007).

Data center operators mostly come from the world of real-estate development and not that of telecommunications. In this new growing digital sector, everything has become concentrated very quickly to win market shares. As for its own technical specificities, the data center became a program initiated by new private actors; spatially, internet infrastructures multiplied, with a whole interconnected group of large and small data centers.[20] According to one former Goldman Sachs employee who later went to work for Digital Realty, a data center operator, the data center is a real-estate product with very high financial profitability, and its location is at the heart of its value.[21]

The digital industry has created new infrastructural groups on a monumental scale. The initially decentralized nature of the internet promoted the emergence of a host of actors in the data storage industry as well as uncoordinated regional development, which did not play in favor of architectural reflection or spatial coherence. Whereas the public telecom infrastructures made regional solidarity a public service principle—the major catch-up of the 1970s consisting of a massive investment to ensure coverage for the whole country—the deployment of optical fiber is still unequal today, despite efforts to cover the "white zones." Data centers are being sited according to real estate and energy opportunities. Many actors, notably the CNIL (National Commission on Computer Science and Freedoms), are demanding a public digital service not only to protect the private life of citizens, but also to bring under consideration the deployment of networks and to anticipate the spatial and energy impacts of this phenomenon whose only compass for this frenzied growth is market demand.

One other change prompted Orange to create new buildings from scratch: the increasing demand for kilowatts per square meter. Thirty or 40 years ago, at a technical facility, there was mostly network equipment and some computing with an average consumption of 200 to 300 W per m2. Today, this figure is over 1 kW per m2 on average. With the increase in internet traffic and electricity consumption, most historic exchanges could no longer be adapted, as the transformation costs would be colossal and the work required to integrate electrical and air-conditioning backup systems extensive. In just a few years and throughout France, Orange divested itself of a large part of the built heritage that came from France Télécom. For the data centers, the company consolidated its facilities, going from 20 to 8 data centers, with the objective for 2025 of concentrating everything in three enormous buildings, two of which have just been built in Val-de-Reuil, in Normandy.

20
Diguet and Lopez, "L'impact spatial et énergétique des data centers sur les territoires."
21
Interview by the author.

The historic telecommunication sites have been transformed by the arrival and liberalization of digital technology, whose actors triggered a new privatization phase, then the sale of a large number of buildings of public interest in France. If the technical function has disappeared, what remains of the public in the spatiality of these infrastructures? Couldn't what remains be transformed for other uses of public interest, or must we simply resign ourselves to the loss of this vocation and the disappearance of these symbolic sites?

The invisibility of these infrastructures makes it as difficult to grasp their existence as their mutation. Yves Stourdzé, a philosopher and sociologist specializing in telecommunications, wrote in *Les ruines du futur* (Ruins of the future): "Maps are lacking for this disappearing territory and no point of reference can be perceived, polarities have dissolved. . . . They are traps, . . . holes that are concealed in the economy in such a way that under the leadership of the industrial standard the procession of pebbles and crumbs, uses and values, can be replayed indefinitely."[22] These exchanges, ghosts of telecommunications, are also those of public service. The spatialization of a territorial technical project and a general interest ring in the echo of these voids.

Today a concern for public well-being is behind many initiatives in the fields of information and communication technologies. As the major digital companies started to amass monopolistic power, movements to reappropiate the internet, as well as network and storage infrastructure, have grown. The calls for a public service based on "commons" (shared land) (ALIX, BANCEL, CORIAT and SULTAN 2018), remunicipalization, and deprivatization on municipal or regional scales are multiplying. There is a growing desire to create the public starting from the local. It is interesting to see that the internet infrastructure (and not only its uses) is also following the reappropriation movement that can be observed in the energy sector, with many citizens opting to choose their energy sources (local and renewable), to return services to municipal management, or to get involved in energy cooperatives. Such collaborative and peer-to-peer efforts are spreading on the small scale. They are led by citizen groups and associations that advocate for control of their data and a more distributed, decentralized, and less energy-intensive internet.[23] Even if the internet access market, like that of hosting, is dominated today by a few major actors, it is important to make room for these associative and cooperative groups, notably for the areas that are not as well served today or for users who lack digital competence or social ties. Making room for them in the digital landscape would allow for more local,

22
Yves Stourdzé, *Les ruines du futur*, 1st ed. (1979, repr., Paris: Sens et Tonka, 1998), 17.

23
There are many examples. See Diguet and Lopez, "L'impact spatial et énergétique des data centers sur les territoires."

better-informed digital management—especially in the hands of its own users, who could opt for more sober, economical practices adjusted to needs. To support citizen and cooperative network spaces is also to support associative, decentralized, and potentially more frugal hosting, favoring local social and economic development and making possible a greater climate resilience in those areas. If the very large companies—the world of banking and finance, which represent a preponderant share of internet traffic and the computing and storage capacities of data centers—are not ready to turn toward this type of distributed infrastructure, opportunities nevertheless exist for civil society, the associations, the municipalities, the social and solidarity economy, to take over this common good that is the internet.

Malta/CCZ:
What are the rights of deep-sea communities to an other-than-human common heritage?

Amy Balkin

What are the rights of deep-sea communities to an other-than-human common heritage?

In a 1967 speech to the United Nations General Assembly, Arvid Pardo, Representative of Malta and "Father of the Law of the Sea Conference,"[1] proposed that the seabed and ocean floor beyond the limits of national jurisdiction ("the Area") be proclaimed "the Common Heritage of Mankind (CHM)."[2] He argued that, along with banning nonpeaceful uses of the ocean floor, the seabed should be mined, with some portion of the profits of the vast mineral wealth used to finance poor nations in a challenge to the "structural relationship between rich and poor countries."[3]

Under the long banner of "the common heritage of mankind," commercial mining of the international seabed appears poised to finally begin, the research, legal, and regulatory phases nearing completion. Fifteen-year contracts have been issued by the International Seabed Authority to sponsoring state/contractor partnerships including the UK/Northern Ireland with UK Seabed Resources/Lockheed Martin[4] for exploration of wide areas of the global seabed, including the Clarion-Clipperton Fracture Zone (CCZ), Mid-Atlantic Ridge, and the Western Pacific Ocean.

This commencement is intertwined with scientific research documenting previously unknown deep-water species and the unsurprising extinction risks of mining for seafloor mineral deposits. Seabed mining, from research dredging to planned hydraulic bucket mining, threatens seamount scavengers and sessile creatures of the abyssal plains where polymetallic nodules are found,[5] produces sediment plumes damaging to life in the water column, and endangers communities around black smoker hydrothermal vents, where seafloor massive sulfides form, and at white smokers, where some scientists theorize life on Earth began.[6]

These scientific discoveries parallel and inform growing global public awareness, pushback, and protest against the irreversible harms of deep-sea extractivism, which are inseparable from the rights of future generations of deep-sea dwellers to an "other-than-human" common heritage.

The rights of nonhuman life of the ocean floor are increasingly recognized in the demands of anti-mining alliances like the Alliance of Solwara Warriors and Kiwis against Seabed Mining, and a growing subject of critical and theoretical investigation and attention.

The question of an other-than-human commons is urgent, as seabed mining, driven by the expansionist imperatives and technological capacities of capital, will produce new extinctions, legitimized under the rubric of common heritage and its framework of multilateral exploitation. What work can be done beyond environmental monitoring and accepting fragmented marine protected areas? Without a ban, a brutal ecocide of the seafloor's desertlike ecologies, vent assemblages, and vertically and horizontally migrating deep-sea species seems inevitable.

While the rights of nature are fought in human courts with both symbolic and practicable outcomes, the rush toward commercial deep-sea mining and the development of its apparatuses quickens, generating documentation and, with it, glimpses for third parties of the stakes of the commons for diverse abyssal life.

The project of seabed mining, with its bathymetric geopolitics and biopolitics of deep-sea research exploration, has left a wake of images documenting seafloor communities, habitats and landscapes, mineral deposits, and mining technology. Due to the inaccessibility of the deep seabed and ocean floor to those other than states, research institutions, and mining companies, images and visual materials available to the public reflect these origins and interests.

1

"Dr. Arvid Pardo, 'Father of Law of Sea Conference,' Dies At 85, in Houston, Texas," United Nations Press Release, SEA/1619, July 16 1999. https://www.un.org/press/en/1999/19990716.SEA1619.html

2

UNCLOS, Article 136.

3

Wikipedia/Pardo A (1984). "Ocean, Space and Mankind." *Third World Quarterly.* 6 (3): 559–569. doi:10.1080/01436598408419785

4

International Seabed Authority, Deep Seabed Minerals Contractors, web page, retrieved June 1, 2020. https://www.isa.org.jm/deep-seabed-minerals-contractors

5

NOAA Ocean Exploration and Research, Deep-Sea Mining Interests in the Clarion-Clipperton Zone, website retrieved June 1, 2020. https://oceanexplorer.noaa.gov/explorations/18ccz/background/mining/mining.html

6a

NASA JPL, Underwater "White Smoker" Vents: Is This Where Life Began?, website, retrieved April 15, 2020. https://www.jpl.nasa.gov/video/details.php?id=1613

6b

M. Dodd et al. "Evidence for Early life in Earth's Pldest Hydrothermal Vent Precipitates." *Nature* 543, 60–64 (2017). https://doi.org/10.1038/nature21377

Cutthroat eels feed at a baited camera on a seamount in APEI 7, a "no-mining" area within the Clarion-Clipperton Fracture Zone (CCZ). The CCZ is a broad area in the Pacific Ocean between Hawaii and Mexico divided into 16 mining claims. It holds billions of tons of manganese nodules.

A remotely operated subsea crawler mines for polymetallic nodules in a promotional video for Royal IHC Deep Sea Mining.

Zinc sulfide hydrothermal vent chimney cross section collected from the Mariana volcanic arc in the west Pacific Ocean by the USGS in 2010.

Credit: James Hein, U.S. Geological Survey Pacific Coastal and Marine Science Center.

Vent snails, shrimp, and crabs on a black smoker hydrothermal vent on the seafloor between Samoa and Tonga. Black smokers form when super-heated, sulfide-rich water solidifies into vents and chimneys, where benthic communities assemble. The Schmidt Ocean Institute, which operates the R/V Falkor, is funded by Google's former CEO Eric Schmidt through the Schmidt Family Foundation.

Credit: FK160322 Virtual Vents expedition. Schmidt Ocean Institute.

Torquaratoridae, from OER's Benthic Deepwater Animal Identification Guide, "a collection of in situ images created from video frame grabs taken from Deep Discoverer (D2) remotely operated vehicle (ROV)."

Black smoker in 2,980 meters of water on the Mid-Atlantic Ridge.

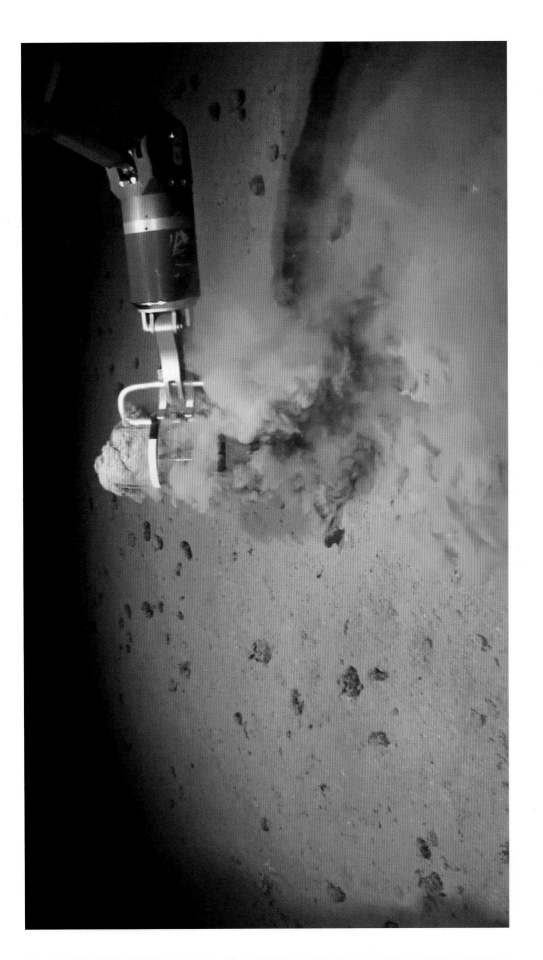

Deep CCZ Expedition: Exploring Abyssal Communities in the Pacific Ocean before Deep-Sea Mining Begins.

Remotely Operated Vehicle (ROV) Lu'ukai collects sediment and microbe/microbial samples from the abyssal plain at 5,000 meters in the CCZ. Manganese nodules can be seen on the seafloor. The project is intended to research the adequacy of the network of nine preservation areas (APEIs) set aside within the planned nodule mining area of the Pacific seafloor, which encompasses over one million square kilometers.

Credit: https://oceanexplorer.noaa.gov/explorations/18ccz/logs/photolog/photolog.html#cbpi=../../media/ccz_video_070518/ccz_video_070518.html

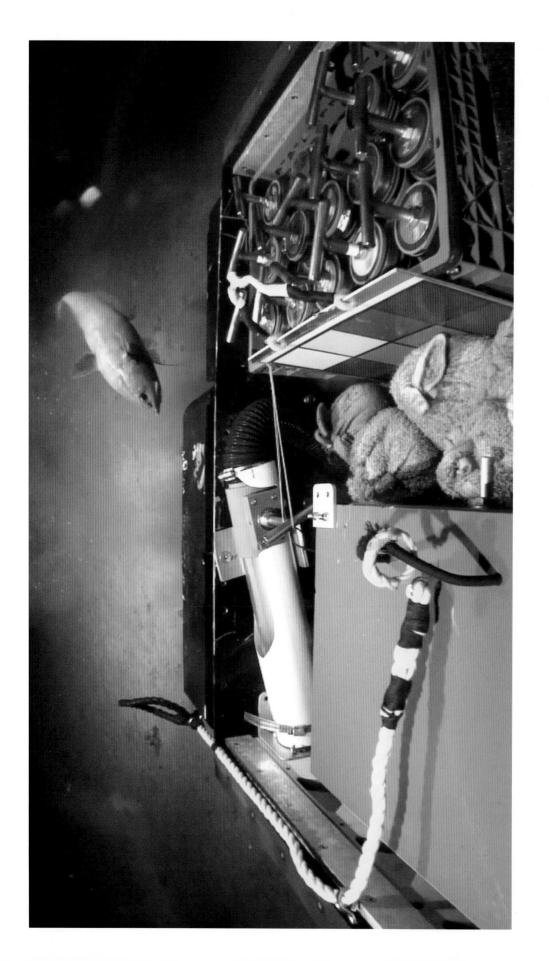

Deep CCZ Expedition: Exploring Abyssal Communities in the Pacific Ocean Before Deep-Sea Mining Begins.
Remotely Operated Vehicle (ROV) Lu'ukai showing interior with color calibration card and rattail fish.

Credit: https://oceanexplorer.noaa.gov/explorations/18ccz/logs/photolog/photolog.html#cbpi=../../media/ccz_video_070518.html

Notes from the Cracks of the Panthéon: On Symbolic Friction and the Possibility of Counterinstitutions

Niklas Plaetzer

Resisting the Enclosures of Theoretical Production

The challenge that the common(s) face under contemporary capitalism does not stop at the privatization of state property. As scholars and activists have shown since the Midnight Notes Collective coined the phrase "new enclosures" in 1990,[1] capital accumulation relies on the commodification of shared activities and spaces, even if their terrain can take radically heterogeneous forms: enclosures occur through the practice of logging in Brazilian Indigenous territories, the privatization of water in Senegal or postal services in the United States, and, not least, through the expansion of capital's "new frontiers" into spaces of digital labor and biotechnology.[2] The very "notion of the common is a result of privatizations, attempts at appropriation, and the complete commodification of the body, knowledge, land, air and water."[3] Paradoxically, an especially thorny problem for resistance against these enclosures arises from the fact that *theories* of "the common(s)" are *themselves* continually drawn into processes of commodification. More dramatically, invoking the commons can today operate as a "call to order," in the sense that Fred Moten and Stefano Harney give to the term: a switch from ongoing, opaque, and dissonant forms of cooperation to the mapped spaces of sovereign control, book projects, and research grants—and hence right back into the circuits of profitable knowledge production. "Critique endangers the sociality it is supposed to defend" rings true as a warning for all those who are committed to common worlds beyond the product life cycles that are proper to critical theory.[4]

At a time when the "sharing economy" is recognized by the European Union as a key to future competitiveness, it can hardly be surprising that discourses around the common(s) have been woven into the fabric of neoliberal governance.[5] There is a great risk involved when "minor-key sensibilities are made major, put right there for all to see yet not caring who the hell is doing the seeing," as Marquis Bey has put it. "Fugitive gatherings and devious assemblages draw the attention of forces of governance and control."[6] Emmanuel Macron, for instance, was able to vacuously declare that "the common is created on the level of a city, a town, a country, or a continent. We share the same adventure because we have decided to do so,"[7] even as the streets of French cities were swept by precarized workers in yellow vests and subsequent clouds of tear gas—every Saturday, for more than 60 weeks. In fact, the Yellow Vest movement (*Gilets jaunes*), which began in November 2018 and only found a provisional ending with the caesura of the coronavirus lockdown, appears emblematic for the contested boundaries of political space.

1
Midnight Notes Collective, *New Enclosures* (Brooklyn, NY: Autonomedia, 1990).
2
Sandro Mezzadra and Brett Neilson, *Border as Method, or, the Multiplication of Labor* (Durham, NC, and London: Duke University Press, 2013), 295.
3
Silvia Federici, quoted in Veronica Gago, "Entrevista: Cuentos de Bruja," *Pagina/12*, April 15, 2011, https://www.pagina12.com.ar/diario/suplementos/las12/13-6441-2011-04-15.html.
4
Fred Moten and Stefano Harney, *The Undercommons: Fugitive Planning & Black Study* (London: Minor Compositions, 2013), 19.
5
European Economic and Social Committee, "Collaborative or Participatory Consumption: A Sustainable Model for the 21st Century," *Official Journal of the European Union*, OJ C 177 (2014): 1–8.
6
Marquis Bey, *Them Goon Rules: Fugitive Essays on Radical Black Feminism* (Tucson: University of Arizona Press, 2019), 53.
7
Emmanuel Macron, "Discours du Président de la République au Cirque Jules Vernes d'Amiens," Elysée Palace, Paris, November 21, 2019, https://www.elysee.fr/emmanuel-macron/2019/11/21/amiens-est-capitale-europeenne-de-la-jeunesse-2020-le-message-demmanuel-macron-a-cette-occasion.

8
"Acte XVIII: Dans toute la France, des convergences entre 'gilets jaunes' et manifestants pour le climat," *Médiapart*, March 16, 2019, https://www.mediapart.fr/journal/france/160319/acte-xviii-dans-toute-la-france-des-convergences-entre-gilets-jaunes-et-manifestants-pour-le-climat.

9
See Linda Zerilli, *A Democratic Theory of Judgment* (Chicago: University of Chicago Press, 2016), 28–29.

10
Miguel Abensour, *Democracy against the State: Marx and the Machiavellian Moment*, trans. Max Blechman and Martin Breaugh (Cambridge, UK, and Malden, MA: Polity Press, 2011).

11
"The Call of Yellow Vests, Commercy Assembly," *Altersummit*, January 27, 2019, http://www.altersummit.eu/IMG/pdf/call_commercy_eng.pdf. For a particularly lucid analysis of the Yellow Vest movement on this point, see Stefan Kipfer, "What Colour Is Your Vest? Reflections on the Yellow Vest Movement in France," *Studies in Political Economy* 100, no. 3 (2019): 209–231.

12
Hannah Arendt, *On Revolution* (London and New York: Penguin Books, 1965), 202.

The Yellow Vests emerged from an opposition to raising taxes on car fuel, but they later marched with radical ecologists to demand government action against climate change.[8] Their meeting space was not the factory floor but the *rond-point* (roundabout), and their movement resonated in areas where deindustrialization and political alienation have gone hand in hand for decades. The Yellow Vests' revolt also spoke to precarized workers in cities—workers for whom the lifeworlds of traditional labor seemed like an antiquated ideal. Party politicians on the Left and Right, as well as union leaders, were taken by surprise when the Yellow Vests hit the streets, giving expression to a changed economy and unruly visions of the future. But what the *giletsjaunisation* of French politics also demonstrated was that a common *space* of political action did not flow from common *interests* or from the nature of public *goods* to be defended. There was no automatism involved as alliances were forged, cut off, and refigured. Common space turned out to be a fragile achievement as actors engaged in unexpected forms of translation between incongruous viewpoints and tried to give permanence to what at all times risked remaining a riotlike sequence of ephemeral events.

How to give institutional expression to the struggle for the commons if one can never determine the shape of political space in advance? How to engage in political action if what is *political* in the first place is never the *object* per se—a public hospital, the French nation, one's burnout symptoms, or the car used for Uber driving—but ever only the *mode* in which actors gather around it?[9] And what form could a struggle for the commons take that does not inadvertently fall back into depoliticized governance? How, in other words, could one avoid the transformation of "insurgent democracy"[10] into routinized "mini-publics," convened so as to *not* disrupt the workings of smooth administration? The question of an *insurgent institutional form* found a response in the Yellow Vests' experiments with communalism, including an "Assembly of Assemblies" that brought together elected delegations from around France.[11] But even within the movement, the deliberative spaces of Commercy and Saint-Nazaire remained at a distance from the riotous experience of impromptu demonstrations, the *manifs sauvages*. Would it be possible to combine the "'revolutionary' act of beginning something entirely new" with a "conservative care, which will shield this new beginning"[12]—give it a framework, without in the same gesture undermining its newness, its radical plurality, and, above all, its opposition to intractable mechanisms of repression and appropriation?

Frictional Spaces:
Gilets jaunes and *Gilets noirs*

If a counterinstitution is to be more than an abstract possibility, it must combine the *permanence* of common space with a *dissonance* that becomes generative for actors from plural standpoints.[13] A counterinstitution of the commons cannot replicate a depoliticized structure of state-administered goods if it aims to challenge an economic system that is very well able to thrive on state ownership and centralized management; neither could such an institution assume the *preexistence* of a common interest or a shared identity, as long as its commitments point beyond national citizenship and the all-too-often violent limitations of "community." Against the logics of administration and identity, the commons as a counterinstitution need to undertake the balancing act of permanence and radical novelty; they become a collective project in need of what José Medina has called "beneficial epistemic friction."[14] Such friction occurs between actors who never assemble around already given objects of concern but constitute these objects *as common* to the extent that their relation also pushes them *to become somebody else*: common space is a space of unsettled selfhood, or it is not common.

In the case of the Yellow Vests, epistemic friction could be observed and experienced when former working-class voters of the extreme right found themselves marching and discussing with feminist and anti-racist activists like Assa Traoré, a leader of the fight against police violence in the *banlieue*.[15] One of the centers of the Yellow Vest movement was La Réunion, in the Indian Ocean, where geographies of center and periphery as much as widely held assumptions about the movement's racial composition became subverted.[16] In the streets of the metropole, too, a yellow safety vest moved from an emblem of sameness to a fluorescent, floating signifier for a constitutively plural phenomenon.[17] It was the simple act of putting on neon-colored, high-visibility clothing that not only meant a shared (though without a doubt racially differentiated) sense of exposure to the physical threat of police control. It also provided a weekly starting point for unscripted encounters with others who were both *equal* and *unlike* one another. At that moment, the yellow vest became a counterinstitution and perhaps the symbol of citizenship itself.[18]

But the most powerful instances of productive dissonance were enacted by those who, in the eyes of the state, were noncitizens: the Black Vests, or *Gilets noirs*. The Yellow Vest demonstrations

13
The question of the institution has (finally) become a central concern in the most recent debates on the commons, providing a counterpoint to an earlier enthusiasm about extra-institutional flows. Michael Hardt and Antonio Negri, *Assembly* (Oxford: Oxford University Press, 2017), 37–39.

14
José Medina, *The Epistemology of Resistance: Gender and Racial Oppression, Epistemic Injustice, and the Social Imagination* (Oxford: Oxford University Press, 2013), 23–26, 50–56.

15
Ludo Simbille and Thomas Clerget, "À la marche pour Adama Traoré: 'Nous sommes des gilets jaunes depuis notre naissance,'" *Basta!*, July 26, 2019, https://www.bastamag.net/A-la-marche-pour-Adama-Traore-Nous-sommes-des-gilets-jaunes-depuis-notre.

16
Christiane Rafidinaviro, "Essor et déclin des 'gilets jaunes' de la Réunion dans l'espace public," *The Conversation*, March 1, 2020, https://theconversation.com/essor-et-declin-des-gilets-jaunes-de-la-reunion-dans-lespace-public-131958.

17
See Félix Boggio Ewanjé-Epée, "Le gilet jaune comme signifiant flottant," *Contretemps*, November 22, 2018, https://www.contretemps.eu/gilets-jaunes-signifiant-flottant/.

18
My analysis draws on Étienne Balibar, who has insightfully discussed the Yellow Vests as a "counter-power" (*contre-pouvoir*). Étienne Balibar, "Gilets jaunes: le sens du face à face," *Médiapart*, December 13, 2018, https://blogs.mediapart.fr/etienne-balibar/blog/131218/gilets-jaunes-le-sens-du-face-face.

19
Plateforme Enquête Militante, "'We will go until the end, on lâchera rien!,' interview with Gilets Noirs," *Verso Blog*, October 31, 2019, https://www.versobooks.com/blogs/4473-we-will-go-until-the-end-on-lachera-rien-interview-with-gilets-noirs.

20
Camille Baker, "A 'Black Vests' Movement Emerges in France to Protest Treatment of Undocumented Migrants," *The Intercept*, October 27, 2019, https://theintercept.com/2019/10/27/france-black-vests-gilets-noirs/.

21
Jacques Rancière, *Disagreement: Politics and Philosophy* (Minneapolis: University of Minnesota Press, 1999), 25.

22
See Ayten Gündoğdu, *Rightlessness in an Age of Rights: Hannah Arendt and the Contemporary Struggle of Migrants* (Oxford: Oxford University Press, 2015).

23
A video recording of *Gilets noirs* speeches (produced by the activist news collective Redfish) can be found online at https://www.facebook.com/watch/live/?v=402005627083378.

24
"'Black Vests' protestors storm Panthéon in Paris," *BBC*, July 12, 2019, https://www.bbc.com/news/world-europe-48969438.

had begun on November 17, 2018, bringing thousands of mostly white working-class protesters to the streets; nine days later, the *Gilets noirs* emerged on the scene of French politics through the occupation of the National Immigration Museum.[19] Many of the *Gilets noirs* had a long-standing involvement with migrant self-organization in the collective *La Chapelle Debout*, which had itself come up in the context of the social movement *Nuit Debout* in 2016. On July 12, 2019, about 700 protesters stormed the Panthéon in Paris and occupied this symbolic space of the French national imaginary for several hours.[20] Most of them were undocumented migrants from Francophone West Africa, working precarious jobs in the Paris metropolitan area. With the occupation of the Panthéon, they brought their claim to be heard to a new level of visibility. Not only did they "invade" one of the most visited touristic sites of France; they also had the audacity to assemble peacefully for hours, sing "La Marseillaise," and draw on memories of French revolutionary citizenship. Their occupation presented itself as what Jacques Rancière calls a "staging of a nonexistent right"—an enactment of precisely the citizenship that they are denied.[21]

The Black Vests did not petition the French state for legal concessions but cast themselves as the most vivid embodiment of its revolutionary principles; they did not ask the Republic to live up to its unfulfilled promises but immediately *performed* its normative contradictions.[22] Under the dome of the Panthéon on July 12, 2019—two days before Bastille Day, *le 14 juillet*—the speeches of the *Gilets noirs* denounced the violence of borders and recounted crushing experiences of racialized dehumanization. But they also, with a sense of dignified irony, referenced Jean-Jacques Rousseau and Victor Hugo, buried just underneath their assembly space. In denouncing the state's impostrous claim to the revolutionary heritage, they configured themselves as its true heirs.[23] As if in confirmation, the *Gilets noirs* were beaten, tear-gassed, and pepper-sprayed by riot police, with 37 arrests made, some (if not all) of which entailed deportation to their respective countries of legal citizenship in Africa.[24]

On the Brittle Grounds of the Panthéon

The *Gilets noirs* enacted the citizenship they did not have, drawing on the symbolic resources of French republicanism, as in the case of the Panthéon occupation, and consciously linking their struggle to the ongoing movement of the *Gilets jaunes*. But they certainly did not affirm any glorious past that could already define the outlines of an existing, supposedly "common" space. During the Panthéon occupation, the *Gilets noirs* instead made reference to memories of colonialism and enslavement—both to the transatlantic slave trade and to the ongoing enslavement of migrants in North Africa, placing their own fight in a larger, non-Eurocentric lineage of marronage and anti-colonial resistance.[25] One can also complicate the singing of "La Marseillaise" as an echo of previous counter-stagings of French republican symbols by Haitian maroons in 1802, as famously recounted by C. L. R. James in *Black Jacobins* (1938).[26] The *Gilets noirs*, assembled in the Panthéon, pointed not only to the tomb of Rousseau but also that of Aimé Césaire.[27] They claimed the principles of revolutionary fraternity in the same moment that they also highlighted the memory of Senegalese *Tirailleurs*—troops who liberated Paris from Nazi occupation in August 1944 but were never publicly recognized—and their performance staged a form of French republicanism that simultaneously broke away from the weight of *laïcité* when demanding access to prayer rooms for Muslim migrants. Finally, their speeches drew a line between the French participation in the historical slave trade, on the one hand, and the European Union's contemporary outsourcing of border control to Libya, which provides the conditions for the dehumanizing of migrants as commodities to be bought and sold on slave markets, as a CNN report showed in 2017.[28]

Historian Michael Rothberg has offered the notion of "multidirectional memory" in order to account for the ways in which historical events resonate with memories from supposedly distinct contexts.[29] Rothberg's work traces perhaps surprising encounters between memories of the Holocaust and those of colonialism: Memory is here no longer imagined as a zero-sum game between mutually exclusive traditions or events to remember. Instead, the politics of memory comes alive through the unforeseen and self-altering encounters between perspectives that are not only plural in their differences but internally: "The archive of multidirectional memory," Rothberg writes, "is irreducibly transversal; it cuts across genres, national contexts, periods and cultural traditions."[30]

Rights claims of migrant movements have been at their most powerful not when they find the most effective legal argument but rather when their action manages to draw on the ambiguities within the symbolic space of the nation-state. In such rights claims, the figures of *the migrant*, *the citizen*, and *the maroon* merge within a dissonant ensemble: a common space is produced through the *creolization* of subjects

25
Niklas Plaetzer, "Fugitive World-Building: Rethinking the Cosmopolitics of Anti-Slavery Struggle with Arendt and Glissant," in Tamara Caraus and Elena Paris, eds., *Migration, Protest Movements and the Politics of Resistance: A Radical Political Philosophy of Cosmopolitanism* (London and New York: Routledge, 2018), 186–204.

26
C. L. R. James, *Black Jacobins: Toussaint L'Ouverture and the San Domingo Revolution* (1938; repr., New York: Vintage Books, 1989), 317–318.

27
See Redfish video material, fn23. On Aimé Césaire's counter-stagings of French citizenship, see Gary Wilder, *Freedom Time: Negritude, Decolonization, and the Future of the World* (Durham, NC, and London: Duke University Press, 2015).

28
"Migrants Being Sold as Slaves," CNN, November 13, 2017, https://edition.cnn.com/videos/world/2017/11/13/libya-migrant-slave-auction-lon-orig-md-ejk.cnn.

29
Michael Rothberg, *Multidirectional Memory: Remembering the Holocaust in the Age of Decolonization* (Stanford, CA: Stanford University Press, 2009).

30
Ibid., 18.

31
Édouard Glissant, *Poetics of Relation*, trans. Betsy Wing (Ann Arbor: University of Michigan Press, 1997).

32
John Drabinski, *Glissant and the Middle Passage: Philosophy, Beginning, Abyss* (Minneapolis: University of Minnesota Press, 2019), 16.

33
Massimiliano Tomba has proposed the notion of "chronotones" (from the Greek, *chronos*, "time," and *tonos*, "tension") to describe "the friction generated by the sliding of different temporal layers." Massimiliano Tomba, *Insurgent Universality: An Alternative Legacy of Modernity* (Oxford: Oxford University Press, 2019), 10.

34
An earlier version of this paper was presented at the Immigration Theory Workshop at the University of Houston Law Center (February 20, 2020), organized by Professor Daniel Morales. My discussion in Houston centered on the generative friction that emerges from the principle of fraternity in the French constitution. I would like to thank Professor Morales for this opportunity and all participants for their generous comments.

who are pushed to relate differently to others and themselves.[31] Such a creolizing interaction of perspectives "refuses to make either the space between or the material sites of contact legible, but rather keeps the opaqueness of the unknown and chaos in motion alongside the known and the ordered."[32] The *Gilets noirs* are a powerful example of this interstitial process insofar as their Panthéon occupation gave rise to an insurgent excess from the crossroads of memories and brought it to bear on the Yellow Vest movement, which, similarly, drew much of its force from an activating relationship to collective memory.

The possibility of counterinstitutions hence does not arise from the space of a radical elsewhere but within the cracks of supposedly stable institutions—which, it turns out, overflow with *frictional* signification: the Panthéon, the law, "La Marseillaise." Where the democratically generative exercise of *epistemic friction* appears as crucial for the production of common space between differently situated subjects, the permanence of political space relies on the *symbolic friction* between the always noncongruent layers of institutionalized memories and collective imaginings.[33] Epistemic friction concerns the plural undoing of deep-seated ways of seeing and looking away, challenging the blind spots that are limiting the social production of knowledge. Symbolic friction, on the other hand, refers to the always tension-ridden interplay of layers of signification in institutional symbols, which animates the production of political space. Such points of symbolic friction designate the sites at which common space is constructed across plural standpoints, precisely through the non-identity of the object held in common—whether it is the built environment of the Panthéon, a yellow safety vest, or perhaps even the page of a constitutional text, understood not as a legal framework but as an overflowing repository of significations that begin to act up.[34]

"La rue elle est à qui ? Elle est à nous !"
("Whose street? Our street!")

If common political space as a counterinstitution never consolidates into a fixed legal framework or objects in the world (that is, as "public goods," of which the "publicness" would be beyond dispute), it would also be naive to think that the *struggle for the commons* could, in any simple way, operate through the *language of the commons*. Here is the paradox: Just like the struggle for universal rights might not always operate most effectively through the discourse of universalism, the struggle for the commons also has to be constantly on the lookout for reversals into domination.[35] The *Gilets noirs* are acutely aware that any demand for "integration" would amount to the consolidation of a nation-state citizenship from which they have been violently excluded. But in publicly staging the excess of citizenship, cracks in the hegemonic imaginary begin to coalesce and open up the space of a counterinstitution. Similarly, the yellow vest was such a massively successful symbol because its signification was both empty and full to the brim: a yellow safety vest with no political meaning up to autumn 2018—but also a symbol of visibility, available to anybody, a symbol that could be interpreted as an homage to the historical sans-culottes.[36]

Where other movements appeared and faded away, the Yellow Vests stayed on and institutionalized themselves as a weekly "fraternal disorder,"[37] laying a claim to common ownership of the streets in French cities. Whereas the excitement about the commons among urban planners in air-conditioned conference rooms might signify danger for popular movements, *Gilets jaunes* and *Gilets noirs* tangled up timelines of collective memory and punctured public spaces. Their appropriation of space was not only a physical takeover but also an act of self-narration in which stories that had silently run parallel now crisscrossed, giving way to multidirectional flows that were experienced as painful and disturbing by privileged actors who had imagined themselves as self-identical and well established. The symbolic friction of *Gilets jaunes* and *Gilets noirs* thereby exposed myths of comfort and tranquility amidst an uprooting whirlwind of political and economic transformations.

"Men fight and lose the battle, and the thing that they fought for comes about in spite of their defeat, and when it comes it turns out not to be what they meant, and other men have to fight for what they meant under another name," wrote the utopian socialist and radical textile designer William Morris in 1886.[38] As the language of the commons is being smoothed out by corporate actors eager to explore the next frontier of a profit-driven "sharing economy," the Yellow Vests can inspire a more serious reflection about the forms that an insurgent practice of the commons might take, so as to resist the seemingly inevitable onslaught of cooptation by a neoliberal governance that runs on "disruption." Building the commons as a counterinstitution is by no means reducible to the exceptional spaces of social movements. Points of symbolic friction also began to form the outlines of a counterinstitution when a curator put up Kehinde Wiley's painting of a black man on a horse entitled "Napoleon Leading the Army over the Alps" (2005)

35
In 1997, Étienne Balibar put the challenge as follows: "Can solidarity emerge from *one single discourse*, or at least a *common discourse*, a *shared discourse*? We must discover the mode of reciprocity not in the abstract but within actual painful experience." Étienne Balibar, "Algeria, France: One Nation or Two?," in *Giving Ground: The Politics of Propinquity*, ed. Joan Copjec and Michael Sorkin (London and New York: Verso, 1999), 163.

36
Sophie Wahnich, "The Structure of Current Mobilizations Correspond to That of the Sans-Culottes," *Verso Blog*, December 9, 2018, https:// www.versobooks.com/ blogs/4160-the-structure-of-current-mobilizations-corresponds-to-that-of-the-sans-culottes.

37
Abensour, *Democracy against the State*, xxv.

38
See Philippa Bennett and Rosie Miles, eds., *William Morris in the Twenty-First Century* (Bern: Peter Lang Publishing, 2010), 1.

39
"Kehinde Wiley rencontre Jacques-Louis David," *Musée national du château de Malmaison*, September 23, 2019, https://musees-nationaux-malmaison. fr/chateau-malmaison/ actualite/c-wiley-rencontre-david-malmaison-du-9-octobre-2019-au-6-janvier-2020.

40
See Medina, *The Epistemology of Resistance*, 309.

41
Decolonial feminist Françoise Vergès engaged with Wiley's painting in her multimedia performance "Les fantômes au musée" on November 17, 2019, putting emphasis on the resonance/dissonance between the figures of Napoléon Bonaparte and Toussaint L'Ouverture.

42
Guy Keulemans, "The Geo-cultural Conditions of Kintsugi," *Journal of Modern Craft* 9, no. 1 (2016): 16.

in the castle of the notorious statesman who, in 1802, reintroduced slavery in the French Empire.[39] Through this curatorial intervention, institutional space is not undone but subverted insofar as the staging of the piece is experienced as uncomfortable by the museum's visitors. If (and only if) they find themselves pushed toward a "kaleidoscopic social imagination" under the impact of disturbance, the curatorial choice has achieved some measure of success.[40] Common space was hence generated, combining the durational time of the museum with perhaps involuntary shifts in the political imagination of visitors across various standpoints.[41]

Dating back to the 17th century, kintsugi, the Japanese art of broken pottery in which the edges of fragments are not fixed but mended with gold, might serve as an image for the dissonance of counterinstitutions. In kintsugi pottery, brokenness is not plastered over and hidden but itself becomes the starting point for a "transformative repair craft" in which "precious metals [are used] to draw attention to the object and transform the object's appearance, in contrast to other forms of repair that attempt to hide a history of damage."[42] What if we were to picture the *Gilets jaunes* and *Gilets noirs* as practitioners of kintsugi, assembling the fragments of French republicanism? And what if architects and urban planners were to become deserters of mapmaking and reinvent their profession as the production of interstices? They would have to learn how to be attuned to incompletion, consciously (if perhaps secretly) hoping to cut open spaces for politics that can never be planned in advance. Perhaps the question of common space stands itself in need of reformulation—beyond the transparency of a research agenda around the commons, which is at risk of a dialectical reversal, feeding dreams of enclosure among corporate architects and state administrators in the very moment one tries to resist them. Designing for the sake of *politicizing commons*, one would have to learn how to attend to fissures within and across collective memory. If one takes Morris's warning seriously, the construction of common space as unruly and constitutively dissonant might thus have to proceed under another name. Or, perhaps, under the *same name* but in *another color:* neither concrete grey nor green-washed, but more like a fluorescent yellow.

Transient Spatial Commoning in Conflict

Taraneh Meshkani

The recent urbanization processes that have been shaped predominantly by the interests of the neoliberal economy are being reimagined through alternative forms of urban appropriations. These responses to capital accumulation and enclosure forces happen either through creative resource management or new modes of organizing. The most frequent examples of both resource management and cooperation practices within the idea of commons in an urban context tend to be the community gardens and squatting. Yet social movements are crucial episodes where, through various spatial practices, the urban space is used to create organizations outside capitalist relations.

A series of political protests erupted at the beginning of the 21st century and escalated into a new wave of social-political movements after the 2008 global economic crisis. Starting with the Arab Spring uprisings in the Middle East, they quickly spawned major regional and global movements such as Occupy Wall Street, Euromaidan, Umbrella Revolution, and the most recent Black Lives Matter movement, among others. The outreach and scale of the recent movements have grown with new forms of digital communication. For example, according to several polls, about 15 to 26 million people participated in the Black Lives Matter movement, making it possibly the biggest civil rights movement in US history.[1]

These expressive forms of collectivism actualize new modes of sharing, cooperation, and social existence in the act of political resistance, forming temporary commons. Even though many recent movements attempted to prolong their presence through the creation of autonomous tent cities that were in one form or another self-sustaining, their commoning practices tend to be mostly transitory. The use of objects of visibility, monuments, and rituals are among such methods. While the social movements and, subsequently, many of these new practices are temporary, they help create the space that nurtures a new culture of common life.

Much of the discourse on commons is centered on external resources, thus excluding the understanding of it as a social and political practice that can (re)produce both resources and social relations. Early discussions primarily focused on the concept of shared resources and its relation to the historical origin of "the commons" in the medieval European feudal system. In 1968 Garrett Hardin published an article in the journal *Science* introducing the "tragedy of the commons."[2] Hardin called into question the concept of commons as a shared but subtractable resource, claiming that, without regulation and private ownership, the individual would exploit and overuse it without limit. The concept

1
Larry Buchanan, Quoctrung Bui, and Jugal K. Patel, "Black Lives Matter May Be the Largest Movement in U.S. History," *New York Times*, July 3, 2020, https://www.nytimes.com/interactive/2020/07/03/us/george-floyd-protests-crowd-size.html.

2
Garrett Hardin, "The Tragedy of the Commons," *Science* 162, no. 3859 (1968): 1243–1248.

of the inevitable destruction of the commons was questioned by Elinor Ostrom, who won the Nobel Prize for Economics by providing empirical examples of efficient cooperation, sharing, and management of resources such as fisheries, grazing lands, forests, by commonslike organizations outside the state and market-driven interventions.[3]

In recent theoretical work written on commons, three elements are often highlighted in defining the concept.[4] For example, according to Massimo De Angelis: "All commons involve some sort of common pool of resources, . . . the commons are necessarily created and sustained by *communities* . . . the third and most important element in terms of conceptualizing the commons is the verb 'to common'—the social process that creates and reproduces the commons."[5] Hence, in relation to the sociopolitical viewpoint of the commons, "it might be better to keep the word as a verb, an activity, rather than as a noun, a substantive,"[6] as stated by Peter Linebaugh. While these discussions of the commons have taken place since the 1960s, the term "urban commons" has become a point of debate only in more recent years. Two key factors have led to this development. The first is rapid urbanization across the world, which has changed the access to resources and the way of life for billions of people. The second is the effect of neoliberal economic policies that have taken hold over the past several decades and have most aggressively exploited cities and created new spatial inequalities.

The urban common space is often interpreted as a physical public space—a square, a street, a park, or a public institution—that is managed by authorities or private entities. Yet it is critical to highlight that commons lie beyond the domains of the public and the private, and thus urban commons is not synonymous with public space. There are limitations to the conception of public space as an open and accessible milieu. The historical forms of public space, even before the emergence of capitalism, have involved some processes of enclosure. This element can be seen everywhere from the male-citizen-dominated agoras to the medieval public spaces, which were owned by lords or kings, to the privately owned public spaces of our time. The inclusive public spaces that are considered a shared resource with access open to all tend not to be the norm, and most examples have some form of limitation on who, when, and where they can be accessed. As stated by David Harvey, "Public spaces and public goods in the city have always been a matter of state power and public administration, and such spaces and goods do not necessarily a commons make. . . . It takes political action on the part of citizens and the people to appropriate them or to make them so."[7]

3
Elinor Ostrom, *Governing the Commons: The Evolution of Institutions for Collective Action* (Cambridge: Cambridge University Press, 1990).

4
The three elements of commons have been referenced in the works of many scholars such as Massimo De Angelis, Andreas Exner and Brigitte Kratzwald, Silke Helfrich, David Harvey, and Elinor Ostrom.

5
"On the Commons: A Public Interview with Massimo de Angelis and Stavros Stavrides," *An Architektur* 23 (2010): 4–27, https://www.e-flux.com/journal/17/67351/on-the-commons-a-public-interview-with-massimo-de-angelis-and-stavros-stavrides/.

6
Peter Linebaugh, *The Magna Carta Manifesto: Liberties and Commons for All* (Berkeley: University of California Press, 2008), 279.

7
David Harvey, *Rebel Cities: From the Right to the City to the Urban Revolution* (New York: Verso, 2012), 73.

8
Henri Lefebvre, "The Right to the City, Writings on Cities," trans. Eleonore Kofman and Elizabeth Lebas (Oxford: Blackwell, 1996), 158.

9
Other writers who expanded on the idea of the "Right to the City" include Neil Brenner, Chris Butler, Margaret Crawford, Mustafa Dikec, David Harvey, Peter Marcuse, Margit Mayer, and Mark Purcell.

10
Peter Marcuse, "From Critical Urban Theory to the Right to the City," *City* 13, nos. 2–3 (2009): 185–197, 190.

11
Michael Hardt, "Politics of the Common," *Contribution to the Reimagining Society Project Hosted by ZCommunications, Boston* 6 (2009).

12
Ruud Kaulingfreks and Femke Kaulingfreks, "The Square as the Place of the Commons," in *Perspectives on Commoning: Autonomist Principles and Practices*, ed. Guido Ruivenkamp and Andy Hilton (London: Zed Books, 2017), 291–325.

Following the distinction between public space and commons, the focus on a sociopolitical perspective to the commons brings forth the discussions on spatial justice and the Right to the City movement. In 1968 Henri Lefebvre underpinned the term "Right to the City" as a "cry and demand,"[8] which was further expanded by David Harvey and Peter Marcuse, among others.[9] According to Marcuse, the right is "a cry out of necessity and a demand for something more . . . an exigent demand by those deprived of basic material and existing legal rights, and an aspiration for the future by those discontented with life as they see it around them, perceived as limiting their own potentials for growth and creativity."[10] The "Right to the City" becomes an essential way to view commoning practices in times of conflict since, more and more, urban public spaces are getting privatized, reconfigured, surveilled, and made inaccessible. Meanwhile, there is also a need for the commons from capital, which should be distinguished from the demands of the public. According to Michael Hardt, "There is emerging a powerful contradiction . . . at the heart of capitalist production between the need for the common in the interest of productivity and the need for the private in the interest of capitalist accumulation."[11] In the same way, there is also a contradiction in how the state constructs and attempts to use major squares, such as Tiananmen Square in Beijing, which was initially utilized for communication between the party leaders and the masses but ended up as a space of protest and occupation.[12]

The public's material and symbolic appropriation of the space can be seen in the demands for social restructuring and imagining utopian future alternatives in times of social movements. While the literature on commons mainly focuses on the stable modes of commoning, social movements create a more transient form of urban commons. This often happens through spatial repertoires of contention that are reutilized, optimized, and in many cases created during the protest actions. These transient repertoires have different life spans. While some are frequently used among various movements, others are unique and reflect local and cultural conditions. The methods can apply at the scale of a building, an urban square, a neighborhood, or even a network of locations. While social media platforms have added a new layer of communication and visibility to the movements, there are myriad existing tactics that are also explored. The following are some case studies that demonstrate these arguments.

In times of conflict, commoners select certain spaces to reappropriate in ways that can meet their political objectives. The transitory nature of these political acts varies depending on the applicable method.

For example, during the 1960 Greensboro sit-ins, the individuals participating in the civil rights protest in the United States maintained their sit-in only as a temporary act during the restaurant's hours of operation. On the other hand, the 2014 occupation of Maidan Nezalezhnosti in Kiev lasted for four months. Throughout the occupation, Euromaidan was built into a fortress that became the epicenter of the movement, with multiple security-force raids that, at some points, resembled a war zone. Yet today the square has returned to normalcy, with little to no resemblance to the days of the occupation. In both cases, space was strategically selected. In the Greensboro sit-ins, protesters selected a space that they did not have the right to access, making the sit-in an act of defiance. In the case of Maidan Nezalezhnosti, the square had previously been utilized similarly during the 2004 Orange Revolution, making it an obvious choice for the new movement. As described, both the method and the spatial setting determined the duration of occupation.

While occupation is one form of reappropriation of space during social movements, many transient commoning strategies have been historically used to disseminate the message of the movement, to create visibility, and to interrupt the "distribution of sensible."[13] While the physical assembly of a large number of people is the most common form of creating visibility, a myriad of techniques can be used to generate the same effect. Use of umbrellas in Hong Kong and yellow vests in Paris, lights from mobile flashlights and candles in Bucharest and Seoul during night protests, the chants of "Allahu Akbar" from rooftops as a sign of defiance by protesters in Tehran, and Black Lives Matter being painted on city streets in the US are among the cases of creating the common space. The use of color can also be a great way to create commonality among the group, something that has been utilized in many political protests and revolutions over the past century. A recent example occurred in 2016 in Macedonia, where protesters used colored paints to tag administrative buildings in acts of defiance. A mobile practice of commoning takes place during rallies and marches that can cover large terrain depending on the number of participants. The March for Our Lives in 2018 in the United States had such a large turnout that it was visible via satellite imagery. On the other hand, the March for Justice in 2017 occurred over a 450 km route that spanned across multiple provinces in Turkey. The act of visibility is a way of marking the space, representing the collective, and creating a sense of unity among the commoners. The marking is ultimately transient since it will be erased once the protest action comes to an end. The spray paints will be washed, furniture and glass pieces will be swept, and the city will look even cleaner than before, with no trace and memory of the rebellion.

13
Jacques Rancière, *Dissensus: On Politics and Aesthetics*, ed. and trans. Steve Corcoran (London, New York: Continuum, 2010), 33.

Black Lives Matter street mural in Washington, DC, 2020.

Occasionally, there are novel and contextual techniques that are applied during social movements. During the 2011 Arab Spring in Cairo, since social media played an instrumental role, protesters installed blogger tents at Tahrir Square to adapt the space for those who were communicating with the outside world. During the 2014 Hong Kong protests, the demonstrators upgraded the amenities offered at the camp. "Freedom Quarter," which was a set of 100 hotel tents, allowed protesters to register at 8:30 PM and check out by noon the next day at no cost. The idea was to encourage more people to participate in the movement. Some of the tents also had addresses such as 2 Democracy Avenue, and protesters even received mail there through the postal services. Since these methods have not been tested and tried, they might be limited to a single occurrence and might work only in a local context.

The spatial aspect of commoning is multiscalar,[14] and with the formation of new technologies that are used as networks of resistance, it can be formed across a variety of geographical scales.[15] During the 1968 Poor People's Campaign, the organizers erected Resurrection City, where thousands of people from across the US occupied the National Mall in Washington with makeshift wooden shanties. Similar to the Poor People's Campaign, the Euromaidan movement started with one location in central

14
Peter Parker and Magnus Johansson, "Challenges and Potentials in Collaborative Management of Urban Commons," in *Multi-faceted Nature of Collaboration in the Contemporary World* (London: Vega Press, 2012).
15
Manuel Castells, *The Rise of the Network Society*, vol. 12 (Chicester: John Wiley & Sons, 2011).

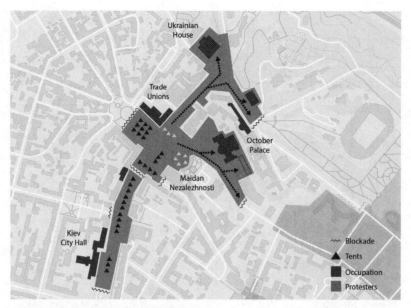

Euromaidan occupation in Kiev, Ukraine, 2014.

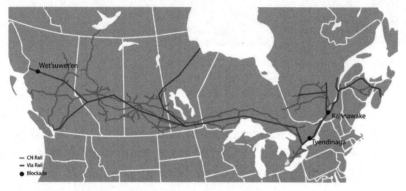

Indigenous anti-pipeline railway blockades in Canada, 2020.

Kiev, but over the course of the occupation, it expanded to multiple government administrative buildings across the city and eventually beyond it. In another incident, once the Lenin statue in Kiev was toppled, it created a ripple effect across Ukraine, with the toppling of hundreds of Lenin statues. In the recent Black Lives Matter movement, a similar ripple effect occurred after a Confederate statue was toppled in Alabama. In Canada in early 2020, during the anti-pipeline protests, Indigenous demonstrators occupied multiple locations on train tracks belonging to Via Rail Canada. While small in numbers and thousands of miles apart, the occupations significantly impacted Canada's supply-chain operations. This was an act that previously occurred during the 1990 Oka Crisis. Perhaps the largest multiscalar protest was the Occupy movement in 2011, which took place in multiple cities across the world, covering every continent except

Antarctica. Through a network of resistance, a movement can spread beyond the initial location and potentially expand its duration.

The practices of commoning in conflict are ephemeral, with events taking place over the span of hours to days and even months on some occasions. But all protests and occupations come to an end regardless of success or failure to achieve the movement's goals. Over time, through symbolism, these commoning practices as repertoires of contention become continuous and ingrained into the culture of resistance. In China, the creation of symbolic statues during the demonstrations has become a trend. During the 1989 Tiananmen Square protests, people built the Goddess of Democracy; about a decade later in Hong Kong, the Umbrella Man was built, and later, in 2019, Lady Liberty was created. In Ukraine, demonstrators first occupied the Maidan during the Orange Revolution of 2004 and repeated the same act during the Euromaidan crisis. The Red Shirts of Thailand are another movement that used color as a symbolic commoning.

Umbrella Man in Hong Kong, 2014.

During social movements, urban spaces become laboratories for experimenting with new forms of organizing and social relations. The formation of temporary commons during insurgencies, whether as spontaneous expressions or mobilized actions, generates new social and political practices beyond the already existing structures. The symbolism of space, repertoires, and even time can unite people across waves of conflict. The symbolic urban spaces help the reclamation process and reinforce the sense of commons. Commoners can pick up the movement where their predecessors left off and create transient common spaces of emancipation that transcend space and time.

Struggles for Housing:
Challenging Dominant Models of Cohabitation through Urban Commoning

Stavros Stavrides

Current struggles for housing, especially in key South American countries, are struggles that explicitly challenge both the predominance of market mechanisms in house production and the priorities of state policies. Those struggles develop demands and practices that actually reclaim the city as commons and connect to traditions of mutual help that have developed in urban populations, especially the poor and the marginalized. It is by struggling for decent housing and by organizing in order to build communities of struggle based on solidarity and sharing that people actively experience urban commoning as a force of social change. With hope for a just society of equals, commoning becomes a shared ethos and a developing matrix of cohabitation rules.

As people build their power and their inspirational momentum on a widely acknowledged feeling of escalating urban injustices, struggles for housing often challenge established stereotypes concerning the "house" and its relation to the city. The demand for decent housing in a "just city" questions the predominance of the privately owned, family-stronghold model, considered as the cornerstone of every housing project. By claiming the right to housing, current movements in Brazil, Uruguay, Mexico, Peru, and other South American countries actually challenge the prevailing individualist ethos and explore the potentialities of sharing and cooperation. They thus directly connect, as we will see, the practices of urban commoning to confrontations with the dominant political system.

For James Holston, an emphasis on "localism and strategic particularism," which valorizes "the constitutive role of conflict and ambiguity in shaping the multiplicity of contemporary urban life," indeed "works against the modernist absorption of citizenship into a project of state building."[1] Although he himself warns us against the dangers of basing planning and design strategies solely on the local (and the "local enactments of democracy" that may "produce anti-democratic results"), he explicitly draws attention to a prevailing social imaginary that cannot go beyond a statist understanding of social organization. Citizenship is indeed a quality and an attribute that can be acquired through practices that challenge dominant modes of governance and dominant urban order. This is how citizenship claims can contribute to a "politicization of the *oikos*"[2] through explicit struggles for the right to the city shaped by demands for decent housing.

As the Brazilian architectural theorist Pedro Fiori Arantes suggests: "The main problem to be faced is not just the deficit of housing units but, above all, the deficit of urban qualities or, simply put, a deficit of the city and, indirectly, a deficit of citizenship."[3] We may relate

1
James Holston, "Spaces of Insurgent Citizenship," in *Cities and Citizenship*, ed. J. Holston (Durham, NC: Duke University Press, 1998), 171.
2
James Holston, *Insurgent Citizenship: Disjunctions of Democracy and Modernity in Brazil* (Princeton, NJ: Princeton University Press, 2008), 312.
3
Pedro Fiori Arantes, *The Rent of Form: Architecture and Labor in the Digital Age* (Minneapolis: University of Minnesota Press, 2019), 230.

this formulation with Henri Lefebvre's approach to citizenship. As he suggests, a new "stipulated, contractual citizenship"[4] is needed in order to establish the fundamental human rights not made explicit in the Declaration of the French Revolution. This kind of citizenship will challenge the omnipotence of the state, opening a process that will "cause the political State to wither away."[5] One of the most important rights included in Lefebvre's redefinition of citizenship is the "right to the city": "The link between 'being a city-dweller' and citizenship is inevitable in societies that are becoming urbanized."[6]

Many housing movements that developed in Latin America (and especially in Brazil, Mexico, and Uruguay, as we will see) have made this connection between the lack of housing for the poor and their expulsion from the "official" city—that is, from the urban conditions that ensure the fundamental rights that constitute citizenship. Demanding decent housing and often forcing authorities to yield to their demands, such movements explicitly refer to the need for constructing communities of cohabitation even prior to the actual construction of their houses. In Mexico, activists talk about the "construction of popular power" through organized housing struggles.[7] And Uruguayan housing "cooperativists" sing an anthem that goes: "houses are just the beginning, not the end."[8]

We may connect this growing awareness of the important link between the right to housing and the reclaiming of citizenship rights by the excluded to a term adopted by the Mexican theorist Gustavo Esteva: *communalidad*. This is not a term to describe the feeling of togetherness only but also, crucially, "the juxtaposition of commons and polity." According to Esteva, through *communalidad* (translated rather unsuccessfully as commonality), a "horizon of intelligibility" is formed in which you learn to "see and experience the world as a 'we.'"[9]

This "we," however, is not the "we" of a homogeneous community. Exactly because such communities are shaped through a common scope—and not through the reproduction of shared identities (racial, national, and so on)—they do not simply tolerate differences but actually profit from them. As Gerardo Meza, a Mexican autonomous neighborhood activist, puts it:

> Here we belong to different cultures. But we all meet in everyday praxis. Voluntary or community work is something common in indigenous communities. But in cities, too, a similar tradition exists, so comrades are used to it. Instead of allowing a culture to dominate all the others we combine them: for example, in

4
Henri Lefebvre, "From the Social Pact to the Contract of Citizenship," in *Henri Lefebvre: Key Writings*, ed. S. Elden, E. Lebas, and E. Kofman (1990; repr., London: Continuum, 2003), 253.

5
Ibid., 254.

6
Ibid., 253.

7
Stavros Stavrides, *Common Spaces of Urban Emancipation* (Manchester: Manchester University Press, 2019), 160–178; E. Torres Velazquez, "A Pancho Villa no lo enterramos, lo sembramos. FPFVI-UNOPII, Comunidad de comunidades en la Ciudad de México," *El Canelazo de la Ciudad* 3 (2014): 102.

8
B. Nahoum, "El Movimiento Cooperativista del Uruguay. Autogestion, ayuda mutua, aporte proprio, propiedad collective," in *Cooperativas de Vivienda en Uruguay*, ed. A. del Castillo and R. Valles (Montevideo: Facultad de Architectura, 2015), 42.

9
Gustavo Esteva, "Hope from the Margins," in *The Wealth of the Commons: A World beyond Market and State*, ed. D. Bollier and S. Helfrich (Amherst, MA: Levellers Press, 2012).

10
Gerardo Meza,
La Polvorilla activist
interviewed by the
author, in Stavrides,
*Common Spaces of Urban
Emancipation*, 164–165.

common feasts many different cultures coexist (mainly those that come from south Mexico). This is how to create a shared culture; we don't think any culture represents absolute truth. Knowledge is produced collectively and through combinations and synthesis. The feeling of belonging to a community is deeply rooted.[10]

The active redefinition of a "we"-in-the-making develops through practices that intersect in circumscribing what is to be shared and how it is to be shared in a specific social context. Within struggles for housing, which aim at producing social relations based on solidarity and equality, the common includes both the future settlement as a world to be shared and the forms of organization that shape the emerging "we." Commoning practices shape the collectively recognized scopes as well as the means to pursue them.

Thus housing movements of this kind politicize commoning in a very specific way. What looks like a set of demands for redistribution connected to a specific good—houses—is essentially a struggle to construct different ways of living together. Spatial practices (or practices of inhabiting spaces while producing them) are being shaped by commoning values but also shape such values. The politicization of the common is performed in space and through space.

Demands and acts that connect the right to housing to the right of being a citizen reveal what is at the core of struggles to define the common: the issue of power. One may focus on problems relating to the legal aspects of the common: central to this approach would be questions concerning property and the rules of goods distribution. One may alternatively focus on problems relating to the economy of the commons: emphasis will have to be put, in this case, on issues of value and exchange and on questions concerning the interests of those involved.

Focusing on the problem of power relations, however, may incorporate these approaches but also transcend them by marking the convergence point of the factors that shape actual commoning practices. It is by directly challenging established power asymmetries that the politicization of commoning may show a possible way beyond unequal sharing and domination. The sharing of power as a target to be pursued through everyday struggles is perhaps the best way to understand the project of developing "popular power" that Mexican housing activists talk about. The sharing of power is the way to establish forms of social organization that may prefigure a liberated society while at the same time developing real changes in the lives of real people.

We may distinguish at least four levels on which struggles for decent shelter connected to struggles for an inclusive and just society may challenge dominant models of housing design and production.

a   Practices of organizing prior to struggle (which actually unfold and develop through struggle) tend to create between future cohabitants social bonds based on solidarity and mutual help.

b   Participation in design and planning processes gives people the means to question stereotypes and to collectively develop solutions that disentangle housing production from developers' or politicians' priorities.

c   The construction site can become a melting pot for acquired habits and preoccupations if future cohabitants participate in building both their homes and the urban shared space that will become the backbone of a "commoned" neighborhood.

d   Keeping alive the forms of participation in decision making and the bonds of cooperation developed through the sharing of duties becomes a crucial stake at issue after the housing complex is completed. Common life is to be organized according to the values of the struggle that produced it.

Let us explore those levels separately:

a   For the Brazilian movement of homeless workers (MTST), pre-paring the subjects of struggle is of utmost importance. Families that express their interest in participating in a land or building occupation meant to promote a demand for decent housing have to become integrated into a community-in-the-making.[11] They have to learn to develop bonds of trust and solidarity, they have to learn how to rotate in duties and how to participate in collective decision processes. Such areas of knowledge, skills, and shared values actually become grounded in practices of cooperation that explicitly transform the everydayness of movement participants. Sharing food, taking care of children collectively, looking after the jobless and the elderly, developing rules of conduct based on gender, culture, and color equality are among the most important ways such practices unfold. Living together in equality and soli-darity is a project that starts even before the demands are stated

11
Afonso Silva, MTST activist, interview by the author.

and pursued through movement action. Movement encampments in occupied land become the first major test of the movement's organized life. In the prospect of grounding their demands on an explicit action that obliges the local state to respond, MTST often chooses to erect, on a large, occupied plot, a temporary miniature city of precarious barracks. In the Marielle Vive II encampment in São Paulo (2018), for example, 3,500 families established their claim for housing when each family erected a small, ad hoc shelter out of wood and plastic covering. The enormous agglomeration of such temporary constructions was not, in most cases, an agglomeration of literal houses (although a few of the most deprived families actually have to live in some of them). A kind of materialized symbolic settlement was sustained by the movement as a strong gesture for reclaiming their right to the city. Scattered among the neighborhoods of this quasi settlement were collective kitchens that provided cooked food every day for the encampment's members but also for those in need from the surrounding neighborhood favelas. Kitchens thus become nodes of a shared everydayness in struggle.

Marielle Vive II MTST encampment in São Paulo.

Marielle Vive II MTST encampment in São Paulo.

b   It has been rightly pointed out that current neoliberalist ideology delegitimizes critical thought, supporting instead an unquestioned compliance to market mechanisms, which are presented as the only means to accommodate the immense variety of individual claims.[12] Forms of regulation and planning that used to be associated with hopes for the construction of a more just future are being equated to totalitarianism. In the face of a highly complex social organization, market—rather than the will of social groups, experts, politicians, and so on—is presented as the mechanism that will reproduce society and ensure its stability.[13]

    Architecture, in such a context, may either embrace the neoliberal orthodoxy and more or less cynically accept its role as the promoter of symbolic and real capital, or engage itself with a renewed social critique based on challenging the dominant spatial practices. In order to distance itself from the neoliberal imaginary, however, militant architecture needs to connect to those who experience the needs and develop the dreams that clash with this imaginary. And this is what happens in the cases of militant participatory planning in which experts support the efforts of housing movements to rethink, reimagine, and thus to redefine housing and

12
D. Spencer,
The Architecture of Neoliberalism (London: Bloomsbury, 2016); M. Foucault, *The Birth of Biopolitics: Lectures at the Collège de France, 1977–78* (New York: Palgrave Macmillan, 2008).
13
Spencer, *The Architecture of Neoliberalism*.

14
S. Stavrides, *Common Space: The City as Commons* (London: Zed Books, 2016), 125–127.

15
USINA, "Processos de projeto como construção de autonomia," in *USINA: Entre o Projeto e o Canteiro*, ed. I. Vilaca and P. Constante (Sao Paulo: Aurora, 2015); P. Arantes, "Reinventing the Building Site," in Vol. 1 of *Brazilian Architecture in the XXth Century* (London: Phaidon, 2004).

cohabitation. Collective inventiveness thus becomes the propelling force and source of practices that reformulate the problem of housing in the context of urban commoning cultures.[14]

We may take as an example the pioneering contribution of USINA, a group of experts in São Paulo who have worked with various homeless movements in support of their efforts to collectively design the social housing complexes meant to house them. Design in those projects first of all has to face problems of communication: how can people and experts communicate, when training, differences in experience and roles, as well as acquired habits erect enormous obstacles? USINA thus tried to devise methods of communication that start from common experiences and not from expert knowledge.[15]

At the same time, giving people the means to form opinions and proposals becomes even more important than simply giving them the opportunity to express those opinions. Commoning knowledge, commoning imagination, commoning memory: These are manifold practices of exchange that neither reduce the complexity of living together to allegedly universal standards (as most modernists did) nor celebrate the variety of differences

USINA designed housing complex (Sao Paulo, Brazil).

in a postmodernist glorification of multiplicity. Specific choices that directly link to design solutions emerge in assemblies aimed at synthesizing different ideas. In the COPROMO complex, for example, in response to a request from the assembly, the stairwell was connected to the balconies of the adjacent apartments in an effort to ensure that common and private spaces are part of a continuum of transitions with no clear borders.[16]

Similar experiences of participatory design took place in the Mexican autonomous neighborhoods. In La Polvorilla neighborhood, created by the Los Panchos movement, the participation of women in the assemblies emphatically guided decisions that prioritized the creation of a small, semipublic courtyard in front of each house. The perforated wall of this small, quasi-open space makes it possible to watch over children playing outside without losing the family privacy that is considered equally important by the neighborhood's inhabitants.[17]

In the case of Tlanezi Calli, another such neighborhood in Mexico City, participating future inhabitants agreed to design their houses by breaking from the predominant stereotypes calling for the kitchen to be separated from the living room. For them,

16
Stavrides, *Common Spaces of Urban Emancipation*, 144–145.

17
Ibid.

La Polvorilla autonomous neighborhood (Mexico City).

18
Sergio Pacheco, a Tlanezi activist, interview by the author.

preparing food and eating are parts of a multifarious and inclusive sociality that is central to family life as well as to the family's openness to visitors.[18]

Participation in the construction process is a factor in shaping the future inhabitants' attitudes toward a shared neighborhood life. Members of the housing cooperatives that constitute the Uruguayan FUCVAM (Uruguayan Federation of Housing Cooperatives through Mutual Help) develop skills and acquire habits necessary for mutual help processes by working together on the construction site.

A FUCVAM project.

c
The "cooperativist" ethos potentially draws from the actual experiences of working together that implicitly orient participants toward a sense of the common. As Pierre Dardot and Christian Laval suggest, "The co-activity that is inherent to all work is always accompanied by a sense of obligations, if only minimally, to the common."[19] No matter how deeply alienated this inherent obligation becomes under the command of capital, it may resurface in cooperation schemes like those developed on the construction sites of *ayuda mutua* (mutual help). Cooperation under such circumstances actually develops and tests the rules and forms of commoning.

19
Pierre Dardot and Christian Laval, *Common: On Revolution in the 21st Century* (London: Bloomsbury, 2019), 333.

Sergio Ferro, a Brazilian architect and theorist, has brilliantly analyzed the conditions that make the construction site an important area of surplus value production in a capitalist economy. But his is not only an economic analysis. He puts an emphasis on the political role of the construction site: under capitalist command, construction is developed through processes that capture the knowledge and skills of workers while at the same time limiting the workers' means to resist and organize.[20]

According to Ferro, design (as a practice and expertise) has gradually transferred building knowledge and decision making to experts who are separated from the construction site itself, where workers and technicians used to have an indispensable role.[21] Arantes sees this process as escalating in today's programmed design with its direct connection to digitally interconnected prefabrication and assembling technologies.[22] Ferro characteristically marks as a turning point in this alienation of construction workers from their work the use of concrete as a structural building material. According to his bold suggestion, concrete became a weapon to destroy the power of organized workers' resistance, as it introduced a technology alien to the various crafts on which the construction process was until then highly dependent.[23]

In direct contrast to the growing alienation of builders from their work, USINA introduces construction methods that give to those engaged in relevant labor tasks a view of and control over the final product: their houses. USINA engineers have introduced the idea of a stairwell structure to be assembled on-site from prefabricated iron parts; this then serves as a scaffold for the rest of the multistory housing buildings. Unskilled workers can be trained to do most of the jobs remaining, especially bricklaying. Thus the actual construction of the building becomes part of the collective experience of working together. Of course, depending on the project, various kinds of skilled workers and technicians contribute to the final product. What remains at the center of this process of cooperation, however, is learning to work together as preparation for being able to live together.

d   Autonomous neighborhoods at the periphery of Mexico City can be taken to concretize the potentialities of a reclaimed citizenship at the level of the organized everydayness of cohabitation. Autonomy in this context seems to define a world of conviviality beyond the total control of the market and the state. "Autonomia seeks to establish new foundations of social life" and is achieved (or, rather, it is sought out in the form of an ongoing project) "by taking back from the State key areas of social life it has colonized."[24]

20
S. Ferro, "Dessin/Chantier: An Introduction," in *Industries of Architecture*, ed. Katie L. Thomas, Tilo Amhoft, and Nick Beech (New York: Routledge, 2016).
21
Ferro, "Dessin/Chantier"; S. Ferro, "Concrete as Weapon," *Harvard Design Magazine* 46 (2018).
22
Arantes, *The Rent of Form*.

23
Ferro, "Concrete as Weapon."

24
A. Escobar, *Designs for the Pluriverse* (Durham, NC: Duke University Press, 2018), 174.

25
R. Zibechi, "Mexico: Challenges and Difficulties of Urban Territories in Resistance," in *Rethinking Latin American Social Movements*, ed. R. Stahler-Sholk, H. E. Vanden, and M. Becker (Lanham, MD: Rowman and Littlefield, 2014).

Autonomous neighborhoods thus develop forms of social relations and organizing principles that attempt to establish solidarity and equality through relations of cohabitation.[25] Claiming urban territory as common and organizing decision-making practices that are grounded in urban commoning—this is what characterizes such neighborhoods. In Tlanezi Calli, home of 109 families that participate in the Brujula Rocha (Red Compass) movement, weekly assemblies decide on the community's priorities and organize the necessary rotation of duties. Apart from solving the everyday problems and concretizing urgent projects related to construction and maintenance (sewage, water purification, alternative energy sources, urban gardening, street cleaning, etc.), Tlanezi Calli commoners develop alternative cultural and educational initiatives that overspill the boundaries of their neighborhood.

They thus become active catalysts of social change not only within their allegedly liberated microcosm but also outside it. "You can see that we share with Zapatistas the same demands and values by observing the names we gave to our streets: Dignity, Work, Democracy, Justice, Liberty, Land, etc."[26] Street names thus become part of a performed and inhabited manifesto.

26
Sergio Pacheco, Tlanezi activist, interview by the author.

Tlanezi Calli autonomous neighborhood (Mexico City).

Autonomous neighborhoods constantly struggle for their survival: The Mexican government (both local and federal) sees them as potential catalysts of popular discontent and thus, depending on the political situation, either directly clashes with their demands and initiatives (that often actively support different urban struggles) or tries to co-opt them with clientelistic policies. Thus autonomous neighborhoods always have to challenge the limits of state power in order to get what will sustain their struggle for collective self-management.[27]

27
Stavrides, *Common Spaces of Urban Emancipation*, 160–178.

In search of a different urban future, housing movements redefine in practice both a scope ("a house for all") and the means to achieve it. They thus connect to the ongoing debates on the nature and characteristics of contemporary cities considered as potential areas of commoning. Their contribution is very important because they develop and test experiences of sharing in equality and solidarity by directly clashing with a predominant individualistic ethos. Debates about the emancipatory prospects of urban commoning may indeed profit from analyzing such experiences and from listening to the voices of the people who make these experiences possible. The politicization of commoning in housing struggles is a great lesson to be learned by all who see in the culture of the common the power to explore a society beyond exploitation and injustice. Because if the emancipatory future is not able to "contaminate" the present, it will never become true. . . .

On the Possibility of Public-Commons Partnerships: Vienna's Coproduction of Housing and the Political Project That Is the City

Stefan Gruber

When the housing question hanging over most global cities raises its head, the example of Vienna inevitably comes up. Over the last century, the Austrian capital has expanded its affordable housing stock even against the backdrops of accelerating urban growth and rampant neoliberalization. The city's widespread success is often attributed to its mythical Red Vienna program, begun in the 1920s, when the newly social democratic municipality built 64,000 communal housing units in just 10 years.[1] As city-owned housing stock has continued to grow, housing 27 percent of Vienna's population to date,[2] the city's modes of affordable housing provisioning, however, have also changed. In many respects, the Red Vienna legacy eagerly upheld by city officials has obstructed the gradual shift from a state to a market paradigm. But if we trace its evolution, we can begin to recognize Vienna's current experiments in participatory planning and collaborative housing developments as forming the outlines of a new possible framework: the commoning paradigm.

Here, commoning is understood as the collective practices structured around the production and stewardship of shared resources and operating beyond the confines of state or market. Commoners form self-defined communities by actively engaging in the governance of material or immaterial common goods. Thus, beyond a mere natural or cultural resource to be extracted, commodified, and consumed, here commoning is understood as an ongoing social practice that creates community and in turn sustains its livelihood and well-being. The focus on the active tense, commoning, directs our attention to the contested nature of continual negotiation through which the commons are produced and reproduced.[3] The key to sustaining the political and pluralistic project that is the city, I will argue, is to design protocols and institutions that turn the conflicts inherent in articulating common interest into agonistic encounters.

1
See Eve Blau, "Revisiting Red Vienna as an Urban Project," in *Urban Change. Social Design—Art as Urban Innovation*, ed. Anton Falkeis (Basel: Birkhäuser, 2017).
2
See Stadt Wien – Wiener Wohnen, *Der Wiener Gemeindebau. Geschichte, Daten, Fakten* (Vienna: Domus Verlag, November 2018), 14.
3
See Stefan Gruber and An-Linh Ngo, "The Contested Fields of Commoning," in *An Atlas of Commoning*, ed. Stefan Gruber et al. (Berlin: ifa / ARCH+ 232, June 2018), 4–5.

Citizens' Initiatives: The Underrated Force in Vienna's Urban Transformations

The 20th-century history of Vienna's urban transformation is defined by the almost uninterrupted rule of the Social Democratic Party. Throughout the years, the expansion of public housing to the middle class has been its most effective and populist tool for sustaining the narrative of the welfare state, as well as staying in power. But in the 1980s, the city gradually liberalized its housing production.

4
Andreas Rumpfhuber, Georg Kohlmayr, and Michael Klein, "Views from Within," in "The Vienna Model of Public Housing Provision–Superblock turned Überstadt," *derive* 46 (2012): 19.

5
See Michael Schluder, *10 Jahre Bauträgerwettbewerbe—Veränderungen im Wohnbau* (MA 50, Wohnbuaforschung, Study July 2005).

6
See Wolfgang Kos, "Vorwort," *Besetzt! Kampf um Freiräume seit den 70ern*, ed. Martina Nußbaumer and Werner Michael Scharz (Vienna: Cernin, 2012).

Meanwhile, it retained indirect control over a large portion of housing developments via land provision, subsidies, and quality management. By international standards, and especially in comparison to unapologetically neoliberal cities, Vienna's use of public-private partnerships achieved a delicate balancing act between maintaining core features of welfare provision and responding to the growing global competition. Nonetheless, the outsourcing of affordable housing to third parties marked an irreversible shift away from centralized government and the tax-funded construction of publicly owned housing, toward a more entrepreneurial mode of governing aimed at improving cost and efficiency as well as expanding the choices available to residents. Backers on either end of the political spectrum argue that Vienna's municipal apparatus, notorious for its overbearing and hierarchical character, would never have reformed from within.[4] Some claim innovation could emerge only from competition via market forces. Others see it as the lesser evil.[5] But most concurred with the need to overhaul an obsolete, paternalistic model in which officials and experts knew best how to care for the wider public, and citizens were muted to passive recipients of welfare in exchange for political complicity.

Despite the general yearning for more self-determination, most accounts of Vienna's urbanization linger in the polarity between the market versus the state, private versus public, and fail to acknowledge the role of citizen-led initiatives as an agent of change. Here, the insights and energies produced around the contemporary commons debate provide an entry point for challenging these binaries. However, rather than framing the commons as an autonomous third sphere, the following argument explores the contested and twisted relation of the commons to the state or market in ongoing processes of claiming and reclaiming. It is precisely through their agonistic relation, I will argue, that citizens have gained agency in shaping Vienna's past and ongoing urban transformations. Be it Vienna's post–World War I Settlers movement or its early Soft Urban Renewal of the 1980s, again and again, grassroots initiatives have sparked imaginations of an alternative society beyond the domination of the state or market. Sceptics have continuously dismissed these citizen initiatives as too marginal to solve broader societal problems. Other cynics scorn their role as one of the critical insider—a toothless position that serves only to rejuvenate dominant power structures. In Vienna, these valid concerns have been fueled by the city government's persistent facility for embracing disobedience and subsequently absorbing the agitators' emancipatory power.[6] As a result, Vienna's citizens' initiatives have often been written out of history, their endeavors declared failures. Meanwhile, alternative accounts of social movement and citizen initiatives describe how their momentum actually pressured city authorities into change. They suggest that their successive institutionalization can also be read as a measure of success.

Settlers Movement Vienna.
Photo: Derbolav-Machovsky, 1921. Copyright: Wien Museum—Siedleramt.

After World War I, widespread famine and homelessness brought about a self-help movement known as the Vienna Settlers movement. From 1919 onwards, settlers self-organized, squatted land for subsistence gardening, built houses and communal facilities, and established a wide range of self-governing associations, cooperatives, and guilds that led to an intricate alternative economy. But interwar historiography has often deemed the "wild" settlements as a marginal movement that ran out of steam and was soon absorbed into the more effective housing program of Red Vienna.[7] By contrast, Klaus Novy has challenged the false dichotomy of bottom-up settlers versus top-down Red Vienna, arguing that the municipal program would not have taken hold without the settlers' achievements.[8] Instead, he describes how the transition from the self-help initiative to comprehensive welfare provision was a gradual one in which the settlers paved the way for a centralized reform.

Similarly, Vienna's Soft Urban Renewal program of the 1970s is often celebrated as a success story in municipal neighborhood

7
See, among others, Eve Blau, *The Architecture of Red Vienna, 1919–1934* (Cambridge, MA: MIT Press, 1999), 129–133.
8
See Klaus Novy and Wolfgang Föster, *Einfach Bauen: Genossenschaftliche Selbsthilfe nach der Jahundertwende, zir Rekonstruktion der Siedlerbewegung* (Vienna: Picus, 1991).

9
See Hannelore Ebner, *Wiener Stadterneuerung – der Weg zur lebenswertesten Stadt* (Vienna: Carl Gerold's Sohn, 2013).

10
See Christiane Feuerstein, "Angaenge der sanften Stadterneuerung," in *Wann Begann Temporär?*, ed. Christiane Feuerstein and Angelika Fitz (Vienna: Springer, 2009).

11
See Helmut Voitl, Elisabeth Guggenberger, and Peter Pirker, *Planquadrat. Ruhe, Grün und Sicherheit—Wohnen in der Stadt* (Vienna: Paul Zsolnay Verlag, 1977).

revitalization.[9] But some of the most catalytic projects for the rediscovery of the historic city, projects introducing notions of participatory design, did not occur with but in resistance to city planning.[10] At Planquadrat, a group of residents fought the demolition of historic buildings to make way for an automobile throughway. They transformed the inner courtyard of a city block into a community-governed public space.[11] Planquadrat's community engagement eventually became a model for revising the municipality's approach to top-down neighborhood renewal and introducing satellite municipal offices for neighborhood care (*Gebietsbetreuung*) across the city. These two brief examples illustrate how citizens' ability to challenge prevailing modes of operating have been instrumental in diversifying the actors involved in coproducing the city. Their hands-on approach to claiming and shaping the built environment around them insists that the common interest should not be determined by authorities but instead shaped by collective action. It is against this backdrop that Vienna's recent experiments in participatory planning and collaborative housing initiatives gain new meaning and may help to outline the possibilities, as well as risks, of an institutional framework for a transformative politics that I will describe as public-commons partnerships, and which provide an antithesis to public-private partnerships.

Participatory design with residents of Planquadrat, Vienna, 1974.
Photo and copyright: Helmut Voitl.

Vienna's Public-Private Partnerships

Since the 1980s, public-private partnerships (PPPs) have proliferated around the world as traditional public procurements struggle to bridge the gap between available public finances and public service or infrastructure development needs. PPPs promise to provide better-quality services at optimal cost and risk allocation by splitting financing, design, construction, operation, management, and/or maintenance between the private and public sector according to their respective strengths. In practice, however, PPPs have become highly contentious, as they tend to socialize risks while privatizing profits. Especially against the accelerating cycles of gentrification and privatization, the relation between public investment and private gain demands further scrutiny. The broad range of cross-sector arrangements in PPPs also make their definition and assessment problematic.

Historically, Vienna's public housing was developed and built directly by the city or by nonprofit housing cooperatives (NPHCs), some of which date back to the interwar period. In Austria, the assets of NPHCs are legally tied to housing projects, and their own funds must be reinvested into the housing sector. Rents or sales for owner occupancy are tightly regulated and audited in exchange for public subsidies, land provision, and tax exemption. These characteristics made NPHCs the predestined partners for early PPPs, when the municipality began to wind down its own housing developments and construction. Then, over the course of the 1980s, the city gradually expanded the field of players involved in the provision of subsidized housing, up until the city withdrew from direct housing provision altogether and opened "housing developer competitions" (*Bauträgerwettbewerb*) to the private sector. Since 1995, all housing developments of 200 dwelling units or more are subject to an open competition in which teams of architects and developers compete for tender. Their proposals are evaluated by an interdisciplinary jury based on economic, ecological, architectural, social quality, and sustainability criteria. The new housing developer competitions have been deemed widely effective in stipulating design innovation and diversifying the types of housing while reducing costs and holding all actors accountable to the same standards in serving public utility or the common interest (*Gemeinnützigkeit*). But this outward success also masked more profound underlying changes in the framing of affordable housing as a common good. While some of these changes resulted from broader sociocultural, economic, and geopolitical influences, others were more calculated.

In 1989 the fall of the Iron Curtain moved Vienna from Western Europe's geopolitical fringe to the center of a reconfigured continent. More broadly, this shift introduced a postpolitical era in which the free world had triumphed over Communism, and the spread of universal liberal democracy in a globalizing world promised a consensus-driven cosmopolitan future free of conflicts. Vienna, after decades of demographic decline, started growing overnight. This new dynamic was further amplified by Austria's accession to the European Union and general economic liberalization. Eager to position itself within a global competition among cities, Vienna used iconic architecture as a catalyst to draw attention to its livability and to attract investments. International and national star architects designing museums or corporate headquarters around the world were lured to Vienna to build distinctive affordable housing—sometimes to great acclaim, other times at the expense of costs, functionality, or residents' well-being.[12] Rather than working in opposition to the market, public housing was now also contributing to promote growth. In line with the postmodern zeitgeist, public housing was no longer to be associated with standardization as an expression of social equality but rather themed around individual lifestyle choices. Sociologists such as Ulrich Beck and Anthony Giddens have described the liberation of individuals from collective ties: unhindered by outdated attachments, they can dedicate themselves to cultivating a diversity of lifestyles as "reflexive modernity."[13] Accordingly, the collective experiences and identities built around communal facilities in the courtyards of Red Vienna's superblocks or its blander postwar counterparts gave way to a palette of unique floor plans as expression of diverse and individualized identities. At the scale of the dwelling, architects' assertion that "no two units are alike" became a badge of inherent quality. But at the urban scale, the aggregate sum of buildings rarely added up to vibrant urban quarters.[14] While the workers' dwellings of Red Vienna's *Gemeindebauten* were complemented with kindergartens, libraries, clinics, theaters, and cooperative stores, the new housing developer competitions focused more narrowly on the provision of dwellings with little incentives for mixed use or the design of public space that would bring the new housing developments to life. Whereas the distinct architectural language of Red Vienna's superblocks rendered public housing legible as an archipelago of islands against the dense urban fabric of 19th-century developments, Vienna's postmodern icons remained self-referential fragments in an incongruous patchwork.

In effect, the new modes of housing production not only changed the architecture of affordable housing but also the very idea

12
See Reinhard Seiß, *Wer baut Wien?* (Vienna: Anton Pustet, 2007).
13
See Ulrich Beck, "The Reinvention of Politics: Towards a Theory of Reflexive Modernization," in Ulrich Beck, Anthony Giddens, and Scott Lash, *Reflexive Modernization,* (Cambridge, UK: Polity Press, 1997).

14
Maik Novotny, "Wiener Bauträgerwettbewerbe: Wohnen macht Stadt," *Die Presse*, June 28, 2020.

of the city and its relation to the common good, or *Gemeinnützigkeit.*
If, until the 1980s, the provision of affordable housing was a political
project aiming at a fairer distribution of wealth and the emancipation
of workers, the subsequent concerns seemed increasingly managerial—
the efficient allocation of municipal resources, cost, and risks. For
the former, affordable housing was a means to a political cause. For the
latter, it had become an end in itself. These divergent approaches are
symptomatic of a broader shift toward a postpolitical agenda. Political
theorist Chantal Mouffe has exposed the dangers of the postpolitical
approach and the implications of disregarding agonistic and adversarial
encounters as the foundation of the political and democratic procedures:

> I contend that the belief in the possibility of a universal ratio-
> nal consensus has put democratic thinking on the wrong
> track. Instead of trying to design the institutions which, through
> supposedly "impartial" procedures, would reconcile all conflict-
> ing interests and values, the task of democratic theorists and
> politicians should be to envisage the creation of a vibrant "ago-
> nistic" public sphere of contestation where different hegemonic
> political projects can be confronted. This is, in my view, the
> *sine qua non* for an effective exercise of democracy. There
> is much talk today of "dialogue" and "deliberation" but what is
> the meaning of such words in the political field, if no real choice
> is at hand and if the participants in the discussion are not able
> to decide between clearly differentiated alternatives?[15]

15
Chantal Mouffe, *On
the Political* (New York:
Routledge, 2005), 3.

Along with Mouffe, I would argue that Vienna's PPPs reframed public
housing and its urbanization at large as a postpolitical project. Driven
by pragmatism and caught between governmental overregulation (as
a result of the legitimate attempt to hold third parties accountable) on
the one hand, and market competition on the other, more often than
not, the differences between housing schemes were flattened to facade
variations. Here, the playful arrangement of exuberant balconies renders the postpolitical as architecture. But their idea of pluralism is
reduced to a shallow image, devoid of the political. How then can the
pursuit of the common good, understood as the articulation of individual interests in such a way as to constitute common interests, be
sustained without a political dimension? While Vienna PPPs succeeded
in continuing to provide affordable housing, they stopped recognizing
the production of space or production of the city as an essential platform for the agonistic encounter of differences. As if the balancing act

between governmental control and market forces had absorbed all the attention, citizens were mostly omitted from the negotiation processes, their political participation reduced to casting a vote every five years. A municipal obsession with evaluating "housing satisfaction" signifies the demotion of citizens to end users.[16]

Vienna's Cohousing Initiatives

It is against these developments, and also fueled by the 2008 global financial crisis and the collapse of the housing bubble, that citizen-led housing initiatives begin to emerge in Vienna at the start of the 2010s. Inspired by the proliferation of cooperative housing in Switzerland and cohousing in Germany, also known as *Baugruppen*,[17] groups of citizens came together to develop housing collaboratively. In contrast to public housing, these groups pursued self-determined forms of living by pooling resources and collective governance. For some, cohousing was an opportunity to move beyond political disenchantment and put into practice their vision of an alternative, more solidary, and ecological society. For others, the reasons were more pragmatic: a patchwork family sought a customized yet affordable dwelling arrangement, or two empty nesters aimed at downscaling while joining a community of collective care and mutual support. Though the motives varied and each group articulated the relation between individuals and the collective on its own terms, they all shared an interest in living in a community beyond the confines of the heteronormative nuclear family—a norm that continues to stifle municipal housing, as well as the housing market, regardless of demographic change. In 2018, almost half of Vienna's households were singles; 10 percent of families were composed of single parents and their children.[18] The cohousing project LiSA focuses on flexible apartment typologies that can adapt, expanding or contracting in response to changing life circumstances. Que[e]rbau is Vienna's first queer cohousing community aiming to support and include "everyone willing to define their own identity."[19] In its description of apartment typologies, the Syndikat habiTAT project deliberately speaks of "family-of-choice rooms." The diversity of social constellation is reflected in the wide range of dwelling types. In cluster apartments, for instance, between 12 and 20 residents form a household, combining smaller private units with a variety of shared spaces. In such a scenario, private kitchenettes are complemented by a larger communal kitchen. Here, the gradation of private and common spaces implies that sharing does not necessarily

16
See, among others, Trendcom, "Lebensgefühl in Wiener Gemeindebauten," April 2008, commissioned by Wohnbauforschung Wien, https://www.wohnbauforschung.at/index.php?id=356.

17
In English the term "cohousing" tends to be associated with Scandinavian intentional communities of the 1960s. The German term *Baugruppe* is broader, as it designates any collaborative and self-governed housing development without the community events, such as shared meals, central to many Scandinavian cohousing groups.

18
Statistik Austria, 2019, "Familien nach Familientyp und Zahl der Kinder ausgewählter Altersgruppen - Jahresdurchschnitt 2019," https://www.statistik.at/web_de/statistiken/menschen_und_gesellschaft/bevoelkerung/haushalte_familien_lebensformen/familien/023080.html.

19
Mission statement, https://queerbaudotat.wordpress.com/welcome/.

come at the expense of privacy. Such trade-offs often also exist at the scale of the building. Many projects share guest rooms, a community garden or roof terrace, an event space, a workshop, music rehearsal rooms, workout or coworking spaces, and in some cases even car- or bike-sharing. The pooling of resources indicates a broader societal shift in which individuals shed the material burden of ownership for accessing shared spaces and experiences on demand. But in contrast to the so-called sharing economy, the benefits of sharing are not commodified by a corporate platform. Instead, they are determined collectively by negotiating the terms of use, access, and stewardship of common facilities. Many groups use sociocracy as a governance model. Constituents make decisions based on consent rather than consensus. In line with Mouffe's notion of the political, consent does not imply the erasure of differences in the process of articulating common interests: "With consensus the participants must be "for" the decision. With consent decision making, they must be not against. With consensus, a veto blocks the decision without an argument. With consent decision making, opposition must always be supported with an argument."[20] Here, the articulation of common interests is an ongoing and active social practice.

20
Mouffe, *On the Political*, 20.

Beyond the resident group, the influence of cohousing projects extends outward onto the urban context. Activities at ground level often spill out onto the streets. In some cases, the neighborhood is invited in and facilities opened to a wider community. With a focus on use value rather than market value, cohousing groups are able to accommodate programs that housing developers are not. Nonprofit programs are sustained through volunteer work, expenses shared among residents or cross-subsidized by the market-rate lease of other parts. Thus the possibility of a corner shop or even a swimming pool is determined not only by its profitability or the lack thereof but by its ability to bring people together. Less dependent on economies of scale, cohousing projects tend to be smaller than typical housing developments and produce a finer urban granularity. Small city blocks and mixed use in turn lead to higher connectivity and more eyes on the street—two key principles from Jane Jacobs's playbook to make neighborhoods safer and livelier.

Ultimately, the positive influence that cohousing projects can have on their surroundings has played a decisive role in changing the municipality's attitude toward citizen-led housing initiatives. They've come to embrace them as strategic instruments in urban developments. Here, the Wohnprojekt Wien project in particular

Cohousing project Wohnprojekt Wien with anarchist graffiti "Bobo shit," 2019.
Photo and copyright: Stefan Gruber.

was a game changer. Founded in 2009, Wohnprojekt Wien is situated in a large-scale brownfield redevelopment in Vienna's 20th district. The redevelopment area contains 3,500 housing units, developed as subsidized housing via housing developer competitions and boasting considerable architectural quality. However, the area remained mostly residential and lacking in public urban life despite the neighborhood public K–12 school campus and a generous park. By contrast, Wohnprojekt Wien became an instant focal point of civic activities in the new quarter. Situated on a strategic site facing the park, its ground floor houses a small café and grocery store, a communal kitchen paired with a kids' playroom and a sunken event space, and the project architect's office. At lunchtime, a group of 25 residents who work and live at Wohnprojekt or nearby take turns cooking in the communal kitchen: "Cooking once means eating 20 times as a guest for 3 Euros."[21] The entrance hall, the communal kitchen, and the kids' playroom are visually connected yet acoustically separated so "as to keep an eye on the kids while cooking but without hearing them scream," explains architect and resident Markus Zilker.[22] Enabling synergies between collective housework, childcare, and socializing, be it as casual chance encounters or intentional gathering, the entrance-kitchen-playroom triad has become a recurring pattern in the architects'

21
Resident interview, "Co-Housing Wohnprojekt Wien," https://simonprize. org/co-housing-wohnprojekt-wien/ sheet/.
22
Markus Zilker, personal interview, October 24, 2019.

growing number of realized cohousing projects. The multipurpose space hosts daily events from seminars to yoga classes, from photo shoots to concerts, and can be rented by third parties. Its inhabitants describe the Wohnprojekt as "a hub for sustainability, collective living, active neighborhood care, and a center for cultural activities."[23]

Beyond the aggregate sum of buildings, cities are the product of social relations and the life unfolding in between buildings. But meaningful social relations take time to build—more time than most constructions, or even the development of an entire neighborhood. In order to develop a sense of place, a sense of belonging, the making of spaces and social relations go hand in hand. Because the residents of Wohnprojekt Wien and other cohousing projects undergo an intensive participatory design process, by the time they move in, they have developed strong bonds. Thus, from day one, cohousing groups bring civic engagement and a commitment to placemaking to new developments, and this is catalytic in nurturing civic life. Robert Temel argues that "cohousing project are places of diversity, and therefore contribute to cultivating the social in cities; they constitute points of crystallization in forming more intensive and neighborly developments."[24] Of course, Wohnprojekt Wien was not Vienna's first cohousing project: notable predecessors include the Sargfabrik, completed in 1996; B.R.O.T. Hernals, in 1990; and Wohnen mit Kindern, from 1984. These projects served as important inspiration for Wohnprojekt Wien. However, burdened with numerous struggles, including municipal obstructions among others, these experiments were long considered singular and difficult to replicate. Meanwhile, Wohnprojekt Wien, supported by a new Red-Green municipal government, marked a tipping point for cohousing initiatives in Vienna and paved the way for future collaborations between citizen-led housing projects and the municipality, which now recognizes cohousing as a possible agent for the common good in urban developments.

From Singular Projects to Collaborative Urban Design

At Aspern Seestadt, a large satellite city for 20,000 residents, the city integrated cohousing initiatives into its masterplan for the first time. Selected in a two-stage request for proposals, five autonomous initiatives are clustered in a city block specifically dedicated to cohousing. The design of the common courtyard was developed in a large participatory

23
Mission statement, https://wohnprojekt.wien/flex.

24
Robert Temel, "Baugruppen und Stadtentwicklung," in *Gemeinsam Bauen Wohnen in der Praxis*, ed. Ernst Gruber (Verein Initiative für gemeinschaftliches Bauen und Wohnen, November 2015), 38–39.

design process, involving stakeholders from all five groups in collective decisions about the landscape design, accessibility, and maintenance agreements. As a result, a large portion of the central courtyard remains open to the general public, rendering the block porous, not unlike Red Vienna's superblocks. But instead of NO BALL GAMES signs, this courtyard shows many traces of spontaneous activities and appropriation. The clustering of multiple cohousing projects allows for the sharing of certain facilities between the groups. Their aggregation also amplifies their presence at the scale of the neighborhood. It provides for diversity and granularity of autonomous midsize buildings, while keeping resident groups small enough for horizontal governance structures. The five initial pilot projects realized at the Aspern Seestadt have boosted the general demand for cohousing in Vienna. Several other initiatives have been or are being implemented across the new town.

Building on the lessons from Aspern Seestadt at the Sonnwendviertel, another large urban brownfield development behind Vienna's central station, the city applied a different approach. In an attempt to maximize the impact of cohousing on the surroundings, here several initiatives were distributed across the entire neighborhood so as to form a network. The four residential projects are complemented by a new typology, the *Quartiershaus* (German for "neighborhood house"). A *Quartiershaus* is a mixed-use building with particular architectural ambitions. The ground-floor lease is predetermined at 4 Euros/sqm in order to encourage a wider diversity of street-level programming and activate the public space. The land for cohousing and *Quartiershäuser* was assigned in a two-stage request for proposals in which teams of architects, developers, citizen groups, and future tenants presented a concept. Besides addressing issues of economic, ecological, social, and architectural sustainability, the bidders were asked to articulate how their project would serve the neighborhood at large.

Mio is a *Quartiershaus* with micro units of 250 to 360 square feet for retail and offices. Designed to minimize fixed costs, the tiny spaces house an independent book and LP store, a health food store, a juice bar, and a radio station—in short, a contemporary version of the mom-and-pop stores that make neighborhoods unique but typically struggle to compete with more substantial retailers. The so-called micro pilots are cross-financed via market-rate housing on the upper floors. Next to Mio, the Haus am Park accommodates a dance school for kids. The third building on the block is a cohousing project, with similarly public programs on the ground floor: an eatery, a music school, and a media workshop. The technical equipment for the event space was crowdfunded. The space will host workshops for youth in cooperation with local TV and radio stations. The cohousing above includes three apartments for refugees that are managed by the Catholic church. All three buildings form an extremely fine grain and porous city block with an unusual mix of programs. The layering of housing, work, commerce, and cultural programs in a single building is reminiscent of the diversity that we cherish in the 19th-century European city but that has become increasingly difficult to achieve in today's market. Beyond the mere curation of programs, here the intertwining of different financing and ownership models is key.

A few blocks away, a newly founded housing cooperative dedicated to collective living and named WoGen is developing a neighborhood house that combines coworking and coliving. The project is organized as two short tower blocks on a common plinth. There is a maker space, or "city-workshop," event spaces, a community kitchen on street level, and a large communal terrace with "the city balcony" on top. Here again, the breaking with modernist separation of living and work, reproductive and productive labor, is an essential feature for weaving the social fabric of the new neighborhood.

Each of these examples put forward a different value proposition. Rather than prescribing a fixed definition of the common interest—as implied by the evaluation metrics for the housing developer competitions—the selection process is designed to set in motion a debate: each project, independent of its financial and ownership model, had to make a case for its contribution to the neighborhood's common interest, be it on a programmatic, spatial, economic, social, or environmental level. Hence the municipality no longer merely attempts to regulate or control market actors but becomes the facilitator of a collaborative and deliberative process in which a diverse range of stakeholders, from housing developers to citizens' initiatives, can take part.

A similar collaborative logic was developed for the overall urban design framework of the Sonnwend quarter. In a new participatory planning process, instead of a single urban designer, six teams were selected to collaborate on the development of an urban design strategy. In the typical market mind-set, innovation and solutions are sought by putting singular authors in competition with one another. At the end, one so-called masterplan emerges as the winner. Negotiations, confrontations, and concessions take place after the fact, often seemingly compromising the original plan. In contrast, the new participatory planning process is designed to encourage agonistic encounters and invites diverse, even conflicting, perspectives to the table early on.

The negotiation between adversary positions is generative and at the core of the design process. Here, urban design regains a political dimension as a symbolic space in which dissent can be articulated and worked through, enacting the complexities and contractions of the city as an expression of a social contract.

Toward Public-Commons Partnerships

Vienna's shift away from a state-market duality toward a third, more collaborative approach has been both gradual and prudent. As a result, the emerging paradigm still awaits designation. Here, the concept of public-commons partnerships (PCPs) seems pertinent. Coined by commons activist Tommaso Fattori in opposition to public-private partnerships, public-commons partnerships aim at not only de-privatizing the public realm, or goods and services of general interest, but also bringing back elements of direct self-governance to local residents.[25] If the state already outsources essential services to third parties, why not to the people on the spot, that is, those who have the strongest incentives for solving the problems at hand and sustaining the commons? PCPs outline the possibility of a more distributed model of governance in which public institutions and commoners work together, enabling citizens to act as collective decision makers in shaping the environment in which they live. Simultaneously, municipal backing and accountability are essential to prevent fragmentation and NIMBYism. But government can also play a more active role in nurturing the commons sector and the type of value that it creates.[26] Support can be achieved through tax exemptions, subsidies, provision of land and infrastructure, or by sharing other public goods or services.

The city of Vienna does not use the term public-commons partnership. But its recent shift in housing provision, as well as its collaborative planning methods, closely align with these ideas. An institutional framework might contribute to better defining its principles and purpose and move the commons-based peer-to-peer production of the city from the margins to the center of the debate on neighborhood planning. At the same time, delineating PCPs from what they are not might also help to address some concerns about commoning in general and cohousing in particular.

Cohousing projects are frequently perceived as a fringe phenomenon because of their exclusive character. In fact, the socioeconomic demographics of many cohousing communities are strikingly

25
Tommaso Fattori, "Public-Commons Partnership and the Commonification of That Which Is Public," in *Living in Dignity in the XXIst Century: Poverty and Inequalities from the Human Rights, Democracy and Commons Perspective* (Council of Europe, 2012), https://commonsblog.files.wordpress.com/2007/10/fattori-commonification-of-that-which-is-public.pdf
26
David Bollier, "The Digital Republic," November 2009, http://onthecommons.org.

homogeneous. But finances are not the only mechanism of exclusion. Participation and direct democracy require time and skills—two privileges not everyone has. In order to lower financial barriers, some cohousing groups have introduced a solidarity fund through which selected dwellings are subsidized and become accessible to a wider range of inhabitants. Many groups explicitly include refugees in their community. But any intentional community comes at the risk of excluding others and, more often than not, the criteria and selection process for cohousing members remain rather opaque. At the same time, borders are essential for constituting a sense of community, defining responsibilities, and sustaining a commons. Economist Elinor Ostrom identifies clear borders as one of eight essential principles for governing the commons.[27] Through PCPs, the government might introduce criteria for defining diversity and inclusion as conditions for municipal support while respecting the group's pursuit of self-determination.

Building on the account of exclusivity, some critics see commoning initiatives as alternative islands, unable to tackle broader systemic issues, such as affordable housing.[28] Just as with PPPs, these concerns call for scrutiny as to who will benefit from public subsidies. When applied to housing, PCPs should focus on long-term decommodification and reject projects that could ever revert to private ownership. However, this doesn't mean PCPs shouldn't remain open to different ownership models and forms of collaboration. Here, the Syndikat Habitat offers a case in point. Modeled after the German Mietshäusersyndikat, the tenement syndicate Habitat is legally defined as a limited liability corporation. Meanwhile, its decentralized governance structure renders the reselling of property nearly impossible and stabilizes rents below market rate. Similar to a community land trust, the syndicate distributes power onto two subordinate bodies that mutually monitor one another while empowering tenants within autonomous projects to collectively determine how they would like to live. The tenement syndicate is a reminder for conceiving PCPs not so much as a fixed institutional form, but rather a series of principles and processes that need to be designed and implemented largely on a case-by-case basis.

Finally, Michael Bauwens cautions us to not confuse PCPs with plans to dismantle the welfare state: "The peer production of common value requires civic wealth and strong civic institutions. In other words, the partner state concept transcends and includes the best of the welfare state, such as the social solidarity mechanisms, strong

27
Elinor Ostrom, *Governing the Commons: The Evolution of Institutions for Collective Action* (Cambridge: Cambridge University Press, 1991).

28
Andreas Rumpfhuber, "Vienna's Housing Apparatus and Its Contemporary Challenges: Superblock Turned Überstadt," in *The Vienna Model of Public Housing Provision—Superblock Turned Überstadt, derive* 46 (2012): 19.

educational systems and a vibrant and publicly supported cultural life. What the British Tories did was to use the Big Society rhetoric to attempt to further weaken the remnants of social solidarity, and throw people to fend for themselves. This was not enabling and empowering; it was its opposite."[29] While PCPs offer a framework for more localized governance and stewardship, they do not discharge the state of responsibility—on the contrary. Conversely, self-governance does not aim at overcoming municipal governance but rather situating democratic procedures more deeply in the everyday. PCPs, then, imply a new type of institution, one whose primary goal does not serve to consolidate power but rather to introduce protocols for the continuous renegotiation and redistribution of power.

Cohousing is no panacea for the housing question. Public housing still has an important role to play and will remain the foundation of housing affordability in Vienna. While cohousing might not be suited to provide housing to those most in need, it might relieve the strained public housing program to shift its focus to those who currently fall through its cracks. At the rate of Vienna's current growth, requiring 40,000 new dwellings a year, and the unlikelihood of the city's return to the scale of public housing provision of the Red Vienna program, a diversification of affordable housing models seems necessary. Rather than a singular solution, PCPs offer a framework for breeding a network of diverse collaborative partnerships and tactics.

In the same vein, Keir Milburn and Bertie Russell argue that PCPs should not be understood as "a mono-cultural institutional form applied indiscriminately, but should emerge as an overlapping patchwork of institutions that respond to the peculiarities of the asset and scale at which the PCP will operate and those individuals and communities that will act together as commoners. The very design of PCPs must therefore be a democratic one which, from the outset, considers the most effective, responsive and equitable institutional processes to facilitate us acting in common."[30]

Just as Vienna's cohousing initiatives have gone beyond the provision of affordable housing and revived civic engagement in the coproduction of the city, PCPs promise to help reimagine the democratic institutions and agonistic processes critically needed for rejuvenating the political project that is the city. David Harvey describes the right to the city as "far more than the individual liberty to access urban resources: it is a collective right to change ourselves by changing the city."[31] Against the backdrop of political polarization,

29
Michael Bauwens, "Blueprint for a P2P Society: The Partner State & Ethical Economy" (Shareable, 2012), http://www.shareable.net/blog/blueprint-for-p2p-society-the-partner-state-ethical-economy.

30
Keir Milburn and Bertie Russell, "Public-Commons-Partnerships" (Schumacher College, October 18, 2019), https://centerforneweconomics.org/newsletters/public-common-partnerships/.

31
David Harvey, Rebel Cities: From the Right to the City to the Urban Revolution (London: Verso, 2012), 4.

the right to the city today conjures images of protest, the occupation of streets and squares, and violent confrontation with state authority. Public-commons partnerships outline the possibility of claiming the right to the city by transforming antagonism into agonism, that is, the centering of practices of urban transformation around the encounter of differences as a means for constituting common interest.

The Struggle to Govern the Commons:
An Institutionalist Engagement of Collective Action and Its Maintenance

Yan Zhang

Since Garrett Hardin postulated the "tragedy of the commons," the struggles of the commons have been at the center of discussions and debates on a sustainable future for mankind. Conceptualizing the commons and its governance dilemma generates three levels of significant discussion. How do human actors cope with uncertainty collectively? Why would people cooperate for sustainability goals? How do people cooperate and sustain collective action in the long run? This paper provides a balanced survey of relevant studies and theories on the commons, organized in the analytical structure of an institutionalized governance process of enduring human cooperation on shared common resources and environment. It takes a critical look at the theories of the commons under the historical development of social-ecological system thinking and reviews the emerging literature on complexity and uncertainty aimed at capturing the dynamics of change over time and across scale when attempting to govern the commons.

Introduction

The future of human civilization is dependent upon linking the prosperity of people and the planet. Interestingly, this linkage also imposes the most fundamental dilemma—growth (human development) versus environment and resources (nature conservation). This article adopts an ontological reasoning approach to explore this fundamental dilemma. Ontological reasoning investigates the nature of reality and/or the social being. The ontological reasoning of collective action and its maintenance investigates trust, rules, and institutions among social beings over the shared resources on which they depend. Therefore, conceptualizing the commons (as the shared resources) and its governance (institutional arrangements) is fundamental. Considering the nature of their subject matter, studies of the commons are mostly examined in social sciences such as economics and political science. A wide range of prior studies largely focused either on managing the resources as commodity under the market mechanism or on protecting nature as a public good by the state. Before the Anthropocene narrative prevailed in the 2000s, the social-ecological systems integration had been entwined, but only recently did it emerge as an interdisciplinary field across earth science, environmental studies, economics, and politics. There are other critical studies examining the commons as the sharing of intangibles, such as the knowledge, language, culture, and even virtual commons on the internet.[1] However, discussions involving institutional engagement

1
Charlotte Hess, "Mapping the New Commons," *Social Science Research Network* (2008); James Boyle, *The Public Domain Enclosing the Commons of the Mind* (New Haven, CT: Yale University Press, 2008).

of the physical commons and its governance remained core to the interdisciplinary studies of sustainable development.

Much broader discussions on the commons, such as in the "multitude framework" proposed by Michael Hardt and Antonio Negri, conceptualized the commons as the public delineation of social structure, or the social production of the commons.[2] The commons represents distinctive understandings of "the public" and "the private" in different disciplinary inquiries. In her 1958 work *The Human Condition*, Hannah Arendt claimed that the term "public" has two meanings. The first is that "everything that appears in public can be seen and heard by everybody and has the widest possible publicity."[3] The second is that "it is common to all of us and distinguished from our privately owned place in it." Thus the public sphere "signifies the world itself," and such "public space . . . must transcend the lifespan of mortal men."[4] In modern individualistic society, however, we might lose the opportunity of being seen and heard by others, which is vital to the public realm because "our feeling for reality depends utterly upon appearance."[5]

Focused on the *zivilgesellschaft* that strives to maintain the living society within the systems built up by the state and the market, Jürgen Habermas described the destruction of the public sphere by the growth of the state in bourgeois society, in which the concept of a public sphere exists as an institutionalized mechanism of communication between the state and civil society. A public sphere thus grew from forces opposed to state/market power and was yet still a part of the private sphere. A public sphere is not created by the state and government but emerges naturally in discussions among equal and free citizens, and the state only confers legitimacy of such publicity generated by equal and free individuals.[6]

In economics literature, the commons dilemma has always been focused on the issue of optimal distribution of resources, as the single overarching principle of efficiency rules all discussion. From this perspective, the "tragedy of the commons" is not an issue for the public realm until it becomes a dilemma that requires rules to institutionalize resource distribution and use. However, human cooperation and trust go beyond a discussion of efficiency and rules, which determined the commons as an issue of dialectical yet nonbinary-opposite dichotomy of the public and the private. Norms, rules, and institutions are gradually fixed along the process of individuals living together, so they represent the public context of interactions between individuals and society. However, the public space to nurture norms, rules, and institutions is not necessarily nonprivate.

2
Michael Hardt and Antonio Negri, *Commonwealth* (Cambridge, MA: Harvard University Press, 2009); Antonio Negri and Michael Hardt, *Multitude* (New York: Penguin, 2005).
3
Hannah Arendt, *The Human Condition* (Chicago: University of Chicago Press, 1958).
4
Ibid., 72, 75.
5
Ibid., 71.

6
Jürgen Habermas, *The Structural Transformation of the Public Sphere: An Inquiry into a Category of Bourgeois Society* (Cambridge, MA: MIT Press, 1989).

A related discussion appears in Antonio Gramsci's writing on the cultural hegemony of the ruling class as the artificial social construct of norms and institutions, forms of consciousness, and political-cultural practices. Within such multilayered social structures, civil society (the public sphere) or the personal common sense of daily life—all exist within a political society, which produced "common sense" to overarch and incorporate personal perceptions of a greater socioeconomic system. Thus, the public sphere is not a benign place where minds can freely discourse. The directive propaganda creating "coercive control" and "consensual control" by mass media is one prominent example. However, people often interrogate the private sphere, rather than the public sphere, dominated as it is by cultural hegemony—dominated, because the greater picture is always too big to be perceived by the individuals. The key bridge is intellectuals, who participate in the process of cultural hegemony's creation and re-creation.[7] Nevertheless, this paper mainly discusses the commons as shared resources within the social-ecological systems, where the focus is on the interactions between social systems and natural systems, as well as the institutional arrangements of managing common resources. The "multitude framework of the commons" can be understood as the larger social and political context of resource governance, which would require further exploration beyond the scope of this paper.

This paper provides a balanced survey of relevant studies and theories on social-ecological systems (SES) integration, organized in the analytical structure of the institutionalized governance process of enduring human cooperation on shared common resources and environment. It takes a critical look at the theories of the commons under the SES framework and reviews the emerging literature on complexity and uncertainty that attempts to capture the dynamics of change over time and across scale. The final section looks into some of the major challenges ahead—the application of various valuation methods without proper location of diverse values in the SES model; the interdisciplinary gap to capture the SES interactions; and the obstacles to practicing SES in reality. The paper aims to contribute to the broader discussion by identifying two interconnected research gaps: systematic understanding of interactions among the social-ecological systems integration (diagnostic explanation) and the development of appropriate scalable and integrated strategies for solving complex problems under SES integration (policy intervention).

The human species developed a complex system with adaptive and self-organizing subsystems, such as a cultural system and an economic system, and that is precisely a major link of successful evolution

7

Antonio Gramsci, *Prison Notebooks*, ed. Joseph A. Buttigieg, vol. 1 (New York: Columbia University Press, 1992).

8

Bryce Morsky and Erol Akçay, "Evolution of Social Norms and Correlated Equilibria," *Proceedings of the National Academy of Sciences of the USA* 116, no. 18 (2019): 8834–8839, https://doi.org/10.1073/pnas.1817095116, https://www.ncbi.nlm.nih.gov/pubmed/30975757.

9

Peter J. Richerson, "Cultural Evolution and Gene–Culture Coevolution," *Evolutionary Studies in Imaginative Culture* 1, no. 1 (2017): 89–92.

10

Karl Polanyi, *The Great Transformation: The Political and Economic Origins of Our Time* (1944; repr., Boston: Beacon Press, 2001); K. Polanyi, "The Economy as Instituted Process," *Trade and Market in the Early Empires* (1957): 243–270.

11

Jianguo Liu, Thomas Dietz, Stephen R. Carpenter, Marina Alberti, Carl Folke, Emilio Moran, Alice N. Pell, Peter Deadman, Timothy Kratz, and Jane Lubchenco, "Complexity of Coupled Human and Natural Systems," *Science* 317, no. 5844 (2007): 1513–1516.

12

M. J. Klapwijk, J. Boberg, J. Bergh, K. Bishop, C. Björkman, D. Ellison, A. Felton, R. Lidskog, T. Lundmark, E. C. H. Keskitalo, J. Sonesson, A. Nordin, E. M. Nordström, J. Stenlid, and E. Mårald, "Capturing Complexity: Forests, Decision-Making and Climate Change Mitigation Action," *Global Environmental Change* 52 (2018): 238–247, https://doi.org/10.1016/j.gloenvcha.2018.07.012.

within the natural, ecological, and biophysical systems. The cultural subsystem is a typical example, that all cultures evolved, more or less, from the natural system in which the community lives. Social norms emerge and evolve among human societies via constant interactions among individuals.[8] The culture construction is not only the way people try to understand the natural environment they depend on, but also the way people try to understand the human species as a part of nature. This process is dual-directional. The coupling of cultural diversity and biodiversity is a good example of gene-culture coevolution.[9] Even within the socioeconomic systems, the subsystem of market cannot be completely disembedded. "Economy" is a dynamic process embedded in a specific social structure, historical tradition, and cultural system. Economic relation is an organic component of society rather than an independent "set of rules referring to choice between the alternative uses of insufficient means."[10] Interestingly, a paradoxical antinomy was raised implying that the market could be created only by society (through social structuring) but once the market starts to operate, society becomes subordinate to allow it to function efficiently. The same logic applies to the social-ecological systems integration—that human systems cannot survive independently from natural systems—a simple yet often ignored fact. The way to organize human capabilities must be related to the interactive context where one operates and the strategy one pursues in that context.

On the other hand, the interdependence of social-ecological systems does not exclude a certain independence of each system. Both are multilevel complex systems with resilience and adaptive capacity. The adaptive capability of the human system and the nature system can adjust to cope with changes, conflicts, and shocks. This feature is core to the coevolutionary processes, where two systems or any subsystems interact with one another and are impacted by feedbacks. To coevolve is to dynamically maintain the stability of social-ecological systems (SES) interdependence.

Complexity theory is the most appropriate tool to interpret this.[11] Complex systems are composed of smaller subsystems, which are composed of units. All units and subsystems interact with one another differently, according to the information they receive and the environment they belong to, within the boundary of the overall system framework. When changes and coevolution (i.e., interactive changes and feedbacks) constantly occur, the system will adjust according to the changing dynamics—and vice versa, the units and subsystems will respond to the system adjustment.[12]

The discussions on complexity of social-ecological changes and related governance approaches signalized an emerging direction of the cross-scale and cross-system research on SES integration. In recent decades, interdisciplinary sustainable development studies have attempted to investigate the interdependence and coevolution of human societies and natural ecosystems, both intertemporally and spatially, as fully articulated in Elinor Ostrom's SES integration theory. The SES framework has endeavored to trace the parallel interactions between human systems (actors) and natural systems (resources).[13] It was important because the theory illustrated a simple mechanism of how the social system of governance and the natural resource system with distractible resource units interact with each other. However, SES theory was also strongly criticized for its inability to analyze cross-scale interactions given its limited explanatory power to interpret above-local systems. The failure to capture the dynamics of the cross-system interactions also hugely undermined its analytical framework. Another difficulty is incorporating the enriched dimension of human development, which has long developed away from narrow measurement of GDP, and the dimension of the biophysical environment, representatively demonstrated in 10 planetary boundaries,[14] as illustrated in Figure 1. Globalization with several megatrends sits in the center of social-ecological systems interaction, particularly in resilience, vulnerability, and adaptation to environmental change.[15] However, SES cannot flexibly reflect these megatrends under globalization.

13
Elinor Ostrom, "A Diagnostic Approach for Going beyond Panaceas," *Proceedings of the National Academy of Sciences* 104, no. 39 (2007): 15181–15187, http://www.ncbi.nlm.nih.gov/pmc/articles/PMC2000497/pdf/zpq15181.pdf; "A General Framework for Analyzing Sustainability of Social-Ecological Systems," *Science* 325 no. 5939 (2009): 419–422, http://science.sciencemag.org/content/sci/325/5939/419.full.pdf.

14
Johan Rockström, Will Steffen, Kevin Noone, Åsa Persson, F. Stuart Chapin, Eric F. Lambin, Timothy M. Lenton, Marten Scheffer, Carl Folke, and Hans Joachim Schellnhuber, "A Safe Operating Space for Humanity," *Nature* 461, no. 7263 (2009): 472–475.

15
Oran R. Young, Frans Berkhout, Gilberto C. Gallopin, Marco A. Janssen, Elinor Ostrom, and Sander Van der Leeuw, "The Globalization of Socio-Ecological Systems: An Agenda for Scientific Research," *Global Environmental Change* 16, no. 3 (2006): 304–316, https://www.sciencedirect.com/science/article/pii/S0959378006000276?via%3Dihub.

INTERDEPENDENCE OF SES SYSTEMS

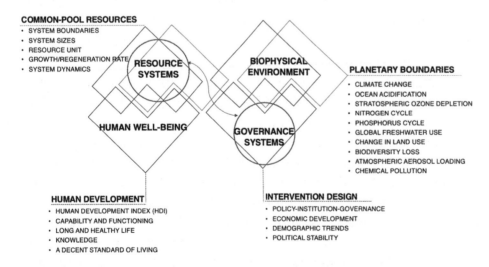

Fig.1: Interdependence of the social-ecological systems. Four social-ecological systems are studied separately as the resource systems, biophysical environment, human well-being, and governance systems. Each school of study represents some core concepts, as illustrated in the figure. All four systems are interdependent.

Drawing the whole picture of such complex, dynamic, and uncertain interdependence and coevolution of SES is extremely challenging, even seemingly impossible. Hence, it makes sense to dismantle this giant into smaller pieces for the convenience of study. However, claiming such studies as the controlled sample of the overall SES integration mechanism to justify their research findings as the answer to SES challenges is problematic. This is precisely why interdisciplinary collaboration is so important, although it remains challenging. The resistance from disciplines being "invaded" by other subjects—or, more generally, between natural sciences versus social sciences—is difficult for interdisciplinary studies.[16]

The Social Dilemmas of the Commons

The commons is an influential social science concept that represents a core dilemma of human cooperation.[17] We need to explore the complex interaction to identify reliable causalities for the institutional design to nurture and to maintain collective actions for common good. We have looked for integrated strategies to adapt to the complex changes. These strategies must include policy trade-offs and institutional fragmentation. How a hierarchy has been built is also important for understanding the impact of dynamics on cooperation.

The discussion of the commons started from the management and governance of natural resources; however, the concept of the commons is defined as commonly shared natural resources, institutional public goods, and cultural sentiments that reinforce each other by constructing the very meaning of the commons as something shared by all, or many.[18]

The origins of collective action on the commons impose the first social dilemma of sharing and free riding—what is the commons? The collective action in the commons depends on the following factors: physical characteristics of the resource (commons); the characteristics of the resource users (collective action); and the institutionalized governance structure of the resource (maintenance). The complex nonlinear interactions between biophysical systems and institutional governance systems travel across vertical levels and horizontal scales.

The characteristics of collective action on the commons impose the second social dilemma of cooperation and conflict—why do people cooperate? The commons' first classical dilemma of free riding and externality is communal sharing and common use of

16
Margaret A. Palmer, Jonathan G. Kramer, James Boyd, and David Hawthorne, "Practices for Facilitating Interdisciplinary Synthetic Research: The National Socio-Environmental Synthesis Center (SESYNC)," *Current Opinion in Environmental Sustainability* 19 (2016): 111–122, https://doi.org/10.1016/j.cosust.2016.01.002.

17
S. Battersby, "News Feature: Can Humankind Escape the Tragedy of the Commons?," *Proceedings of the National Academy of Sciences USA* 114, no. 1 (2017): 7–10, https://doi.org/10.1073/pnas.1619877114, https://www.ncbi.nlm.nih.gov/pubmed/28049815.

18
Yan Zhang, *Governing the Commons in China*, ed. Peter Nolan, Routledge Studies on the Chinese Economy (London: Routledge, 2017).

limited resources (tragedy of the commons); it then leads to the second social dilemma of why people cooperate—the origins of collective action such as trust and altruism. Altruism has been long debated.[19] Humans evolve as social beings and do present altruistic preferences, even if they are inherently composed of the "selfish genes."[20] People give up individual freedom/interest for the common good, which for various reasons is motivated beyond rationality. However, developing a clear awareness of the common interest (asymmetric information) remains a challenge for people.

Humans are changing the course of evolution. Whether consciousness serves an evolutionary purpose is still fiercely debated, but the dynamics of coevolution have been widely recognized. The public sphere and the private sphere are associated with discussions about key concepts of human evolution and the natural system in the Anthropocene epoch—the planetary boundaries and carrying capacity of nature. Arendt claimed that social evolution, from family-oriented "natural associations" to societies with a state and *polis*, imposed two "orders of existence": the private and the public.[21] For instance, the concept of private property provides the line that separates the private and the public spheres. Property rights are often interpreted as being inherent in the nature of resources themselves, rather than an institutional arrangement. However, institutionalists believed that "property rights do not refer to relations between men and things, but to the sanctioned behavioural relations among men that arise from the existence of things and pertain to their use."[22] The social structure influences the emergence and maintenance of cooperation. Human critical capacities are underlaid by two characteristics: complex scenario building and exchange of ideas with others. People can cooperate flexibly with very large numbers of people because of their social structure and imagination for fictional storytelling, as in ideology and religion. Objective global ecology depends on the subjective human imaginary fictional reality of power and politics. Therefore, the sociopolitical structure is essential for human behavior and cooperation.

The maintenance of enduring collective action on the commons imposes the third social dilemma of trust and rule—how to maintain/promote cooperation? The maintenance of collective action on the commons requires the mobilization and continuation of such cooperation and long-term sustainability of resource systems. There are different pathways to sustainability that involve different institutional arrangements and governance structures. Policy tools and their implementation are subject to the institutionalized governance structure/process.

19
David Sloan Wilson, *Does Altruism Exist?: Culture, Genes, and the Welfare of Others* (New Haven, CT: Yale University Press, 2015).
20
Richard Dawkins, *The Selfish Gene* (Oxford and New York: Oxford University Press, 1989).
21
Arendt, *The Human Condition*.
22
Eirik G. Furubotn and Svetozar Pejovich, "Property Rights and Economic Theory: A Survey of Recent Literature," *Journal of Economic Literature* 10, no. 4 (1972): 1137–1162.

Human behavior is influenced by past interactions and environmental changes. The dynamic mechanism, which consists of interactive actions and different actors with different capabilities and accountabilities, does not concern only the goal/result of the cooperation. What does the good governance of the commons look like? The Great Leviathan of the state (coercive force under the state authority) or the invisible hand of the market (imposition of private property rights and price mechanism) or Ostrom's third way of self-governance by the community (internalization of commitment)?

The study of the commons and its social dilemmas has progressed for three generations.[23] Each generational theoretical framework depicts a more accurate representation of real human-nature interactions. In this part, these theories are reviewed to introduce the latest SES framework.

23
Arun Agrawal, "Studying the Commons, Governing Common-Pool Resource Outcomes: Some Concluding Thoughts," *Environmental Science & Policy* 36 (2014): 86–91, https://doi.org/10.1016/j.envsci.2013.08.012.

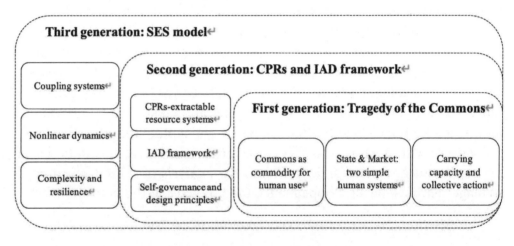

Fig. 2: Three generations of the theory of the commons. Layers of boxes represent the steady progress of each generational theory developing on the foundation of the previous one. Three boxes in each generational framework respectively represent sharing the resource/nature; governing system; and core mechanism to maintain such governance.

Tragedy of the Commons under a Simple Human-Nature Relationship

24
Benjamin Jowett, ed., *The Politics of Aristotle*, trans. B. Jowett (Oxford: Clarendon Press, 1885); Hardin, "The Tragedy of the Commons."

The commons' social dilemma of sharing, from Aristotle to Hardin,[24] focused on the pessimistic inability of humans to cooperate. The commons is still regarded as a kind of commodity (imposition of property rights or valuation to monetize resources), so only a simple human system of two organizational forms was discussed: state and market. However, the commons tragedy has never been perfectly overcome, not to mention the maintenance of cooperation on the commons. Economics tried to tackle the issue by analyzing the externalities and free riding, and hence prescribed solutions of Pigouvian tax/subsidy and assignment of property rights.[25]

The dilemma of human cooperation from a biological perspective debated whether humans as a species can cooperate. The discussions ranged from mutual aid versus the selfish gene to *homo economicus* against *homo reciprocans*. But do humans act as individual agents of rationality or as social animals? The cooperation dilemma from a social point of view sees it as a problem of asymmetric information, moral hazard, and disorganization. Prisoner's dilemma and game theory further modeled human behaviors of cooperation. A lack of trust, asymmetric information, and moral hazard can push people to make strategic choices that favor their self-interest.[26] Arrow's impossibility theorem further argued that individual preferences under rationality do not necessarily lead to the aggregate social choice and general social welfare.[27]

Collective action theory developed from group theory and organization theory and investigates cooperation at the organizational level, not at the individual level.[28] New Institutional Economics (NIE) decoded the commons dilemma from an institutional perspective.[29] NIE provided solid foundations for the second-generational studies by providing an institutional analytical framework and a conceptual tool to connect individuals with organizations. The call for incorporating "institutional arrangements and cultural factors" into the analysis of shared-resource management has never stopped since the "tragedy of the commons."[30]

Common-Pool Resources (CPRs), Institutional Analysis, and Development Framework

The commons can be seen as resource systems with subtractable resource units—common-pool resources (CPRs)—rather than a type of goods. CPRs are defined by two key features: the access control of potential users is problematic (either impossible or too costly); the resource system is subtractable, with each user able to withdraw from the welfare of others.[31] Conceptualization of CPRs deconstructed a resource as an entity in a simple human system; now it becomes a subsystem of units, actions, and rules in the complex human-nature system.

The relaxed Neo-Classical hypothesis of rationality makes it more accurate to observe human behaviors in the real world, which are analyzed in the action arena under the Institutional Analysis and

25
Arthur Cecil Pigou, *The Economics of Welfare* (London: Macmillan, 1952).

26
Joseph E. Stiglitz, *Economics of the Public Sector*, 3rd ed. (New York: W. W. Norton, 2000).

27
Kenneth Joseph Arrow, *Social Choice and Individual Values* (New York: Wiley, 1963).

28
Mancur Olson, *The Logic of Collective Action: Public Goods and the Theory of Groups* (Cambridge, MA: Harvard University Press, 1965).

29
Ronald Coase, "The New Institutional Economics," *American Economic Review* 88, no. 2 (1998): 72–74, http://www.jstor.org/stable/116895; Oliver E. Williamson, "The New Institutional Economics: Taking Stock, Looking Ahead," *Journal of Economic Literature* 38, no. 3 (2000): 595–613.

30
David Feeny, Fikret Berkes, Bonnie J. McCay, and James M. Acheson, "The Tragedy of the Commons: Twenty-Two Years Later," *Human Ecology* 18, no. 1 (1990): 1–19, https://link.springer.com/content/pdf/10.1007%2FBF00889070.pdf.

31
Ostrom, *Governing the Commons*.

Development (IAD) framework of enduring rules and institutions. By analyzing successful and failed cases with meta-analysis, eight design principles for successful CPR management were proposed. Because rules-embedded institutions can influence human behaviors and decision making on CPRs, we need to nurture accommodating institutions to maintain sustainable resource governance.

IAD theory uses institutions to deconstruct human behavior and decision making as actions being constrained by norms and rules at multiple levels. The aim is to adapt institutions to overcome commitment issues in order to nurture long-term trust and then promote cooperation behavior. Second-generation theory acknowledged bounded rationality, asymmetric information problems, preferences originated from norms, trust, and altruism, and heuristic rules. It built micro-situational analysis into a broader context, linked external rules to the internal action arena, and built a multiscale model from individual decision making to society.

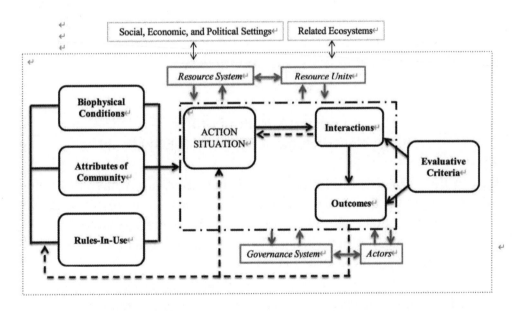

Fig. 3: Institutional Analysis and Development (IAD) Framework. This adaptation of Ostrom's IAD framework includes the wider tiers of backgrounds in which human behaviors are deeply embedded. Start with the micro-operational level of action arena (in the center), which maps out diverse actors and a sophisticated action situation. The second step is to identify resulting patterns of interactions and outcomes. The evaluation should be on both the interactive process and the outcomes. This helps us to understand the evolving dynamics and possible institutional/policy alternatives. The next step is to draw out direct causal links and feedbacks between the evolving dynamics and the resource system and governance system over a longer period of time. Biophysical conditions, local attributes, and rules in use are external factors, but they too have direct impacts on the action arena. The interactive patterns would also have feedbacks toward those external factors, for instance, changing the rules in use. Global settings and interdependent ecosystems could also influence the entire process through underlying divergent or convergent values. For instance, the profound neoliberal logic of free market and privatization. Adapted from Ostrom[32] and Zhang.[33]

32
Ostrom, *Understanding Institutional Diversity*; Ostrom, "A Diagnostic Approach for Going beyond Panaceas."
33
Zhang, *Governing the Commons in China*.

The IAD framework is designed to analyze diverse human situations from an institutional perspective.[34] As Figure 3 shows, the central part of analysis is the action arena, in which actors practice their actions according to various conditions, such as the position they hold, their characteristics, and more complicated issues, with the outcomes affected jointly. Actions can be interpreted as the specific set of choices made by the actors at specific nodes in a decision tree, which then lead to intermediate or final outcomes. A key point of IAD is that actions and outcomes interact, and such interactions have a meaningful impact on the allocation of costs and benefits related to actors' choices. IAD is a useful tool to assess various policies adopted for the governance of natural resources (i.e., the commons/CPRs). It tackles three important aspects of resource governance—complex motivational structure and capability of a diversity of actors; possible and desirable institutional design to bring out the best of humans; explanation of interactions between actions and outcomes at multiple levels. IAD, however, has limitations on two fronts. First is its isolation of the "internal" action process from "external" variables such as the attributes of the community and biophysical conditions of the resource system. Second is its constraint on explaining larger and more diverse empirical cases, apart from fisheries, irrigation, grassland, and forestry.

Looking into the Future:
The Social-Ecological Systems (SES) Model

Back in the 1970s, C. S. Holling argued that ecosystems have multiple points of equilibrium to continue functioning in spite of disturbances.[35] Ecological resilience is therefore defined as the degree to which the system can withstand disturbances without changing its fundamental processes and structures.

The third-generational social-ecological systems theory recognized that nonlinear ecological dynamics and complex human decision making need to be coupled. In the last 20 years, much more advanced explorations have been conducted in complexity studies of social network, especially computational complexity studies. In 2007, Ostrom prescribed "a diagnostic approach" to analyze SES integration.[36] Accepting the complexity of social-ecological systems' interaction and outcome, the SES approach provided a multilevel framework to map out diverse variables from the resource system and governance system. The SES framework is an expanded version

34
Ostrom, *Understanding Institutional Diversity*.

35
Crawford S. Holling, "Resilience and Stability of Ecological Systems," *Annual Review of Ecology and Systematics* 4, no. 1 (1973): 1–23.

36
Ostrom, "A Diagnostic Approach for Going beyond Panaceas."

of the IAD framework; the former provides a tool for analyzing four internal systems embedded in two external systems (resource and governance), while the latter focuses on rather narrow sets of variables set in a single level of a single system. The SES model opened a door to the new world of understanding complex social-ecological systems interaction and integration. It tackled the complexity of both systems and their interactions, with a clear objective to diagnose why and how some systems are more resilient than others. Based on a large number of empirical case studies, yet still overwhelmingly constrained to small-size fishery, irrigation, grassland, and forestry, the SES approach concluded that sustainable governance of common resources is possible via polycentric self-organization designed and evolved within a specific institutional framework.

The SES model is a complex adaptive system wherein interactions of its many parts are not deterministic or mechanistic but instead follow the feedbacks from heterogeneous agents on multiple scales. Such interactions and feedbacks can be both positive and negative. In the classic cases of irrigation systems and forest management, positive outcomes can be induced by certain institutional arrangements. On the other hand, combating global climate change—or the more recent COVID-19 pandemic—presents more complex challenges for positive cooperation. Through a process of self-organization, SES can exist in different stable states throughout various stages of an adaptive cycle. The third-generational SES theory extended largely away from previous studies on natural resources and started to bridge with other scholarly discussions on, say, the Anthropocene and sustainability science.[37]

On the other hand, Ostrom herself once said: "The theory of collective action is the core of the justification of the state."[38] There are needs of a higher-level state: "to threaten to impose a solution, . . . to provide a source of relatively neutral information, . . . to provide an arena for negotiating, . . . to help monitor compliance and sanction defection in implementation."[39] Identifying a series of adaptive institutions that can nurture trust and long-term cooperation is essential for the institutionalized governance process. The adaptive capability of certain institutional frameworks is equally, if not more, important than polycentricity to improve system resilience. Another issue that is often neglected in the discussion of the SES model and the commons is, who designs the policy intervention? Is decision making dominated by technocrats and politicians or by the general public? Is the technocracy up against democracy? Although this topic goes beyond the scope of this paper, it stands as one of the key aspects of a sustainable future.

37
Amy R. Poteete, Marco Janssen, and Elinor Ostrom, *Working Together: Collective Action, the Commons, and Multiple Methods in Practice* (Princeton, NJ: Princeton University Press, 2010).

38
Elinor Ostrom, "Beyond Markets and States: Polycentric Governance of Complex Economic Systems," *American Economic Review* (2010): 641–672.

39
Jane Mansbridge, "The Role of the State in Governing the Commons," *Environmental Science & Policy* 36 (2014): 8–10, https://doi.org/10.1016/j.envsci.2013.07.006.

A major undertaking for sustainable development research and practice is to acknowledge, account for, and govern the new context of intertwined, cross-scale, and dynamic SES of the Anthropocene. However, recognizing the system structures, processes, and values underpinning sustainability outcomes requires a significant reconfiguration and research effort into how sustainable development, resilience building, and other sustainability investments are monitored, from the local level to the global level. An immediate methodological challenge would be analyzing from causalities to complexity. Overall, the social-ecological systems theory enabled us to understand the world we live in as a holistic entity. However, as human systems are changing rapidly, the theory has to adapt to these changes and to examine the design of human systems. Nevertheless, the ultimate mission for mankind, not to mention the planet we live on, is surviving drastic transitions essentially caused by mankind. We need to shift our thinking from seeking the best practice to searching for the best fit.

Value, Waste, and the Commons Fix

William Conroy

. . . but unproductive in relation to whom and to what mode
of production?
—Antonio Gramsci, *The Prison Notebooks*

In March of 2014, the City of Chicago decided to do something surprising: it decided to give away its land. Under the auspices of a program known as Large Lots, Chicago initiated a land sale program to move vacant, residentially zoned parcels into private hands for the flat fee of one dollar. In the city's telling, Large Lots was (and remains) a "neighborhood stabilization initiative"—a revalorization strategy aimed to create "more attractive estates" in rapidly depopulating areas.[1] As such, its pilot phase targeted the South Side neighborhood of Englewood—a neighborhood that is 97 percent Black and a hotspot for vacant lots. Since then, the program has expanded, stretching to encompass a number of high-vacancy neighborhoods across the city's Black South and West Sides: areas defined by the "whites-only character of the charter documents of the US middle class,"[2] and, more recently, by the expropriative logics of neoliberalization. Under Large Lots, only a few formal caveats apply: lot applicants must already own property on the block of their purchase; they must have no outstanding "financial obligations" to the city; and they must maintain their lot according to the city's municipal code, taking care of weeds, fencing, and annual property taxes.

And yet, through conversations with planners and their partners, a subtle feature of the program emerges. Because of these racialized geographies' long "predatory inclusion"[3] in the capitalist urban fabric, their "stabilization" and revalorization are seen as particularly complicated; "knitting together" the local and the global through the material production of the built environment—while still important—will likely not suffice.[4] Therefore, Large Lots encourages, among other practices, commoning—or, more or less collective and egalitarian forms of use and management—on these one-dollar parcels. Through online guides, public outreach, and grant-funded projects, city planners and their nonprofit partners actively encourage new owners to pursue the production of commonly managed gardens and shared green spaces, as well as collective practices of ecological regeneration on this nominally residential and ostensibly "valueless" land. In the process, Chicago's planners and their partners imagine that a new sociality will emerge, one that is legible to hypermobile (and anti-Black) real estate capital. According to those close to the city's planning agenda, Large Lots and comparable projects can help create a collective subject that "take[s] leadership" and practices "on-the-ground community building," thus staving off "negative

1
City of Chicago (website), "Large Lots Program," https://www.chicago. gov/city/en/depts/dcd/ supp_info/large-lot-program.html; see also Large Lots, "Five-Year Housing Plan / Green Healthy Neighborhoods: Large Lots Programs," City of Chicago (website), https://largelots.org/static/ images/large_lot_overview. pdf.
2
Walter Johnson, "What Do We Mean When We Say, 'Structural Racism'?" *Kalfou* 3, no. 1 (2016): 36–62.
3
Keeanga-Yamahtta Taylor, *Race for Profit: How Banks and the Real Estate Industry Undermined Black Homeownership* (Chapel Hill: University of North Carolina Press, 2019).
4
See Rachel Weber, "Selling City Futures: The Financialization of Urban Redevelopment Policy," *Economic Geography* 86, no. 3 (2010): 251–274.

5

These comments were collected through interviews with Chicago planners and their nonprofit partners during the summer of 2017.

6

Ben Anderson, *Encountering Affect: Capacities, Apparatuses, Conditions* (London: Routledge, 2014), n.p. [e-book].

7

Antonio Negri, *From the Factory to the Metropolis* (Cambridge, UK: Polity Press, 2018), n.p. [e-book].

8

See Neil Brenner, "Is 'Tactical Urbanism' an Alternative to Neoliberal Urbanism?," *POST* (2015).

9

Vinay Gidwani, "Six Theses on Waste, Value, and Commons," *Social & Cultural Geography* 14, no. 7 (2013): 776.

10

Vinay Gidwani and Rajyashree Reddy, "The Afterlives of 'Waste': Notes from India for a Minor History of Capitalist Surplus," *Antipode* 43, no. 5 (2011): 1627.

11

Mazen Labban, "Rhythms of Wasting/ Unbuilding the Built Environment," in Fallow, ed. Michael Chieffalo and Julia Smachylo, a special edition of *New Geographies* 10 (Barcelona: Actar, 2019), 36.

perceptions of violence . . . [and] low-income socio-economic culture."[5] Land revalorization is thus understood as intimately linked to the production of an "affective quality"—a new "disposition towards oneself, others and the world";[6] it involves the coordination of a racialized structure of feeling, as well as the "capitalist capture of the processes of social [re]production."[7]

In these ways, Large Lots is not unique. Similar "tactical, acupunctural projects" of socio-spatial reorganization have recently been developed across the racialized, deindustrializing United States.[8] And yet what remains striking across such "acupunctural" projects is the extent to which they subvert received wisdom on the relationship between value, waste, and the commons. The Marxist tradition has long identified how the commons have operated as the economic and moral "other" of value: as ideologically conflated with waste and at odds with the notion of property. The commons, we have rightly been told, retain a logic that "stymies the accumulation of property *qua* capital."[9] In such a view, waste "haunts the modern notion of 'value'" and its realization,[10] not simply due to the fact that capitalist production "proceeds without regard [for] social needs or effective demand"[11]—producing crises of overaccumulation and devaluation—but also because of capital's incessant need to subsume the "commons-as-waste" in the name of enclosure and valorization or, as it is often put, "improvement" and "productivity." (In this context, geographer Vinay Gidwani has suggested that Marx's formula of M-C-M' is perhaps better transcribed as W-(M-C-M')-W'.) By contrast, in contemporary landscapes of racialized devalorization—in contemporary *"wastelands,"* like those targeted by Large Lots—the commons seem to appear as anything but waste; commoning is encouraged for the sake of enclosure and monopoly rent extraction, even if the contemporary regime of accumulation *maintains* the waste/value dialectic of previous moments.

To make sense of this seemingly disjunctive condition, this essay will make three closely related moves. First, it will draw on recent work within Marxist theory that attempts to rethink the value form, so as to identify the logics that animate the contemporary geography of "wasteland" in the United States. Then, and against that backdrop, it will discuss the structural function of the commons in such racialized and devalorized landscapes—developing a specific understanding of the "commons fix" in the process. Finally, it will close with two notes on the articulation of resistance in the face of this historical-geographical conjuncture, drawing especially on post-Polanyian theories regarding the (im)possibility of complete commodification.

Rethinking Value

In order to situate the contemporary production of "wasteland" in the United States, we must turn to recent efforts within Marxist theory to rethink the value form under capitalism. The most compelling of these recent efforts—for our purposes—move beyond the wage relation, underscoring the expropriative/appropriative aspect of contemporary and historical capital accumulation.[12] This literature, which has its roots in long-standing feminist, Black, and ecological Marxisms, has attempted to suggest that the capitalist value form relies on the ongoing expropriation of a host of non-commodified (or minimally commodified) spaces and forms of work. In relation to feminist critiques, such scholars suggest that the unwaged and gendered work of "provisioning, caregiving, and interacting" is integral to the social reproduction of capitalism, and thus to waged exploitation itself.[13] It is argued that these forms of work—which largely occur in the "domestic" realm and which are thus seen as spatially and theoretically constituting a "hidden abode" of capital—cannot be waged under the contemporary mode of accumulation. In much the same way that capital can never fully pay for the "value it withdraws" from waged exploitation,[14] it also requires these unwaged forms of gendered work.

In a similar register, a number of contemporary theorists have forcefully argued that the "foundation of capitalism requires a consideration of the 'hidden abode of race': the ontological distinction between superior and inferior humans—codified as race."[15] Marx himself underscored this relation through his writing on primitive accumulation, and in reference to the "pedestal" of slave labor upon which European industrial production stood.[16] So, too, did Rosa Luxemburg, in her work on capital's dependence upon a noncapitalist "strata." More recent scholars have developed far more theoretically sophisticated insights on this point, through work on variegated forms of racialized accumulation by dispossession.[17] In these accounts, accumulation by dispossession is not simply found in those moments wherein the onto-epistemology of private property and the material act of enclosure are imposed on "rural" or "noncapitalist" settings. While such historical and contemporary sites remain important for our understanding of how capital initiates its violent "cuts" through relational space,[18] they are not enough. Racialized expropriation persists, this literature maintains, in a range of "everyday" domains throughout the Global North (and the United States more specifically): in the subprime debt economy; (indirectly) through municipal fee and fine farming; and in the form of "offender-funded criminal justice 'services'" and forced carceral labor.[19]

12
Much of this work uses "expropriation" and "appropriation" in closely related, if not nearly identical, ways. Here, I use expropriation to connote the extraction of a "surplus product" from the unpaid or underpaid work of people *and/or* ecologies. See, for context, John Bellamy Foster and Brett Clark, "The Expropriation of Nature," *Monthly Review* (2018).

13
Nancy Fraser and Rahel Jaeggi, *Capitalism: A Conversation in Critical Theory* (Cambridge, UK: Polity Press, 2018), 31.

14
Richard Walker, "Value and Nature: From Value Theory to the Fate of the Earth," *Human Geography* 9, no. 1 (2016): 1–15.

15
Michael Dawson, "Hidden in Plain Sight: A Note on Legitimation Crises and the Racial Order," *Critical Historical Studies* 3, no. 1 (2016): 147.

16
Walter Johnson, "The Pedestal and the Veil: Rethinking the Capitalism/Slavery Question," *Journal of the Early Republic* 24, no. 2 (2004): 299–308.

17
Jackie Wang, *Carceral Capitalism* (Cambridge, MA: Semiotext(e), 2018).

18
Nicholas Blomley, "Cuts, Flows, and the Geographies of Property," *Law, Culture and the Humanities* 7, no. 2 (2010): 206.

19
Wang, *Carceral Capitalism*, 76.

20
Ibid., 71.
21
Fraser and Jaeggi, *Capitalism*, 41.
22
Michael McIntyre and Heidi Nast, "Bio(necro) polis: Marx, Surplus Populations, and the Spatial Dialectics of Reproduction and 'Race,'" *Antipode* 43, no. 5 (2011): 1466.

23
Sharad Chari, "The Blues and the Damned: (Black) Life-That-Survives Capital and Biopolitics," *Critical African Studies* 9, no. 2 (2017): 156.
24
Jared Sexton, "People-of-Color-Blindness," *Social Text* 28, no. 2 (2010): 36.
25
See, by way of comparison, Andreas Malm, "Against Hybridism: Why We Need to Distinguish between Nature and Society, Now More Than Ever," *Historical Materialism* 27, no. 2 (2019): 156–187.
26
Richard Walker and Jason Moore, "Value, Nature, and the Vortex of Accumulation," in *Urban Political Ecology in the Anthropo-obscene: Interruptions and Possibilities*, eds. Erik Swyngedouw and Henrik Ernston (London: Routledge, 2019), n.p., [e-book].
27
Ibid.
28
Thomas Purcell, Alex Loftus, and Hug March, "Value-Rent-Finance," *Progress in Human Geography* 44, no. 3 (2020): 440.

Of course, these racialized forms of expropriation "have a highly spatialized character."[20] This is a point that numerous geographers have taken up, rendering visible the ways in which racialized and anti-Black dispossession—and the "differential valuation" of nonwhite work—concomitantly involves the production of "inherently expropriable" spaces.[21] With this view, capitalism always moves through "racially ontologized hierarchies of space."[22] Much as historical forms of primitive accumulation relied on the dual ideology of commons-as-waste and commoners-as-waste, contemporary forms of accumulation simultaneously render some people and their spaces as ontologically devalued. Of course, "ontology" here is not meant to suggest permanence; following Sharad Chari, this "ontologization" of both people and space is always fraught, and subject to circumvention and refusal.[23] These forms of devaluation represent a "political ontology," not a "metaphysical notion," which is always available to "historic challenge through collective struggle."[24]

Such insights regarding the "expropriability" of particular spaces lead us directly into the realm of ecological Marxism. These scholars are often concerned with the ongoing expropriation (see note 12) of non-commodified or undercapitalized resource frontiers and their centrality to capital accumulation during moments of overaccumulation and under-production. Emergent work in this register builds on, and ostensibly transcends, the literature on "metabolic rift" and the "second contradiction" of capitalism, chastising its purported Cartesian binarism in the process.[25] Much like feminist and Black Marxist accounts, this work posits a negative dialectic: "The valuation of paid labour is simultaneously the devaluation of unpaid work—the work of 'women, nature, and colonies.'"[26] At their most bold, these theorizations attempt to posit a new value theoretical nomenclature altogether. Richard Walker and Jason Moore have recently proposed the notion of "unified labor-nature time," which attempts to name the ways in which labor time is "fundamentally shaped by [the] unpaid work of humans and nature as a whole."[27]

Of course, in raising these critiques of capitalism and its value form, my point is not to adjudicate the relative merits of these various perspectives or the authors behind them. I have clearly elided significant disagreements within this broad discourse, not least regarding the distinction between "productive" and "unproductive" (or value-producing and non-value-producing) labor; the relation between value and price; and, perhaps most important, the extent to which *value itself* represents a critical category that must be overcome or abolished,[28] or to put this final point differently, the extent to which these theories presume that "the problem [with capitalism] is ultimately not that all value comes from labour, and is expropriated from its rightful owners, but that labour in capitalism is condemned to the production of value."[29]

Rather, my simple goal in the context of this short intervention is to sketch out the ways in which these value-theoretical literatures allow us to make sense of the contemporary production of vacant and devalorized "wasteland" in the United States. One overwhelming point becomes explicit in reference to the above summary: contemporary US capitalism depends upon various forms of racialized (as well as ecological and gendered) expropriation; and these forms of expropriation are spatialized and territorialized, such that whole swathes of Black (urban) space can be marked as ontologically "lootable."[30] Here, the production of vacant, devalorized land in Black neighborhoods (like those targeted by Large Lots) makes "logical" sense. Increasingly sophisticated forms of racialized accumulation by dispossession—such as subprime lending and the extension of high-risk credit at the scale of the city[31]—only build on past strategies and regimes of expropriation, such as redlining and blockbusting. Each historical articulation of expropriation was (and is) integral to capitalist valorization, and each "naturally" targeted (and targets) Black people, spaces, and resources. The uneven racial geography of wasteland thus appears as the residue (though not necessarily as the inevitable outcome) of this logic.

The "Commons Fix"

Not only does the (re)emergent literature on value help us to recontextualize the production of "wasteland" in the United States, but it also repositions those strategies that have been developed in recent years to recommodify land in those geographies, in the form of policies like Chicago's Large Lots. As noted, these efforts often use the commons or commoning in order to open the gap between capitalized ground rent and potential ground rent,[32] specifically in Black communities where existing modes of sociality and collective engagement are considered illegible to rent-seeking urban capital. Capital's reliance on the commons—and on what Massimo De Angelis has called the "commons fix"—has been identified by several scholars in other contexts (as has capital's reliance on local forms of "non-market coordination," which, like urban planning more broadly, function as the "collective guarantor of production and reproduction relations"[33]). Work in this vein often underscores capitalism's dependence on "the

29
Geoff Mann, "Value after Lehman," *Historical Materialism* 18 (2010): 176.

30
Wang, *Carceral Capitalism*, 79.

31
Ibid., 112.

32
Neil Smith, *The New Urban Frontier: Gentrification and the Revanchist City* (London: Routledge, 1996).
33
Aram Eisenschitz and Jamie Gough, "The Contradictions of Neo-Keynesian Local Economic Strategy," *Review of International Political Economy* 3, no. 3 (1996): 434; Michael Dear and Allen Scott, "Towards a Framework for Analysis," in *Urbanization and Urban Planning in Capitalist Society*, eds. Michael Dear and Allen Scott (London: Methuen, 1981), n.p., [e-book].

34
Massimo De Angelis, "Does Capital Need a Commons Fix?" *Ephemera* 13, no. 3 (2013): 610.

35
Ibid., 612.

36
Alvaro Sevilla-Buitrago, "Capitalist Formations of Enclosure: Space and the Extinction of the Commons," *Antipode* 47, no. 4 (2015): 1001.

37
McKenzie Wark, *General Intellects* (New York: Verso, 2017), n.p. [e-book].

38
Samuel Stein, "The Housing Crisis and the Rise of the Real Estate State," *New Labor Forum* 28, no. 3 (2019): 52–60.

39
Neil Brenner, *New Urban Spaces* (Oxford: University of Oxford Press, 2018), 61.

40
I develop this concept in my essay "The Biopolitical Commons: A Revised Theory of Urban Land in the Age of Biopolitical Production," *Planning Theory* 18, no. 4 (2019): 470–491. As a phrase, "biopolitical commons" suggests a relation to work on biopolitical production, and to the work of Michael Hardt and Antonio Negri in particular, without repurposing or redefining one of their key terms. "Biopolitical common[s]" does, however, appear in their work at times (to connote something other than what is described here). According to my most recent count, it appears twice in *Multitude* and three times in *Time for Revolution*, as well as in some of the secondary literature on biopolitical production.

41
Ibid.

ability of people . . . to engage in commoning" due to the low wage rate, and/or the social reproductive burdens of contemporary financialized neoliberal capitalism.[34]

And yet, the commons fix identified here—pursued in the midst of racialized urban devalorization—is more specific than that which has been identified in these previous accounts. It is not about momentarily resolving the contradictions that arise due to hyper-exploitation, nor is it even solely about enlisting the commons in a "divisive, competitive process" of urban entrepreneurialism.[35] Rather, it is specifically about mediating the relationship between *racial* capitalism's expropriative dimension and (anti-Black) urban real estate capital's drive to preserve the accumulation of monopoly rents. Thus, this commons fix—which has as its ultimate goal the "movement of spatial abstraction and commodification"[36]—operates in concert with McKenzie Wark's observation that "the global urban crisis is a witness to the exhaustion of [the] positive externalities upon which capital has depended."[37] Municipal government—as part and parcel of the "real estate state"[38]—emerges as a key actor in the mediation of this crisis, even if the resultant commons fix is always a "coalescence, or 'meshing,' of multiple sociospatial . . . struggles."[39]

Moreover, the commons that emerge in the context of this fix are perhaps more accurately described as *biopolitical* commons.[40] To make that distinction is to underscore the fact that the city and regional planners behind this commons fix often work to nurture subjectivities, affects, and collective socialities that are legible to urban real estate capital, in addition to simply encouraging collective forms of land use and management; such planners seek to socialize *commoners* due to the anti-Blackness of urban property markets. In making a related argument, I have previously engaged in a sympathetic reading and critique of the autonomous Marxist literature on biopolitical production.[41] That literature is useful here—in defining the notion of the biopolitical commons, and its relation to the commons fix—given its contention that contemporary urban capitalism revolves around the "destruction of the common" and the expropriation of social cooperation.[42]

Put more directly, the autonomous Marxist literature on biopolitical production is useful in our understanding of the commons fix given its recognition that the valorization of urban space is today (more than ever) integrally linked to both the commons and subjectification. And yet this literature remains insufficient for our purposes. For one, such autonomist Marxist theorizations generally presuppose a linear model of urban enclosure—one that is at odds with the more dialectically evolving commons fix sketched here, which implies contradiction and determinate negation. This linear model of urban enclosure allows theorists of biopolitical production to argue that contemporary urban processes are part and parcel of the unidirectional "real subsumption of society under capital";[43] the extraction of urban rent appears as "perfectly analogous to pulling oil from shale," given the necessarily reactive (or, following Mario Tronti, "subordinate") character of the capitalist class.[44] In making such claims, this literature obscures the active organization of social cooperation and subjectification that is often undertaken by today's city and regional planners—particularly in those landscapes marked by a racialized "condition of ontological lack."[45] (Michael Hardt and Antonio Negri's recent work on the formal and real subsumption of race within capitalist society productively speaks to some of these concerns; that work, however, is beyond the compass of this short intervention.[46])

Of course, this is not the only way in which the image of the commons fix sketched out here diverges from work on biopolitical production. Three others remain:

1   Work on biopolitical production often attempts to suggest that processes of contemporary urban enclosure underscore the general hegemony of "immaterial" production to capitalism today. In doing so, these authors negate the fact that "there is no place for the material-immaterial distinction" in Marxist thought given that "everything relates through material practices and forms of exchange."[47] In contrast, the abovementioned commons fix— which seeks to revalorize racialized urban "wasteland"—remains tightly linked to deeply extractive, material forms of production that stretch far beyond the bounded geography of the city itself. Put tersely: the commons fix cannot, in the last instance, be considered apart from the "planetary mine."[48]

2   Work on biopolitical production often reproduces a false distinction between the "natural" and "social" commons, with the understanding that the former is defined by a "logic of scarcity," while the latter is defined by its reproducibility.[49] In our current conjuncture this contention is increasingly difficult to accept: commons are surely always "more-than-human."[50] As such, those commons that emerge through the commons fix are best understood as socio-ecological.

42
Michael Hardt and Antonio Negri, "Following in Marx's Footsteps," in *Reflections on Empire* (Cambridge, UK: Polity, 2008), 181.
43
Antonio Negri, *The Porcelain Workshop: For a New Grammar of Politics* (Cambridge, MA: MIT Press, 2008), 23.
44
Michael Hardt and Antonio Negri, *Assembly* (Oxford: Oxford University Press, 2017), 169.
45
Matthew Wilhelm-Solomon, Peter Kankonde, and Lorena Núñez, "Vital Instability: Ontological Insecurity and African Urbanisms," *Critical African Studies* 9, no. 2 (2017): 143.
46
Michael Hardt and Antonio Negri, "The Multiplicities within Capitalist Rule and the Articulation of Struggles," *tripleC* 16, no. 2 (2018): 444.
47
Joel Wainwright, "Commonwealth," *Human Geography* 4, no. 2 (2011): 117.
48
Martín Arboleda, *Planetary Mine: Territories of Extraction under Late Capitalism* (New York: Verso, 2020).
49
Michael Hardt, "Two Faces of Apocalypse: A Letter from Copenhagen," *Polygraph* 22 (2010): 26; see also Sara Nelson and Bruce Braun, "Autonomia in the Anthropocene: New Challenges to Radical Politics," *South Atlantic Quarterly* 116, no. 2 (2017): 223–236.

50
Patrick Bresnihan, "The More-Than-Human Commons: From Commons to Commoning," in *Space, Power, and the Commons: The Struggle for Alternative Futures*, eds. Samuel Kirwan, Lelia Dawney, and Julian Brigstocke (New York: Routledge, 2016), 93–112.

51
Hardt and Negri, "Following in Marx's Footsteps," 181.

52
See Stuart Hall, "Race, Articulation and Societies Structured in Dominance," in *Black British Cultural Studies: A Reader*, eds. Houston Baker, Manthia Diawara, and Ruth Lindeborg (Chicago: University of Chicago Press, 1996).

3   Work on biopolitical production undertakes a radical rewrite of Marxist value theory, rejecting many of its key insights for contemporary political economic analysis. Building on a reading of Marx's "Fragment on Machines" in the *Grundrisse* (1939), such scholars claim that under post-Fordist "immaterial" production, "the temporal unit of labour as the basis for measuring the creation of value is by now a nonsense."[51] As a general theory of contemporary production, such a claim remains highly dubious, even if such forms of ostensibly "immaterial" social production operate as an "articulated combination" in particular geographies.[52] The commons fix sketched out here resists claims regarding the general "crisis of measurability" and the "becoming-rent" of profit on a planetary scale.

Resistance: Two Notes

This presentation of the commons fix—understood here as a conjunctural fix to the contradiction between the expropriative dimension of racialized capitalism and the ongoing accumulation of urban monopoly rents— may not inspire much hope for those interested in imagining and producing a more egalitarian city. It appears as if the commons have become completely regressive. However, my point is not that all urban commons are necessarily implicated in the commons fix; it is, rather, that we must be aware of the ways in which we make commons, and of their relation to the circulation of capital. Therefore, by way of concluding, I will underscore two points for those interested in the articulation of resistance in this historical-geographical conjuncture. First, we must common with an acute spatiotemporal perspective. In the case of land-based commoning, we must view the parcel not as "detachable," "emptiable space," but rather as "relational" and "emplaced" within a de- and re-territorializing multiscalar political economy.[53] Further still, we must understand the land itself as embedded in a *longue durée* history in which "the concept of the human" has not been borne equally by all, producing strikingly uneven relations to property and capital accumulation.[54] Such a view is not, on the surface, particularly radical; nevertheless, it is only with a rejection of the notion of time as a series of instants, and of space as an "abstract, calculable and extensible surface,"[55] that we can produce commons attentive to their positionality in relation to the planetary geography of racial capitalism. That is, it is only with such a relational ontology that we can see the "interconnections that liberal capitalism seeks to obscure."[56]

53
Nicholas Blomley, "The Territory of Property," *Progress in Human Geography* 40, no. 5 (2016): 600–601.

54
Brenna Bhandar, *Colonial Lives of Property: Law, Land, and Racial Regimes of Ownership* (Durham, NC: Duke University Press, 2018), 13.

55
Blomley, "The Territory of Property," 599.

56
Keith Feldman, "Blackness and Relationality: An ACLA Forum," *Comparative Literature* 68, no. 2 (2016): 111.

The second point that we must consider, if we are to effectively articulate resistance in the face of the commons fix, is more theoretical. It stems from the Polanyian contention that "fictitious commodities"—such as land, labor, and money—pose difficulties to capital. That claim is based on the understanding that to include these "fictions" "in the market mechanism [would] subordinate the substance of society itself to the laws of the market";[57] and, implicitly, on the notion that capitalism always entails the "restless drive to reproduce and expand the scale and scope of commodification."[58] This understanding of capital, and of the so-called double movement, goes a long way in identifying the forms of resistance that might arise should the commons fix succeed in its aim of land recommodification in racialized urban geographies and "waste-lands." And yet this Polanyian logic also sits uneasily in relation to the value-theoretical critiques that opened this essay. In reading feminist, Black, and ecological Marxisms together, we come to see that deepening commodification not only provokes normative countermovements but also represents a practical and theoretical impossibility under capitalism; in fact, *complete commodification is not even in the interest of capital itself.* Capitalism relies not necessarily on Luxemburg's "non-capitalist strata," but on the existence of "noncommodities," even if the boundaries that define these noncommodities are always being reworked through political contestation.[59]

What, then, does this mean for those mobilizing in the face of the commons fix? To begin, it means that any form of resistance—any attempt to produce a countercommons in such contexts—cannot solely function in opposition to recommodification. As we produce counter-commons, we must be aware of the ways in which noncommodification, too, can serve the imperatives of global capital. Second, this observation should alert us to the fact that the revalorization of racialized urban space, as pursued through the commons fix, cannot do away with spatialized expropriability; it can only move it around. Racial capitalism's expropriable zones will persist somewhere—unless, that is, we more broadly reject capitalism and its political ontology of anti-Blackness.

57
Karl Polanyi, *The Great Transformation* (Boston: Beacon Press, 1957 [1944]), 71.

58
Scott Prudham, "Commodification," in *A Companion to Environmental Geography*, eds. Noel Castree, David Demeritt, Diana Liverman, and Bruce Rhoads (Oxford: Wiley Blackwell, 2016), 127.

59
Nancy Fraser, "Can Society Be Commodities All the Way Down? Post-Polanyian Reflections on Capitalist Crisis," *Economy and Society* 43, no. 4 (2014): 544.

Acknowledgments
Many thanks to Sai Balakrishnan, Neil Brenner, Álvaro Sevilla Buitrago, Kelly Christina Mendonça, Mojdeh Mahdavi, Alex Vasudevan, and Liang Wang for their comments on earlier versions of this essay.

The Space Created
by the COVID-19 Pandemic

Rachel Cobb

On March 12, 2020, my husband, our son, and I came down with coronavirus. We were in the very first wave of people who contracted it in the US. Many were taken by surprise by how swiftly the virus invaded the city. News that was applicable in the morning was outdated by the day's wrap-up. We, too, were caught unprepared. We had not stocked up on food, we had only the usual supply of Tylenol (not enough to counter the raging fevers we developed), and not a single thermometer in our home had a working battery. In normal times, these things would have been easily remedied, but in the first wave of COVID-19, they became real obstacles. Even if we could have gone to a store—instead of quarantining—supplies had already been wiped out. When my husband had to be admitted to an emergency room, we had no other means of transport than an ambulance because, like many New Yorkers, we did not own a car.

A few weeks later, when I was still recovering, I began photographing throughout New York City. I went out every day and night for months, exploring the city that had been transformed by lockdown.

Was this the place I'd lived in for more than three decades?
At night I saw only deliverymen, ambulances, and homeless people.

I documented New York City from the time when it was the deserted epicenter of the pandemic, with refrigerator trucks used as makeshift morgues, through the summer, when it was bursting with protesters.

During lockdown there was literally more space on New York City's streets as people remained indoors. At 9:38 PM, I didn't pass a single other car in the Midtown Tunnel.

JFK Airport had more personnel than passengers.

Restaurants were shuttered.

Red tape cordoned off a tented outdoor triage area at SUNY Downstate Medical Center.

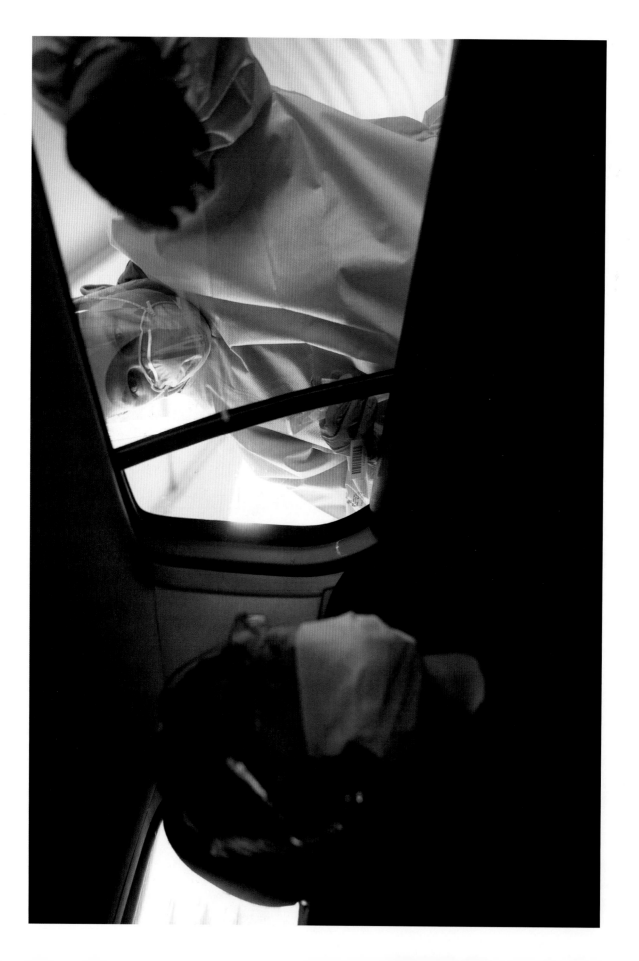

For a time, COVID tests, nearly impossible to get, were limited to those in cars.

As schools were closed, homework assignments were left in boxes outside.

With the city so empty, Times Square became a kind of playground where people would skateboard or ride bikes the wrong way up the street, police be damned.

In warm weather people gathered in parks, inside prescribed socially distanced white circles.

Kids went for joyrides on their bikes and sat in the middle of the street, photographing one another.

Little by little New Yorkers reclaimed the streets, which is to say, their space.

On Memorial Day, the traditional start of summer, George Floyd was killed, and a convulsion of social justice protests quickly followed. "Whose streets?" "Our streets!" protesters shouted as police followed along behind. People expanded their personal space through the act of protest by holding signs aloft, leaning into barricaded spaces, and standing on traffic barriers,

Protesters took a knee in busy crossroads.

Police, struggling to maintain order, cordoned off symbolic sites like Rockefeller Center to prevent protesters from entering.

By late June, a sit-in turned City Hall Park into a police-free zone where street barricades went up at night.

The movement, which caught on globally, had an especially urgent energy after months of pandemic confinement, months spent in enclosed space.

Inside the Zone, outside the Commons: London's Waterfront Redevelopment as Enclosure

Alan Wiig

London's ascendancy to the top of the global urban hierarchy has propelled the metropolis even further into an elite, exclusive, international concentration of financialized capital.[1] And yet the city's long and diverse history of labor, protest, and struggle for the right to the city remains in pockets of "convivial multiculture."[2] Contemporary London's resulting geography charts a splintering terrain[3] that operates in a constantly evolving relationship between the enclosures of capitalist urbanization and unfolding efforts at cultivating an urban commons.[4]

In this paper, I focus attention on the enclosure of East London's Royal Albert Dock, a publicly held deindustrialized waterfront site among the eight square miles of historic docklands, sited in the borough of Newham and transformed into a business enclave controlled by a Chinese real estate developer. If cities are "a key location in the struggle for the commons," enacted within "public space, sidewalks, access to parks and recreation areas, infrastructure like public transport, the provision of roads, the supply of energy or water, an environment that is free of waste, air pollution, or noise, or even public culture,"[5] then the enclosure of spaces like the Royal Albert Dock provides a productive case for considering these matters at the interface of commoning also found in East London's neighborhoods, such as in the struggle for affordable housing,[6] the provision of civic infrastructure,[7] and the control over redevelopment.[8] Here, the politics of large-scale urban transformation operate as contemporary enclosure[9] of what was publicly owned, vacant industrial land, transferred to private control without democratic debate, foreclosing the possibility of expanding the commons beyond existing public spaces and actions. In framing the dock's redevelopment as enclosure,[10] I recognize that London's waterfront has always been a globalized and privatized economic space; in making this argument, my aim is to draw attention to the ways that enclosure-as-urbanization can constrain or limit the geographies within which London's residents and civil society can advance ambitions for a more inclusive, more "common" city. As geographer Doreen Massey explains,[11] London's potential futures have been narrowly focused on the pursuit of capital at the expense of expanding its existing multicultural, transnational commons.[12] Additionally, in advancing this argument, I draw attention to the discrepancy between the idea of the commons as localized relationships that run contrary to globalized cities and the spaces and infrastructure of multinational capital. In so doing, my intent is to inform a systematic problematique of our understanding of urban commons and commoning more generally today.

1
R. Atkinson, *Alpha City: How London Was Captured by the Super-Rich* (New York: Verso, 2020).
2
P. Gilroy, *After Empire: Melancholia or Convivial Culture?* (Abingdon: Routledge, 2004); see also R. Moore, *Slow Burn City: London in the Twenty-First Century* (London: Picador-Pan Macmillan, 2017).
3
S. Graham and S. Marvin, *Splintering Urbanism: Networked Infrastructures, Technological Mobilities and the Urban Condition* (New York: Routledge, 2001); A. Jeffrey, C. McFarlane, and A. Vasudevan, "Rethinking Enclosure: Space, Subjectivity and the Commons," *Antipode* 44, no. 4 (2012): 1247–1267.
4
S. Bunce, "Pursuing Urban Commons: Politics and Alliances in Community Land Trust Activism in East London," *Antipode* 48, no. 1 (2016): 134–150; T. Gillespie, K. Hardy, and P. Watt, "Austerity Urbanism and Olympic Counter-Legacies: Gendering, Defending and Expanding the Urban Commons in East London," *Environment and Planning D: Society and Space* 36, no. 5 (2018): 812–830.
5
M. Kip, "Moving beyond the City: Conceptualizing Urban Commons from a Critical Urban Studies Perspective," in *Urban Commons: Moving beyond State and Market*, ed. M. Dellenbaugh et al. (Basel: Birkhäuser, 2015), 43.
6
Bunce, "Pursuing Urban Commons."

Background:
East London Today

7
J. McGuirk, "Urban Commons Have Radical Potential–It's Not Just about Community Gardens," *Guardian*, June 15, 2015, https://www.theguardian.com/cities/2015/jun/15/urban-common-radical-community-gardens.

8
P. Watt, "It's Not for Us," *City* 17, no. 1 (2013): 99–118.

9
B. Christophers, *The New Enclosure: The Appropriation of Public Land in Neoliberal Britain*, http://search.ebscohost.com/login.aspx?direct=true&scope=site&db=nlebk&db=nlabk&AN=1995210; S. Hodkinson, "The New Urban Enclosures," *City* 16, no. 5 (2012): 500–518.

10
The enclosure of the dock site is in actuality the reenclosure, given the walls that would have enclosed the Royal Docks originally but are no longer standing. See P. Linebaugh, *Stop Thief!: The Commons, Enclosures, and Resistance* (Oakland, CA: PM Press, 2014), 26–27.

11
D. Massey, *World City* (Malden, MA: Polity, 2007).

12
See P. Linebaugh and M. Rediker, *The Many-Headed Hydra: Sailors, Slaves, Commoners, and the Hidden History of the Revolutionary Atlantic* (New York: Verso, 2000).

13
P. Hall, *Urban and Regional Planning*, 4th ed. (London: Routledge, 2002).

14
Massey, *World City*.

15
Watt, "It's Not for Us."

16
Ibid., 103.

After decades of deindustrialized abandonment and decline, East London's Thames River waterfront, and the enclosed waterway of the Royal Docks, has seen significant transformation since the 1980s.[13] As jobs and employment opportunities shifted to information, creative, and finance sectors,[14] today the diverse, working-class neighborhoods that make up the greater area are geographically proximate to, but socially and economically distant from, the primary nodes of global capitalism in the city, namely Docklands-Canary Wharf and the city of London.[15] The greater area is home to long-term poverty brought about in large part by the decline of manufacturing, the rise of containerized shipping, and the subsequent closure of the docks where many workers were employed. Throughout East London today, these disinvested neighborhoods sit alongside gentrification, global finance, remnant sites of the 2012 Olympics, and transit-oriented, shopping center retail. The disenfranchisement of East London's diverse, historically working-class boroughs is ongoing, where "despite their sometimes spectacular physical impacts (as in London Docklands), [large-scale redevelopment has] had at best only modest success in raising the economic and social well-being of deprived local populations."[16] East London's waterfront has been subject to attempts at regeneration since the 1970s,[17] moving east and downstream from Canary Wharf, which sits closer to the city center, toward the Royal Albert Dock and the surrounding borough, Newham. A full examination of the 1,100 acres that comprise the three royal docks—Albert, Victoria, and George V—is beyond the bounds of this paper, although certainly a topic worthy of study.

With the Royal Albert Dock, London's speculative plans for economic growth merge with China's ambitions to align the transcontinental infrastructure and logistics networks of the Belt and Road Initiative. The delineation of this zone into a space of Chinese investment signaled the United Kingdom's desire to reshape trade geographies resulting from the long decline of North Atlantic capitalism and the more recent geopolitical and economic turbulence emerging from the Brexit vote to separate from the European Union. Alongside the wider, ongoing restructuring of the entire royal docks' waterfront and quayside, the Royal Albert Dock materializes as a globalized enclave integrated into China's vision for a world economy pivoted toward Asia. These spaces and the global infrastructure they rely on concentrate the systems and networks that prioritize the circulation of particular bodies, goods, and information with precedence given to the faraway over the nearby,[18] layering quick accessibility to airports and regional transportation with premium municipal services, policing and security, and telecommunications among corporate real estate and worker amenities.

Today, staunching the economic decline of the 1970s and 1980s is no longer the priority: if anything, London is overdeveloped.[19] London's centrality to global finance is undisputed, but the city's urbanization strategies strongly favor attracting multinational capital over local residents' immediate, documented needs for, for instance, anti-poverty programs such as workforce training, built-environment and infrastructure regeneration, and affordable housing schemes.[20] While the fallout from Brexit may challenge the city's position if banks and other firms move their headquarters into cities within the European Union, for now London's key problem remains the unaffordability of housing, even for the middle class.[21] Long-standing efforts at creating inclusive urban commons exist in East London, from the creation of participatory, community-driven plans for the dockland regeneration[22] to community land trusts ensuring affordable housing,[23] but the embedded political structure in support of capitalist urbanization remains intact. The attractive, cosmopolitan atmosphere, proximity, density, and diversity that London provides, and that many residents are priced out of,[24] are produced as much through investments in the city—by public and private money—as through the city's commons themselves, even as the city becomes more and more exclusive and unaffordable.

Pivoting to the East:
Royal Albert Dock as Chinese Urbanism

Below, I critique the dock's redevelopment as the enactment of a narrow vision that limits the potential of commoning to peripheral or minor spaces in the proverbial and literal shadow of the Alpha City's towers and office blocks.[25] With this critique, I do not mean to imply that the dock would inherently have turned into the commons otherwise, but instead to highlight the constraints faced by those advancing the commons when large-scale urbanization proceeds through narrow visions for investment and growth-above-all-else like those discussed here.

Upon announcement of the project in 2013, Royal Albert Dock was described as an "Asian Business Port," a potential location for East Asian financial firms seeking a location in central London.[26] Over this same period, China established a banking presence in overseas financial markets, including those in the city of London as well as Canary

17
F. Brill, "Playing the Game: A Comparison of International Actors in Real Estate Development in Modderfontein, Johannesburg and London's Royal Docks," *Geoforum* (2018), https://doi.org/10.1016/j.geoforum.2018.05.015.
18
A. Wiig and J. Silver, "Turbulent Presents, Precarious Futures: Urbanization and the Deployment of Global Infrastructure," *Regional Studies* 53, no. 6 (2019): 912–923.
19
Atkinson, *Alpha City*.
20
Guardian readers and F. Perry, "'This Is East London, Not Park Lane': Stratford's Regeneration, in Your Words," *Guardian*, August 15, 2014, https://www.theguardian.com/cities/2014/aug/15/stratford-regeneration-your-stories-olympic-legacy.
21
A. Minton, *Big Capital: Who Is London For?* (London: Penguin, 2017).
22
S. Brownill, "The People's Plan for the Royal Docks: Some Contradictions in Popular Planning," *Planning Practice & Research* 2, no. 4 (1988): 15–21.
23
Bunce, "Pursuing Urban Commons."
24
Minton, *Big Capital*.
25
Atkinson, *Alpha City*.

26
J. Pickford and E. Hammond, "Boris Johnson to Seal £1Bn Docks Deal with Chinese Developer," *Financial Times*, May 28, 2013, https://www.ft.com/content/f7b5599c-c7b0-11e2-9c52-00144feab7de; J. Pickford and E. Hammond, "China Investor Waits to Tie Up at Quays of Old British Empire," *Financial Times*, May 10, 2013, https://www.ft.com/content/138bb0fa-b99a-11e2-bc57-00144feabdc0.

27
L.-M. Töpfer and S. Hall, "London's Rise as an Offshore RMB Financial Centre: State–Finance Relations and Selective Institutional Adaptation, *Regional Studies* 52, no. 8 (2018): 1053–1064.

28
See, for instance, D. Lidington, "Writing a New Chapter in the Global Era," https://www.gov.uk/government/speeches/writing-a-new-chapter-in-the-global-era.

29
L. Hughes and J. Ford, "UK-China Relations: From 'Golden Era' to the Deep Freeze," *Financial Times*, http://www.ft.com/content/804175d0-8b47-4427-9853-2aded76f48e4.

30
L. Henneke and C. Knowles, "Conceptualizing Cities and Migrant Ethnicity: The Lessons of Chinese London," in *Routledge International Handbook of Contemporary Racisms*, ed. J. Solomos (New York: Routledge, 2020), 38.

31
ABP (Advanced Business Parks), "ABP Royal Albert Dock London," *Quarterly Review*, 2017, http://www.abp-london.co.uk/assets/Brochures/Quarterly-Review/ABP-Quarterly-Review-01-October-2017.pdf.

Wharf.[27] The contract to redevelop the dock was signed before the vote to separate from the EU. Post-Brexit, the intensifying economic imperative to attract non-European enterprise has become a key element of London's—and the UK's—pivot to Chinese trading partners as part of a "golden era" for UK-China relations.[28] However, in summer 2020, as the COVID-19 public health pandemic took its toll on the UK's economy, geopolitical relations with China deteriorated due to the UK's ban of Huawei's 5G cellular infrastructure from the country and the support of Hong Kong's protests over Chinese rule. The implications of both the pandemic and geopolitical turbulence for Chinese investment in London are uncertain at best, raising the potential for misalignment between the two countries' respective economies,[29] with projects like the Royal Albert Dock stuck in the middle.

The Royal Albert Dock may at some point house firms related to or adjacent to Chinese banking and global finance, although this has not yet been the case. Broadly, the zone aligns London to the emergent transcontinental trade, exchange, and circulation of the Belt and Road Initiative, including the movement of freight trains over 7,500 miles of railway between London and Yiwu, China, beginning in 2017.[30] Conceptualizing the Royal Albert Dock amid China's transcontinental infrastructure corridors recognizes that global infrastructure deployment is occurring not only in the emerging economies of the Global South or the periphery of Europe. This infrastructural deployment and resulting urbanization stretch beyond the newly delineated corridors, both symbolically and physically, into the center of already hyperdeveloped London.

The vision for redeveloping the Royal Albert Dock into a hub of "New Silk Road" Chinese urbanism[31] exemplified the desire of then mayor, now prime minister Boris Johnson to create a speculative third node of global capitalism in the city, one intended to be a "gateway" to Asian markets.[32] The dock shifted from a publicly held but derelict site into what the zone's architect describes as "a vibrant 24/7 district on London's waterways,"[33] owned by, financed by, constructed by, and intended primarily for Chinese enterprise.[34] Although the project began before Brexit, it has been hailed as a post-Brexit "success."[35] The contract to sell the Royal Albert Dock's site to Advanced Business Parks (ABP), a China-based developer that had never worked in the UK, was announced in 2013.[36]

The choice of ABP was unexpected; the 2011 declaration of invitations for development proposals did not list the firm.[37] Investigative reporting from the UK's Channel 4 television news uncovered a significant lack of transparency verging on what opposition politicians condemned as low-level corruption in Johnson's handling of the bidding process. This reporting noted in particular that, in 2010–2011, no less than £162,000 in donations to Johnson's Conservative political party originated from the Anglo-Chinese wife of a Conservative politician with ties to ABP's leader.[38] ABP's tender to redevelop the site was not terminated because of these revelations; the planning process for the site, once shifted to involve the local council and ABP's design partners and contractors, proceeded largely without community input.[39] The multiple levels of opacity present in the planning of the Royal Albert Dock draw attention to the contentious, elite-driven, and globally oriented politics of large-scale redevelopment in London—politics that, I argue, have sidestepped local input and democratic engagement.

Upon intended completion in the early to mid-2020s, the dock will be a 3.5-million-square-foot zone specifically for Asian businesses to expand into the UK and European markets.[40] This speculative process will transform an obdurate, deindustrialized space into a newly globalized space with the potential to expand London's centrality to Asian financial firms. The now completed £1.7 billion first stage of this project was funded by four Chinese banks and one Thai development fund.[41] For this vision of the future of the docks to succeed, the area had to be delineated into privileged and prioritized connective spaces through transport infrastructure and the construction of offices and amenities for workers. Following the inland edge of the node are three nearby stops on the Docklands Light Rail as well as a stop on the Crossrail train that, upon opening, will significantly cut travel time to central London and Heathrow Airport.[42]

The dock's transformation encapsulates the logic of enclosure. This globalized redevelopment privileges the far over the near as it realigns what was port and docklands for the London region into a space operating between the economies of China and London, where ABP intends "to run [the zone] as a 24-hour mini-city to accommodate the needs of Asian businesses focused on Beijing time, which is eight hours ahead of London."[43] This shift of clock time away from Greenwich Mean Time has not happened. Regardless, through political decisions, economic ambitions, and infrastructural connections, the dock has produced a space apart from surrounding neighborhoods, acting as an enclave within the city. The area becomes a space to deploy global connections within the demarcations and circulations demanded by multinational capitalism.

While other, adjacent developments in the royal docks offer housing, including some affordable housing, overall the zone's ambition is to harness public investment in the built form and transport

32
"East Meets West at Royal Albert Dock," *South China Morning Post*, http://www.scmp.com/presented/business/topics/connecting-asia-europe-east-london/article/2120236/east-meets-east-royal; Pickford and Hammond, "Boris Johnson to Seal £1Bn Docks Deal."

33
Farrells, "Projects: Royal Albert Dock," https://farrells.com/project/royal-albert-dock.

34
Henneke and Knowles, "Conceptualizing Cities and Migrant Ethnicity," 43–44.

35
Henneke and Knowles, "Conceptualizing Cities and Migrant Ethnicity."

36
Pickford and Hammond, "Boris Johnson to Seal £1Bn Docks Deal."

37
https://madisonbrook.com/article/top-developers-aim-to-build-new-royal-albert-docks/76.html.

38
M. Crick, "Big Questions for Boris over Billion Dollar Property Deal," *Channel 4 News*, November 13, 2014, https://www.channel4.com/news/boris-johnson-london-propery-deal-china-albert-dock.

39
M. Kennard and A. Caistor-Arendar, "Selling the Silverware: How London's Historic Dock Was Sold to the Chinese," *Pulitzer Center*, http://pulitzercenter.org/reporting/selling-silverware-how-londons-historic-dock-was-sold-chinese.

40
Pickford and Hammond, "Boris Johnson to Seal £1Bn Docks Deal"; Pickford and Hammond, "China Investor Waits to Tie Up at Quays of Old British Empire."

41
G. Parker, J. Evans, and L. Hornby, "Theresa May Welcomes £1.7Bn Chinese Project in London's Docklands," *Financial Times*, November 10, 2016, https://www.ft.com/content/23372450-a693-11e6-8898-79a99e2a4de6.

42
Already delayed from 2018 to 2021, the Crossrail's opening has again been postponed due to COVID-19; a new date is unknown. *Guardian*, July 23, 2020, https://www.theguardian.com/uk-news/2020/jul/23/crossrail-opening-delayed-again-due-to-coronavirus.

43
Pickford and Hammond, "Boris Johnson to Seal £1Bn Docks Deal."

44
https://www.royaldocks.london/.

45
https://rad.london/masterplan.

46
HM Government, "London Mayor Announces 10 Chinese Businesses to the Royal Docks Enterprise Zone," https://enterprisezones.communities.gov.uk/london-mayor-announces-10-chinese-businesses-royal-docks-enterprise-zone/.

47
https://www.royaldocks.london/articles/first-tenant-in-royal-albert-docks.

48
Farrells, "Projects: Royal Albert Dock."

infrastructure to strategically reshape the relations underlying London and China's vision for the world economy.[44] Post-Brexit, it remains to be seen if this reurbanization strategy will succeed. Plans to continue building out the Royal Albert Dock are on hold.[45] Additionally, in lieu of securing at least some of the 10 Chinese firms that pledged to take office space in 2013,[46] ABP shifted to promote the potential of the dock as a "high-tech hub."[47] The first tenant was announced in December 2019, and instead of an Asian financial institution, it was the UK offices of Advantech, a Taiwanese Internet-of-Things firm. It is still possible the original vision will return and the entire development will be built out, but given the economic uncertainty facing the UK over the coming years and decades, there is the potential that this investment will fail in its integration of new circulations of multinational capital into the city, while also failing to achieve localized benefits.

As of September 2019, construction on the first phase of the zone was nearing completion, although tenants had yet to move in. Walking into the area from a nearby light-rail stop, one could see signage on construction siding proclaiming LONDON'S NEXT BUSINESS DISTRICT and BREATHING LIFE INTO A WORLD-FAMOUS DOCK. This first stage of construction consists of five buildings holding 21 commercial units, totaling about 700,000 square feet of office space. Upon completion, the masterplan calls for "3.7 million square feet of high quality work, retail and leisure space, including 2.5 million square feet of offices" intended to cultivate "a rich mix of both Asian and indigenous businesses to develop and thrive."[48] The design of the project gestures toward the industrial waterfront's warehouses: five-story rectangular volumes of brick and glass cluster tightly together, with narrow passageways between buildings and parking on the perimeter. Ground-floor units will contain cafés and shops, with offices above.

On that visit in September 2019, a few pedestrians walked along the quayside paving, an electric Lamborghini was plugged into a charging station, and two security guards watched over the site, diligently observing passersby, including this writer. Freestanding and wall-mounted security cameras blanketed the public space, looking down on park benches, recently planted trees, and landscaping contained in rusting Cor-Ten steel planters. A newly paved but vacant parking lot on the far side of the development sat on land slated for future construction. Stainless-steel signage was etched with the classic x'ed-out circle demanding NO LITTERING/BIRD FEEDING. Other, smaller signs noted NO SMOKING and informed people that CCTV was in operation. Crows circled above the surveillance system, swooping down from the rooftops, while across the marina, planes constantly, loudly landed and took off from City Airport's single runway. Temporary flags encouraged the few passersby to #jointhedocks for an already-past summer jazz festival. In a locked storefront with no one present, an effort at creative placemaking encouraged passersby to come view a *Doodling the Docks* art exhibit on Friday and Saturday afternoons for the month, with paintings propped on sheet music stands.

The way in which the development is situated against the wider area materially and symbolically suggests a separation of the zone from the existing neighborhoods. In Newham's established neighborhoods, there is significant poverty, the second-highest in London at 37 percent of the borough's population.[49] Unemployment is high, and among those with jobs, 32 percent of workers are employed in low-paying ones.[50] At the same time, housing is expensive and the borough has the highest rate of homelessness in the city. These statistics highlight the juxtaposition between globalized zones, facilitating a space largely separated from its surroundings, more integrated into international circulations than the needs of its neighbors.

This does not inherently mean the dock development forecloses the local and proximate per se. Newham's government exercises a degree of oversight over the redevelopment and has encouraged ABP's hiring of local workers.[51] However, without making a strong effort to involve local residents in considerations of the design and use of the space, and without integrating specific provisions for local economic development, workforce education, or other benefits like affordable housing, Newham's and London's governments prioritized the potential of investment from afar over their residents' documented needs. The lack of local pushback or demands made on the developers—from community groups, civil society, or borough government—whether that be in the form of defined job creation for nearby residents or investment in needed civic infrastructure—speaks to the challenges faced by those working toward commoning: large-scale urbanization proceeds apart from efforts to retain or increase these spaces and relations belonging to all.

The dock's redevelopment has opened the adjoining quay to passersby, increasing needed public open space in a borough without a large urban park or other everyday places of well-being.[52] Yet, like many of London's waterfront developments, it does so under the gaze of private security guards on privately held land.[53] In Newham's government offices next door on the waterfront, the very fact of the dock's redevelopment reflects positive change and a net-increase in economic opportunity for Newham, but by its very design the space is aligned to

49
A. Tison, C. Ayrton, K. Barker, T. Barry-Born, O. Long, "London's Poverty Profile," Trust for London (website), https://www. trustforlondon.org.uk/ data/.
50
Ibid.

51
ABP, "ABP Royal Albert Dock London," 4.

52
N. T. Dines, V. Cattell, W. M. Gesler, and S. Curtis, *Public Spaces, Social Relations and Well-Being in East London* (Bristol, UK: Published for the Joseph Rowntree Foundation by Policy Press, 2006), 5.
53
J. Shenker, "Privatised London: The Thames Path Walk That Resembles a Prison Corridor," *Guardian*, February 24, 2015, https:// www.theguardian.com/ cities/2015/feb/24/ private-london-exposed- thames-path-riverside- walking-route.

globally facing connections, routes, and circulations. No amount of creative placemaking and community events can change that.

The political decisions that aligned this land with China's Belt and Road global infrastructure deployments sidestepped civic debate regarding the future of what was, at 35 acres, among the largest intact land parcels in the central city region, one with the additional benefit of close access to multiple forms of quick transport, as well as the business-class flights out of London City Airport. Because the Royal Albert Dock was publicly held land, its sale without oversight becomes an enclosure, the result of "finding new urban outlets for capital accumulation, controlling the use and exchange value of urban space or shutting down access to any urban space or sociality—commons—that offers a means of reproduction and challenging capitalist social relations."[54] The plan to redevelop the Royal Albert Dock site embodies capitalist, entrepreneurial planning[55] to facilitate and prioritize a vision for the city that is privatized, highly securitized, and aligned beyond the local and proximate communities: the commons remain outside globalized Alpha London. This sort of speculative urban redevelopment pivots large areas of the city into spaces for multinational economic growth and overseas ambitions amid a local economy based on property ownership and real estate speculation.[56] In this case, the result is that the commons (and those invested in expanding the commons) are circumvented and effectively removed from efforts to plan London's future at scale. London's transformation into an Alpha City[57] remains largely incompatible with efforts to grow the commons in the same city.

Conclusion:
Whose Commons in What City?

Ultimately, the dock must be understood in geographic relation to the deployment of China's global infrastructure and the enclosure of publicly owned land to redevelop the dock site. For London, the speculation through global infrastructure is novel: this effort is financed, planned, built, and controlled by Chinese interests for Chinese and East Asian multinational firms. The decision to turn the dock into a node owned and occupied by Chinese firms speaks to the political imperatives underpinning post-Brexit urban transformation, even as those imperatives are thrown into disarray by geopolitics. London enclosed a centrally located, highly networkable but unoccupied waterfront and pivoted it toward new networks of connection and exchange. While the proximity to London's financial markets and consumers matters for

54
S. Hodkinson, "The New Urban Enclosures," *City* 16, no. 5 (2012): 515.

55
Hall, *Urban and Regional Planning.*

56
Minton, *Big Capital*, 111.

57
Atkinson, *Alpha City*; Moore, *Slow Burn City.*

the choice of this location, the economic logic underlying this development is driven by China's overseas business interests. Ultimately, the Royal Albert Dock's position in the Belt and Road Initiative may expand London's status at the center of global finance, but the relationship of the dock to the surrounding city also matters, tying the current definition of the area into historic legacies of industrial work, industrial decline, and the further fragmentation of contemporary London into an exclusive city, unaffordable and inaccessible for many residents.

As an alternative to enclosure, commoning opens the possibility of crafting a more inclusive city that does not rely on real estate investment or global infrastructure deployment controlled by distant interests and demands. This is not to imply London should or even could turn away from its cosmopolitanism (although Brexit certainly complicates this), but that, in times of economic crisis such as that brought about by the COVID-19 pandemic, the commons could support the city and its residents' needs much more than another enclave of the Alpha City. For decades, London's large-scale waterfront redevelopments have fundamentally sidestepped community participation in the planning process.[58] Beyond this lack of participation in redesigning the waterfront, efforts to advance the urban commons in East London are constrained by investment in infrastructure and a built environment intended to prioritize flows of multinational capital, curtailing opportunity for the city's residents.

Forty years ago there were few potential ideas for revitalizing London's docklands, but today this is no longer the case. In the context of the commons, it is notable that recently initiated efforts by a local civil society organization in Barking and Dagenham, adjacent to Newham, are not focusing on producing, for instance, another people's plan to present to the city government.[59] They are instead working with residents on building small-scale communal infrastructure such as planting urban orchard trees, grocery shopping for neighbors, sorting out permits for street parties, facilitating shared childcare, or connecting residents for skill sharing, including bicycle repair.[60] With COVID-19, this organization and others have partnered with the two borough governments to organize volunteers to distribute food and other supplies to residents in need, co-creating a version of a commons during an extremely challenging time.[61] As Kip argues, "Just as urbanization keeps expanding and capital latches onto new externalities, urban commons can only survive if they keep expanding as well."[62] While efforts at expanding the commons will continue, the intrusion of large-scale redevelopment and global infrastructure into the material and social landscape of the city curtails this process.

58
Brownill, "The People's Plan for the Royal Docks."

59
Ibid.

60
https://static1.squarespace.com/static/59fe22186957da47865ee364/t/5ef314cf9cd88370a4fd9270/1592988966456/.

61
T. Britton, "Tomorrow Today Streets," *Medium*, May 30, 2020, https://medium.com/@TessyBritton/tomorrow-today-streets-2a6159ee78f0 and https://www.compassonline.org.uk/wp-content/uploads/2020/05/BDCAN_FINAL.pdf.

62
M. Kip, "Moving beyond the City: Conceptualizing Urban Commons from a Critical Urban Studies Perspective," in *Urban Commons*, 44.

Acknowledgments: This paper draws on the author's collaborative work with Jonathan Silver on global infrastructure and urbanization. In addition to Jonathan, I want to thank Renee Tapp for support in drawing the disparate theorizations together, Dillon Mahmoudi and Conor Moloney for feedback, and Regan Koch and Wayne Wang for both their hospitality in East London and their ongoing support of this research, as well as David Imbroscio and Neil Brenner for the invitation to present a version of this work at the American Political Science Association's 2018 annual meeting in Boston. Lastly, this paper benefited immensely from Mojdeh Mahdavi and Liang Wang's editorial advice.

Commoning as a Force in Urban Design

David Bollier

The design of cities is often regarded as a challenge requiring experts to blend various commercial and financial interests, functional needs, aesthetics, social dynamics, and other factors. Often known as "development," this capital-driven model prioritizes the interests of real estate and corporate players, the affluent, politicians, municipal bureaucracies, and recently, tech platform businesses such as Airbnb and Uber. Partly in reaction to this model, however, especially in world cities, a new set of players—commoners—is entering the field with an insurgent perspective. Empowered by digital networks and an open-source sensibility, ordinary people are stepping up to create new types of collaborative urban spaces, social services, governance systems, and infrastructures. Their acts of commoning generally emphasize fairness, access to collective resources, nonmarket cooperation, personal responsibility linked with entitlements, and transparency. These initiatives can be reasonably seen as calls for a new and different type of society.

Because commoning is a system of collective action that functions in a bottom-up, emergent fashion, mostly outside state and market regimes, it remains largely invisible to mainstream political ideologies and modern culture. That's partly because urban commons sidestep the familiar binary choice of "public" versus "private" approaches and disdain public-private partnerships that tend to exclude the interests of ordinary people.[1] Instead, self-styled commoners are demanding greater control over discrete urban spaces and systems so that peer-organized associations of commoners can accomplish work directly. They generally seek to invite broader civic participation, assure fair, inclusive access and use, and privilege nonmarket forms of exchange and cooperation. They rely on their own vernacular practices and "convivial tools" as a community[2]—and in so doing, tend to engender a greater sense of belonging, ethical commitment, and long-term stewardship of shared wealth.

This article offers an introduction to the commons paradigm as a robust, emerging template for urban design, policy, and social life.[3] It also describes some notable commons-based projects that point to a larger vision of change, and to special challenges in developing the commons as a new sector of provisioning and governance.

1
The corruption and inefficiencies of private-public partnerships have been well documented by the nonprofit group In the Public Interest, among others. See https://www.inthepublicinterest.org/tools-and-guides and https://www.inthepublicinterest.org/governing-for-the-common-good.

2
Convivial tools, as described by Ivan Illich, do not prescribe narrow ways of doing things, but rather unleash personal creativity and autonomy to pursue work to meet one's own needs and circumstances. Illich, *Tools for Conviviality* (New York: Harper & Row, 1973).

3
Besides a surge of experimentation and projects based on the social dynamics of commoning, there is a growing literature focused on urban commons. See, for example, Shareable [organization], *Sharing Cities: Activating the Urban Commons* (San Francisco: Shareable, 2019), https://www.shareable.net/sharing-cities. See also Sheila R. Foster and Christian Iaione, "The City as a Commons," *Yale Law & Policy Review* 34, no. 2, article 2 (2016), http://digitalcommons.law.yale.edu/ylpr/vol34/iss2/2.

I. Commoning as Living, Emergent Design

The idea of the commons as a useful, generative tool in urban design would have been ridiculed or ignored 20 years ago. That was before the internet had insinuated itself into the global political economy and culture, demonstrating the impressive power of bottom-up, emergent creativity and cooperation among ordinary people.[4] Over the past 20 years, too, an eclectic network of activists, cooperatives, digital projects, and others have embraced the commons as a fresh framework and discourse for pursuing personal, social, and political emancipation. Many were inspired by the work of the late political scientist Elinor Ostrom, whose fieldwork and theorizing about the commons earned her the Nobel Prize in Economics in 2009.

Fed up with the shortcomings of conventional politics, state bureaucracy, and market capitalism, self-identified commoners have launched a wide variety of projects—open-source software, platform cooperatives, community-supported agriculture, alternative currencies, citizen-science networks, open-access scholarly journals, community-managed forests, fisheries, arable land, and water, and so on.[5] Each is a gambit to imagine and build a better future without relying on existing market structures dominated by large corporations or state institutions and politics. The basic goal is to enable groups of people to meet their needs more directly, on their own terms, through collective provisioning systems.[6]

Much of the conventional economics and social science literature sees commons as unowned resources at best and a "tragedy" [of the commons][7] at worst—the commons as a noun, a vestigial form that requires supervision by either private property owners (i.e., corporations) or the state. This article regards commons as living social systems: the commons as a verb. This perspective represents an important interpretive shift—a shift in the ontological premises and epistemology in how one understands the commons.[8]

The full dimensions of this "OntoShift" are too complicated to go into here; suffice it to say that a change of perspective is needed to shift the focus from individual self-interest and calculative rationality in managing "resources"—the premise of standard economics and public policy—to a worldview in which cooperation, social solidarity, and holistic, systemic behaviors are seen as more important. We must shift our perspective from a world of separation—of humans from nature; of individuals from each other; between our minds and bodies—to a world of mutuality and relationality.

Instead of seeing subject and object as separate, for example, and causality as a mechanical and linear process, commons invite us

4
See, for example, Clay Shirky, *Here Comes Everybody: The Power of Organizing without Organizations* (New York: Penguin Press, 2008).

5
For a wide-ranging review of dozens of contemporary commons, see David Bollier and Silke Helfrich, *Patterns of Commoning* (Amherst, MA: Off the Commons Books, 2015), http://www.patternsofcommoning.org.

6
"State Power and Commoning," Chapter 9 in Bollier and Helfrich, *Free, Fair and Alive: The Insurgent Power of the Commons* (Gabriola Island, BC: New Society Publishers, 2019), 283–316.

7
Economics has long embraced this parable, as set forth by Garrett Hardin, "The Tragedy of the Commons," *Science* 162, no. 3589 (December 1968): 1243–1245.

8
Bollier and Helfrich, "The OntoShift to the Commons," Chapter 2 in *Free, Fair and Alive*, 29–50.

to see the world as a web of dynamic interdependency. Individuals are actually nested within ecosystems and communities ("the Nested-I"), for example, and cannot be seen in isolation. Rationality strives for an alignment of individual and collective needs ("Ubuntu Rationality"), and not just maximization of individual gain. Design can be seen as a social process through which commoners contribute to emergence (as posited by complexity theory) as they interact with each other, their context, and environment.[9]

Much more could be said about this OntoShift, but for our purposes here, the important point is that commons are practical, peer-driven venues for the development of fair provisioning and trusted peer governance. The more salient dimensions of commons are *social and relational.* Their overriding goal is not economic growth, profit, or capital accumulation. It is to enact more humane, responsible stewardship of care-wealth and more secure, empowered ways of life. Commoners want to generate new ways of doing, being, and knowing that are generally impossible within the affordances of contemporary capitalism and even liberal, democratic polities.

This is a key reason why many cities and towns around the world are exploring the potential of commoning. They are often frustrated with existing systems that are dysfunctional, cumbersome, or corrupt, and attracted to the freedom, flexibility, fairness, and conviviality that commoning invites. In this sense, commoning represents a powerful design tool for (re)organizing governance, provisioning, and social practices. It is a "social technology" that can mobilize creativity and collective energies; elicit contextually sensitive knowledge in addressing design challenges; and assure greater levels of trust and legitimacy in design outcomes. Commoning may arguably contribute to "design justice," as some have called it, by empowering communities "to seek liberation from exploitative and oppressive systems."[10]

As such, commoning offers an organic participatory process for growing (not fabricating from expert designs) new types of institutions. Part of the point is to avoid the structural limitations of state power (elite dominance of politics and law, bureaucratic universalism and inflexibility, overreliance on "experts," etc.) and the anti-social aspects of capitalist markets (the compulsion to privatize and marketize collective assets, the commodification of nature and social relations, unfair allocations of market benefits, etc.). More affirmatively, commoning is about creating participatory platforms to fulfill specific needs for the benefit of members. Their social practices, values, traditions, and collective wisdom are "baked into" the institutional structures and culture that result.

9
An excellent overview of how complexity theory and emergence apply in economic contexts is found in Eric D. Beinhocker, *The Origin of Wealth: Evolution, Complexity, and the Radical Remaking of Economics* (Cambridge, MA: Harvard Business School Press, 2006).

10
Design Justice Network Principles, https://designjustice.org/read-the-principles. See also Sasha Costanza-Chock, *Design Justice: Community-Led Practices to Build the Worlds We Need* (Cambridge, MA: MIT Press, 2020).

II. Commoning in Cities:
Do-It-Together Forms of Social Emancipation

It is helpful to speak in particulars because each commons, as a matter of theory and practice, is a world unto itself. There is no master blueprint or abstracted ideal to which every commons must conform or aspire. Each bears the indelible imprint of its particular members and its unique history, culture, practices, geopolitical factors, landscape, and more. That is why it is problematic to assert a typology of urban commons; they are simply too idiosyncratic and varied. In addition, at this time, urban commons are more a field of experimentation than a mature theoretical discipline.

That said, a number of major cities—such as Barcelona, Amsterdam, Seoul, Bologna—and dozens of smaller cities are self-consciously experimenting with new types of collaborative governance and peer provisioning. This work, when combined with a reinter-pretation of familiar models, is giving rise to a new discourse about urban commons. For example, Community Land Trusts (CLTs) for affordable housing and citizen-managed community gardens are well-established ways for groups of people to collaborate for their collective benefit. By accenting how these groups are propelled by citizen participation, operate independently of government, and decommodify land that is otherwise part of the real estate market, we can see how CLTs and community gardens are better understood as species of commons. Figure 1 below shows Forest Row, a neighborhood of 18

Fig. 1: Community Land Trusts for Affordable Housing.
Photo by Schumacher Center for a New Economics. Used with permission.

Forest Row, a neighborhood of 18 households on a 21-acre site owned by the Community Land Trust in the Southern Berkshires, in western Massachusetts.

David Bollier

191

households on a 21-acre site owned by the Community Land Trust in western Massachusetts. The CLT has made housing more affordable in a region with relatively high housing costs.

One of the more remarkable housing commons in an urban setting is Mietshäuser Syndikat, a federation of residential real estate in Germany that is peer-managed by residents.[11] At the end of 2018, 136 residential buildings were affiliated with the syndicate. What's special about Mietshäuser Syndikat is that residents collectively own all of the buildings together, while at the same time paying an affordable monthly (nonmarket) "rent" to themselves and to the federation to keep the whole system going. Not only have the buildings been effectively taken off the real estate market, avoiding the risk of rising rents and possible eviction, a portion of everyone's "rent" payment goes into a pay-it-forward fund that helps the federation acquire more buildings. Unlike cohousing or housing co-ops, Mietshäuser Syndikat is legally structured to prevent residents from selling out or liquidating their property holdings; it is permanently inalienable. Figure 2 depicts the "moralized" facade of Grüuenberger 73, an apartment building in Berlin owned and managed by the Syndikat.

11
This account is taken from Bollier and Helfrich, *Free, Fair and Alive*, 252–257.

Fig. 2: Mietshauser Syndikat.
Facade of Grüuenberger 73, an apartment building in Berlin owned and managed by Mietshäuser Syndikat. Photo from Mietshäuser Syndikat website.

Decommodifying land is one important goal of urban commons; another is to give residents some important measure of self-determination and "ownership" over urban spaces. Rather than rely on "starchitects" and real estate developers to design city spaces, commons privilege the use-value of those spaces by inviting residents to play primary roles. That is more or less what the City Repair Project in Portland, Oregon, has done. Founded by activist planners in the late 1990s, the group helps residents beautify their streets and neighborhoods (through "intersection painting," for example), build housing for the homeless, teach urban permaculture, and in other ways make the cityscape their own ("place-making").[12] Operating on its own agenda but with the consent and support of city government, City Repair has used commoning to develop a homegrown vision for the city of Portland that would not have emerged otherwise.

A recurring theme in urban commons is the grit and determination of residents to make a place their own, whether or not the politicians or city government wish to assist. The remarkable community gardens that flourished in New York City in the 1990s were a case in point. As hundreds of abandoned lots throughout the city filled with debris, junked cars, prostitution, and drug dealing, a group of self-styled "green guerrillas" began to assert control over the sites in the 1980s. "We cut fences open with wire cutters and took sledgehammers to sidewalks to plant trees," said one early activist. "It was a reaction to government apathy."[13]

Over 800 community gardens sprang up through the five boroughs, and with them, an economic and social revival of the neighborhoods. The commoners were able to deliver what the private market alone could not—the civilizing of blighted neighborhoods through non-market means, at minimal cost. As property values rose, in part because of the gardens, the city government sold off the land to condo developers. (The tax-delinquent properties were still technically owned by the city.) Dozens of gardens were saved only because of last-minute interventions by the Trust for Public Land and donations by wealthy celebrities.

A similar ethic was at play in Todmorden, England, when a woman planted vegetables in her front yard and extended an open invitation to "help yourself." The effort resulted in an urban gardening project that shares the food that it grows and encourages local self-sufficiency in agriculture. It has stimulated great community pride, as suggested by this locally produced mural celebrating the project (fig. 3). The initiative has spurred the creation of 100 Incredible Edible groups across the UK offering "open-source food" to the hungry and passersby.[14] Similarly, in Amsterdam, the I Can Change the World with My Two Hands commons (fig. 4) organizes numerous projects to promote local food production, local composting, and rainwater collection in the city. Here, participants transport compost to a new green space planted and maintained by the group. In Cambridge and Somerville, Massachusetts, a network of individuals invented a scheme to harvest from urban trees the

12
https://cityrepair.org.

13
Anne Ravner, "Garden Notebook: Is This City Big Enough for Gardens and Houses?" New York Times, March 27, 1997, C1.

14
Incredible Edible network, at http://www.incredibleediblenetwork.org.uk; and Incredible Edible Todmorden, www.incredible-edible-todmorden.co.uk.

fruit that would otherwise fall to the ground and rot. Their efforts to map the locations of more than 100 trees and arbors, harvest the fruit (with permission by owners, as needed), and preserve the fruit, produces about 5,000 pounds of jam, ciders, and preserves every year.[15]

15
League of Urban Canners, http://www.leagueofurbancanners.org.

Fig. 3: Incredible Edible-Todmorden.co.uk
Photo by Sludge G, via Flickr. Licensed under a Creative Commons Attribution-ShareAlike 2.0 Generic License. https://creativecommons.org/licenses/by-sa/2.0.

This mural was painted on a "billboard" near the Rochdale Canal in Todmorden, England, to showcase the activities of Incredible Edible Todmorden, an urban gardening project that shares food that it grows and encourages local self-sufficiency in agriculture.

Fig. 4: Urban gardening in Amsterdam
Photo © by Niels Dortland. Used with permission.

The "I Can Change the World with My Two Hands" commons in Amsterdam organizes a variety of projects to promote local food production, local composting, and rainwater collection in the city. Here, participants transport compost to a new green space.

A theme in urban commons starts to come into focus: ordinary people see a problem and social need, then take direct action with others, often in innovative ways, to develop effective solutions. This approach can apply in countless, unlikely circumstances, which is why it is problematic to define commons based on a specific type of "resource." The crucial ingredient is people with the imagination, motivation, and capacities to work together. These often emerge in unpredictable places.

In an outlying neighborhood of Barcelona, Spain, the problem was lack of affordable wireless access to the internet. A tech engineer, Ramón Roca [fig. 5], decided in 2004 to hack some off-the-shelf routers and built a jerry-rigged mesh network–like system connected to a single DSL line used by municipal governments. The new system, dubbed Guifi.net, quickly caught on. Soon volunteers and donations helped build a larger infrastructure—a commons-based Wi-Fi system with more than 35,000 nodes extending over the entire region.[16] It now provides far better broadband service and lower prices than can be had in the US, for example. It is another example of how mutualizing costs and benefits in a commons regime can enable us to become less reliant on money and therefore more free from the structural coercion of established markets (*while* serving people that conventional markets have ignored as insufficiently profitable).

16
Guifi.net, http://www. guifi.net. Dan Gillmor, "Forget Comcast. Here's the DIY Approach to Internet Access," *Wired*, July 20, 2016, http:// wired.com/2016/07/ forget-comcast-heres-the-diy-approach-to-internet-access. See also http:// www.freifunk.net.

Fig. 5: Photo of Ramón Roca, an engineer who hacked together a jerry-built mesh network in 2004, which evolved into a Wi-Fi commons, Guifi.net, with more than 30,000 nodes in Catalonia, Spain.

Photo by TedX Madrid 2011. Licensed under a Creative Commons Attribution-NonCommercial, NoDerivs 2.0 Generic License. https://creativecommons.org/licenses/by-nc-nd/2.0/

One can replicate this dynamic in many registers: Commoners in many cities have created time-banking systems (service-barter) for meeting their needs without money. The scheme is enormously helpful to poor people, the elderly, and others without a steady income.[17] In various towns and cities, people have created their own neighborhood-based health insurance systems,[18] tool libraries for household equipment, little book libraries, and even local currencies.[19] In some cities in the Netherlands, a peer-run, neighborhood-based homecare system avoids the industrialized, productivity-driven "care" preferred by businesses and state bureaucracies.[20]

Makerspaces and Fab Labs have been incubators for a new type of localism by empowering amateurs and professionals, young people and experienced technical experts, to come together to tinker, invent, and co-learn from one another. Their guiding ethic is one of "think it, make it, share it," as this T-shift from Fab Lab Adeleide declares. Fab Labs are open spaces filled with a variety of machines for crafting creative artworks, electronics, and other flights of the imagination (fig. 6).

17
TimeBanks US, https://timebanks.org. See also Jukka Peltokoski et al., "Helsinki Timebank: Currency as a Commons," in Bollier and Helfrich, *Patterns of Commoning*, http://patternsofcommoning.org/helsinki-timebank-currency-as-a-commons.
18
Artabana at https://alisphere.wordpress.com/2017/05/18/artabana.
19
The Schumacher Center for a New Economics is a pioneer in this realm with its BerkShares currency used in the Berkshires region of western Massachusetts. See also the interview with Will Ruddick, "How the Bangla-Pesa Tapped the Value of an Informal Community," in Bollier and Helfrich, *Patterns of Commoning*, 199–203, http://patternsofcommoning.org/how-the-bangla-pesa-tapped-the-value-of-an-informal-community.
20
"Home Care by Self-Governing Nursing Teams: The Netherlands' Buurtzorg Model," The Commonwealth Fund, May 29, 2015, http://commonwealthfund.org/publications/case-studies/2015/may/home-care-nursing-teams-netherlands.

Fig. 6: Fab Lab hosted by Waag Society, Amsterdam.
Photo by Rory Hyde, via Flickr. Licensed under a Creative Commons Attribution-ShareAlike 2.0 Generic License. https://creativecommons.org/licenses/by-sa/2.0.

21
Vasilis Kostakis et al., "The Convergence of Digital Commons with Local Manufacturing from a Degrowth Perspective: Two Illustrative Cases," *Journal of Cleaner Production* (2016), http://dx.doi.org/10.1016/j.jclepro.2016.09.077. See also P2P Foundation wiki entry, "Design Global, Manufacture Local," http://wiki.p2pfoundation.net/Design_Global_Manufacture_Local. *Patterns of Commoning* on Wikihouse.

22
Dorn Cox, "Farm Hack: A Commons of Agricultural Innovation," in Bollier and Helfrich, *Patterns of Commoning*, 145–150. See also Open Source Ecology and Farm Hack.

23
Tristan Copley-Smith, "The Growth of Open Design and Production," in Bollier and Helfrich, *Patterns of Commoning*, 154–158. See also Open Desk at https://www.opendesk.cc.

24
Wikispeed car, http://wikispeed.org/car.

25
Copley-Smith, "The Growth of Open Design and Production," 154–158, http://patternsofcommoning.org/the-growth-of-open-design-and-production.

26
The idea that resources themselves dictate the type of social management of them is explored in Silke Helfrich, "Common Goods Don't Simply Exist—They Are Created," *The Wealth of the Commons: A World beyond Market and State* (Amherst, MA: Levellers Press, 2012), 61–67, http://wealthofthecommons.org/essay/common-goods-don%E2%80%99t-simply-exist-%E2%80%93-they-are-created.

As these spaces have proliferated globally, a new type of "cosmo-local production" has arisen, outside of conventional supply chains and corporate control. The system allows "light" design and knowledge to be shared and improved by commoners, open-source style, while the production of "heavy" physical things can be done at the local level using nonproprietary, less expensive local materials.[21] Cosmo-local production techniques have been applied to farm equipment,[22] furniture,[23] motor vehicles,[24] and houses,[25] among other things.

III. Two Key Challenges in Building Urban Commons

It is tempting to treat these various innovations in commoning as something that can be encouraged through law and policy alone. But in fact two challenges need serious attention in order to nurture urban commons. First, we must support the *inner social dynamics of commons*, which are the animating, stabling force of any commons. And second, we must devise *new sorts of state structures* (law, policy, institutions) that take proper account of commons as living social systems having their own peer dynamics and quasi-independent authority.

Recognize That Commoning Arises from Within

In our book *Free, Fair and Alive* (2019), Silke Helfrich and I came to realize that the standard economistic framings of commons fail to deal adequately with their social and ethical dynamics.[26] Commons don't simply exist as inert resources, as economists generally believe; they need to be created. They are living systems. But this immediately raises a question. If commons vary immensely and develop in unique contexts, can we possibly identify common features in their social and political ecologies?

To tackle this challenge, we took inspiration from Christopher Alexander, the iconoclastic architect and urban planner who developed the idea of "pattern languages" to identify design regularities amidst great diversity.[27] By carefully reviewing scores of commons, my colleague and I identified more than two dozen patterns that tend to be present in successful, durable commons. As described in our book *Free, Fair and Alive*, we call these patterns in the social life, provisioning practices, and peer governance of commons the "Triad of Commoning."[28] We regard them as cross-sectoral social dynamics that are foundational in how commons function.

The idea behind our Triad of Commoning framework is to make visible the behaviors that tend to be present in commons without resorting to reductionism. Patterns help identify regularities while acknowledging the role of situated knowledge—people's experiences, know-how, and intuition. The Triad shifts attention to the whole human being *in situ* and moves away from the idea of the commons as only an economic institution, a collection of self-interested, utilitarian individuals. We learned that patterns resemble DNA, a set of general instructions that is underspecified so that it can adapt to and coevolve with local circumstances. We regard the patterns themselves as eminently open and amenable to additions and revisions.

27
Christopher Alexander, *The Nature of Order* (London: Taylor & Francis, 2004).
28
Bollier and Helfrich, *Free, Fair and Alive*.

While there is not space here to review the Triad of Commoning at length, the important point is to realize how these inner aspects of commoning are critical to successful cooperation. The patterns for the Social Life of Commoning, we concluded, suggest that commoners embrace certain precepts: they cultivate shared purpose and values, ritualize togetherness, and practice gentle reciprocity. They must also strive to trust situated knowing and preserve relationships in addressing conflict, among other behaviors. Peer governance patterns suggest that commoners must create semi-permeable membranes around their commons, so that beneficial relationships and energies can come into a commons while excluding forces that wish to appropriate shared wealth or disrupt it. Commoners must also ensure transparency in a sphere of trust, share knowledge generously, and assure consent in decision making.

Develop Mechanisms to Support the State-Commons Relationship

The modern bureaucratic state has its ways of doing things, and its mindsets and methods are often at odds with the vernacular practices and norms of commoning. A key question for our times—given the ubiquity of distributed culture on the internet, the loss of trust in centralized institutions, and the jealousy with which states protect their authority—is how to conjoin state action and commoning in constructive ways.

This can be particularly challenging for politicians who, as guardians of the market/state system, reflexively wish to promote economic growth. This premise can make it difficult for politicians to support commoning; they may not, in fact, truly *understand* commoning. State power is committed to a static, individualistic worldview, after all, at least in liberal democracies allied with market capitalism. Individual rights, economic liberty, and private property rights are the cultural priorities. But commoning enacts a very different vision of a human being, one that is based on sociability, cooperation, and relationality in general.

So if we wish to take the commons idea seriously, we have to fundamentally rethink how state power might be used strategically to advance commoning. This is a daunting task. Without aspiring to be comprehensive here, I wish to cite a number of fascinating experiments attempting to bridge the ontological and operational divide separating state institutions (law, policy, bureaucracy) and commons.

One of the most interesting experiments is being advanced by the activist-minded Barcelona en Comú (Barcelona in Common) movement, which is attempting to reinvent city government to foster greater civic participation in decision making and implementation. Several charters issued by the city administration outline bold ambitions to "do politics differently" by opening up new spaces for the "co-production of politics" between residents and city government. There is a keen recognition that municipal government must enable and facilitate citizen engagement, not just hand down policies and deliver services.

Helfrich and I have dubbed many of these approaches "commons-public partnerships" because they blend the on-the-ground social dynamics and authority of commons with the traditional administrative systems and politics of the liberal state. A notable model of commons-public partnership has been developed by the city of Bologna and other Italian cities, in which city bureaucracies work in tandem with neighborhoods and other citizen groups. It started when a resident of Bologna wanted to install a bench in a public space in her neighborhood, but the city government had no formal procedures for even considering such a request. From this seed, law scholar Christian Iaione and others worked with the city bureaucracies to develop the Bologna Regulation for the Care and Regeneration of Urban Commons, a formal initiative to invite and facilitate commons-public partnerships.

The Bologna Regulation is a "regulatory framework outlining how local authorities, citizens, and the community at large can manage public and private spaces and assets together. It is a sort of handbook for civic and public collaboration, and also a new vision for government."[29] Scholarship about new forms of government-citizen (or state-commons) collaborations has surged in recent years, particularly with the founding of an Italian LabGov—an "urban commons governance lab"—and its replication in Washington, DC, Costa Rica, São Paolo, New York, and elsewhere [fig. 7].

City governments may be the most promising nexus of commons experimentation because they are more proximate to citizens than national governments and are less ideologically driven. Too, the smaller scale of cities makes it easier to innovate there. Some city governments

29
See the LabGov website, http://labgov.city; and LabGov Georgetown website, https://labgov. georgetown.edu/ about_labgov/#.

LABORATORY FOR THE GOVERNANCE OF THE COMMONS

Fig. 7: LabGov Georgetown.
Fair use of logo of LabGov.

LabGov projects are a series of applied research laboratories that bring together international scholars from various disciplines to "explore innovative forms of stewardship and governance of shared urban resources."

have sought to develop infrastructures that can enable citizen action (but not necessarily commoning), for example, by building accessible Web infrastructures (Web hosting, e-mail, open data).[30] Others are supportive of platform cooperatives that provide commons-friendly, locally accountable apps for ride-hailing and Airbnb-style rentals. Ride Austin in Texas and COOP Taxi in Seoul, Korea, are two examples. In such cases, the state acts as an enabling force—through legal recognition, technical support, and political validation—for self-organized "pooling economies" (commons) to arise and flourish.

Leveraging the Potential of Urban Commons

Urban commons hold great potential for helping us reimagine governance at local and regional levels while meeting needs more effectively. They also hold out the promise of reimagining citizenship itself as a form of commoning. The point is to provide people with the ability to take actions and responsibilities that generate shareable benefits. The beauty of so many urban commons is that they are socially convivial forms that can adapt to changing circumstances. They engender a sense of belonging and social engagement at a time of social alienation and distrust, while meeting real needs in flexible, non-bureaucratic ways.

While guardians of state power may prefer to annex and assimilate commons as part of the larger state apparatus—a strategy for bolstering credibility and trust in government—there are risks in domesticating commons in this way. Part of the vitality and success of commons depends on people having the perceived and actual freedom to invent their own solutions. They must be able to develop authentic, quasi-independent cultures of collaboration, devise innovative provisioning systems, and reap direct benefits from their commitments. For these reasons, the fate of commons-public partnerships may depend on finding new ways to bring the interests of the state and commoners into a constructive alignment.

30
Open Commons Linz,
https://opencommons.
linz.at.

Laboring Together

Neeraj Bhatia

As contemporary cities increasingly become the sites for extracting capital and organizing forms of dominant power, questions arise about the spaces of urban life that might resist such forces and produce new opportunities for the appropriation of the city. We might consider this to be the role of public space—whether parks, squares, or streets more generally—which contemporary planners and architects often employ as a vehicle to gather people together. More often than not, however, public space is managed and controlled by particular authorities that act in the name of community while tending to limit the liberating potential of such spaces.[1] In a very direct way, we notice that (with decreased government funding) these spaces are increasingly reliant on implicit or explicit forms of commodification. In a subtler manner, public space is often accompanied by latent social norms as well as values and thereby does not necessarily relate to all of us equally. This process of normalization seeks to mold social relations and behaviors that are repeatable and predictable, using space as one means to do so.[2] These direct and indirect techniques have positioned public space, and the public goods within, as areas of power and administration for the continued development of capitalism.[3]

Against this backdrop, reframing the notion of the commons as an "urban commons" might offer a useful alternative organization to resist such dominant forces and enable the appropriation of the city through laboring together and sharing. Going beyond simply the sharing of a physical resource, the urban commons brings diverse groups together around forms of labor and action. In the case study that follows, the urban commons and the act of *commoning* are positioned as critical agents to enable the empowerment of urban dwellers. In particular, the practice of commoning, which involves *laboring together*, operates as a crucial tool to overcome differences and focus on shared collective goals. Laboring together becomes the glue of the commons, as it involves both the management and governance of the common resource as well as the processes and mechanisms that allow for the ongoing negotiation between commoners. This is a process that is made and remade, constantly evolving, and a form of continual social labor that defines the values, aims, and voice, or "politics," of a group. Not only do these forms of labor provide a platform for the individual within a collective, they also produce new forms of agency that can resist the dominant forces of contemporary urbanization. The following case study examines San Francisco, where the highest housing and rental costs in the United States have revealed the deep inequalities produced through advanced capitalism. One of San Francisco's last frontiers of gentrification is the Southeast Waterfront, a series

1
Stavros Stavrides, *Common Space: The City as Commons* (London: ZED Books, 2016), 4.
2
Ibid., 14–15, 40. Stavrides posits, "Dominant institutions legitimize inequality, distinguishing between those who know and those who do not, between those who can take decisions and those who must execute them and between those who have specific rights and those who are deprived of them. Thus, dominant institutions focused on the production and uses of public space are essential forms of authorization which stems from certain authorities and aim at directing the behaviors of public space users" (40).
3
David Harvey, *Rebel Cities: From the Right to the City to the Urban Revolution* (New York: Verso, 2012), 73.

of neighborhoods with a scarcity of open space yet whose history holds lessons for the production of the urban commons. In the abbreviated history that ensues, I expand on two moments—separated by over 200 years—wherein a completely different system of economics and politics plays out. The pendulum swing from the shared commons to the crisis of inequity created by private property suggests that alternative ways of empowering people in space is not only urgently required, it is the only way to return the city to be a space of politics.

Common Resources

While the commons might seem like a utopian fantasy in today's society, historians and legal theorists have suggested that, prior to European colonialism, commons were the rule rather than exception for much of the globe.[4] The commons revolves around a shared resource, which is managed and governed collectively by a community.[5] Some of the earliest examples included land for herding or raising livestock. Not only was the land often held in common, each person was also an equal stakeholder in the land and its resources (known as the "common good" or "commonwealth"), and thereby in its success. This had effects on the maintenance of the commons—inherently creating a stewardship of the shared resource.

The Southeast Waterfront was in fact first urbanized as a commons by the Spanish missionaries who used it for grazing cattle between 1776 and the 1820s (the end of Spanish rule). These lands were organized as a commons known as Potrero Nuevo (New Pasture). Because of the natural boundaries—Mission Creek to the north, Islais Creek on the south, Potrero Hill on the west, and the bay on the east—this site was ideal for a pasture. Built by the neophytes[6], new boundaries in select areas were demarcated with adobe and stone walls.[7] Potrero Nuevo was set up as an *ejido*, or land that could be used by anyone through usufruct rights. As a productive and shared resource, this land was able to sustain the soldiers, priests, and neophytes.

Mexico won its independence from Spain in 1821 and reestablished this land as a Mexican land grant—with its 1,000 acres spanning from Potrero Point to Mission Creek in the north and Islais Creek in the south. The land grant also included Rincón de las Salinas y Potrero Viejo, a 4,446-acre plot that comprised Rincón de las Salinas (Corner of a Salty Marsh) and Potrero Viejo (Old Pasture). Rincón de las Salinas covered what is now Bernal Heights, Excelsior, Crocker-Amazon, and the Outer Mission, while Potrero Viejo encompassed the present-day

4
Derek Wall, *The Commons in History: Culture, Conflict, and Ecology* (Cambridge, MA: MIT Press, 2014), 9.

5
Massimo De Angelis, *Omnia Sunt Communia: On the Commons and the Transformation to Postcapitalism* (London: ZED Books, 2017), 10.

6
Neophytes were largely Indigenous Groups who had converted to Christianity. It is beyond the scope of this paper to unpack this complex history, but it is worthwhile to not romanticize this situation as many neophytes were forced into these conditions.

7
City and County of San Francisco Planning Department, *City within a City: Historic Context Statement for San Francisco's Mission District* (San Francisco, 2007), 13.

Drawing of the Mission San Francisco de Asis by lithographer Captain William Smyth, 1839.
Credit: Digitally reproduced by the USC Digital Library. From the California Historical Society Collection
at the University of Southern California.

Plan drawing of the Mission San Francisco de Asis, 1840. Land case map B-819.
Map shows the conceptual enclosure of the Mission and the landscapes it encompassed.
Credit: United States District Court (California: Northern District). Land case. 381.
Digitally reproduced by the Bancroft Library, UC Berkeley.

neighborhoods of the Bayview and Hunters Point. These lands were used for a variety of things, including the raising of cattle, sheep, and horses that were farmed by Swedish, German, and Irish immigrants. Under the provisions of Mexican land governance, the land could not be subdivided or rented, and any public roads that crossed through the property had to remain open. Most important, the land was required to be open for common use for all residents of the pueblo.[8] The Treaty of Guadalupe Hidalgo, marking the end of the war in 1848, also entailed new mechanisms for evaluating and parceling land into private ownership, a process that accelerated with the exponential population growth incited by the Gold Rush of 1849.

8
Ibid., 15.

Photograph of a sketch depicting the city of San Francisco, looking toward Telegraph Hill, 1849. Clusters of workers houses and buildings occupy the land mostly between the mountains and near the bay, while land in the foreground remains unplatted.
Credit: Digitally reproduced by the USC Digital Library. From the California Historical Society Collection at the University of Southern California.

During the roughly 75-year period of Spanish and Mexican rule, much of the land in the Southeast Waterfront centered on the shared resources that the land provided. In his influential essay of 1968 on the so-called tragedy of the commons, Garrett Hardin attacked these types of commons, arguing that the self-interest of individuals would eventually deplete the common resource.[9] More recently, Elinor Ostrom's empirical observations, as well as game theory modeling, have refuted Hardin's simplistic conclusions. Ostrom's documentation of several enduring common-pool resources reveals the integral role that communities have in establishing the rules, agreements, enforcement, and conflict-resolution mechanism around the commons.[10] The overlooked social and political dimensions between a resource and its commoners are now understood as central to the

9
Garrett Hardin, "The Tragedy of the Commons," *Science* 162, no. 3859 (December 13, 1968): 1243–1248.
10
Elinor Ostrom, *Governing the Commons: The Evolution of Institutions for Collective Action* (Cambridge, UK: Cambridge University Press, 1990), 90.

Neeraj Bhatia

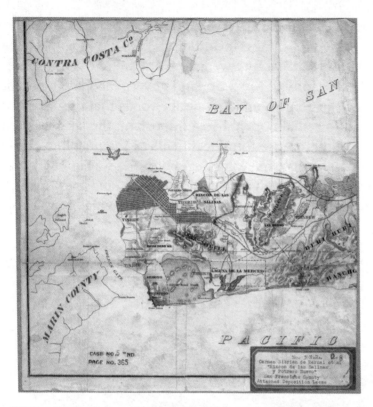

Map of San Francisco, 1853 (North to the left). Potrero Nuevo and Rincón de las Salinas visible in the middle of the map and remain unplatted.
Credit / Permission: United States District Court (California: Northern District).
Land case. 5. Digitally reproduced by the Bancroft Library, UC Berkeley.

development and long-term maintenance of the commons. Not only does this expand the "dichotomous choice between state and market,"[11] it expands the definition of commons to include the shared resource as well as its community of commoners and governance structure. The glue that binds this process between commoners is the act of laboring together.

11
Harvey, *Rebel Cities*, 69.

Estrangement

In the 100-year period following the Treaty of Guadalupe Hidalgo, the Southeast Waterfront witnessed successive waves of industry—gunpowder, steel- and ironworks, and shipbuilding, among others. Serviced by diverse groups of migrant and immigrant laborers, these neighborhoods were brought together by an atmosphere of making and working together that bonded people despite cultural differences. Most of these laborers resided in the inexpensive lands adjacent to the industrial

View of the Southeast Waterfront, 1892. Waterfront lands are occupied by industry, while workers housing begins to fill the platted lands.
Credit / Permission: H. S. Crocker & Co., 1982. Digitally reproduced by the Bancroft Library, UC Berkeley

waterfront, which were platted into private properties. In the past decades, as these industries have slowly relocated outside the city core, the industrial lands have remained dormant—making them a primary target for development. Currently five massive development projects along the waterfront will add over 16,500 new residential units, 5.5 million square feet of commercial space, as well as an NBA stadium. The key concessions within these developments to mitigate displacement and maintain the culture of the larger Southeast Waterfront include ample public parks and modestly higher ratios of affordable units. Joining these developments along the fragmented waterfront is the Blue Greenway, a recreational path that weaves through the parks. If Hardin's "tragedy of the commons" was instrumental in advocating for private property, today's housing crisis and associated gentrification in San Francisco might suggest a renewed role for the commons.

Gentrification could be identified through an uneven allocation of a city's resources and thereby a scarcity of quality urbanism in particular neighborhoods.[12] The potential value capture derived through this unevenness often directly and indirectly drives out longtime residents. This is primarily due to forms of estrangement—spatial, social, cultural, economic—between a neighborhood's existing residents and their physical and social community. Spatial alienation is largely due to policies

12
The term was first coined by Ruth Glass, a Marxist sociologist who witnessed the working quarters of London transforming as the gentry moved in and the proletariat vacated, "until all or most of the original working class occupiers are displaced and the whole social character of the district is changed." See Ruth Glass, *London: Aspects of Change* (London: MacGibbon & Kee, 1965).

Neeraj Bhatia

that redefine the character of space and extend its implicit/explicit privatization. This also extends to the shaping of collective identities that eliminate the impurities of social antagonism and rather stage a form of "publicness" and its associated lifestyle. As such, these large development projects tend to become enclaves of total planning and surveillance through the programming of life.[13] Gentrification could be seen as the emblematic project of advanced capitalism reified in urban form, as posited by Stavros Stavrides:

13
Stavrides, *Common Space*, 25, 142.

> Gentrification may be publicized through rhetoric of diversity and plurality but it is essentially a highly selective set of interventions that establish strict rules of public space uses. Gentrification is explicitly connected to displacement acts directed against all those who are stigmatized for their misery or their "unruly" behaviours and especially against those who inhabit areas that may become "developed" in the interest of real estate investors. Gentrification, thus, is a specific set of policies that shapes the revanchist city as both an aggressively homogenized urban order and rhetorically shaped world of individual opportunities and safe consumption of differing lifestyles.[14]

14
Ibid., 139–140.

Framed in a promise of connection and access, projects such as the Blue Greenway or the large mixed-used developments reveal and produce only a particular form of urbanism along the waterfront. This limited narrative further estranges longtime residents from the waterfront, the enclave developments, and their own neighborhoods. By silencing these voices, it diminishes the potential for alternative relationships based on cooperation, negotiation, and sharing, characteristic of commoning.[15]

15
See, for instance, Harvey's discussion on the High Line in New York, which has similarities to the Blue Greenway. Harvey, *Rebel Cities*, 75.

Commoning as an Act of Laboring Together

The urban commons is a relatively new notion and involves a shift in understanding the commons not simply as shared resources but also as a relational social framework. The expansion of the noun "common" to the verb "commoning" entails active participation in the mechanisms of sharing, including shaping the rules that sustain the commons and exploring the emancipating potentials of sharing.[16] As such, commoning is a practice that is continually evolving, made and remade by the subjects involved in the commons. Through an ongoing process of working together, negotiating, and organizing, these practices produce

16
Guido Ruivenkamp and Andy Hilton, *Perspectives on Commoning: Autonomist Principles and Practices* (London: ZED, 2017), 1, as well as Stavrides, *Common Space*, 32.

17
Stavrides, *Common Space*, 35.

18
De Angelis, *Omnia Sunt Communia*, 11.

19
De Angelis, *Omnia Sunt Communia*, 207, and Stavrides, *Common Space*, 272.

20
De Angelis, *Omnia Sunt Communia*, 210.

21
See, for instance, Eizenberg's research on community gardens in New York: Efrat Eizenberg, "Actually Existing Commons: Three Moments of Space of Community Gardens in New York City," *Antipode* 44, no. 3 (2012).

22
See Richard Sennett, *The Uses of Disorder: Personal Identity and City Life* (New York: Knopf, 1970) and Amanda Huron, "Working with Strangers in Saturated Space: Reclaiming and Maintaining the Urban Commons," *Antipode* 00, no. 0 (2015): 7.

23
Michael Hardt, *Thomas Jefferson: The Declaration of Independence* (New York: Verso, 2007).

24
Stavrides, *Common Space*, 54.

what is to be named, valued, used, and symbolized in common. Ultimately, these practices create forms of social life—highlighting new forms of living, working, and being in common.[17] Precisely for the empowerment offered by these acts, they are always under continual threat of enclosure by the forces of capitalism as they attempt to transform society's common wealth.

The social systems produced by commoning and between commoners are a continuous form of social labor.[18] As profit, expropriation, and competitiveness are not dominant influences, the social force formed around cooperation, negotiation, and sharing is distinct, as it centers on solidarity.[19] Massimo De Angelis identifies two types of social labor enacted during commoning—communal labor and reciprocal labor. Communal labor is the labor that commoners gather around toward common objectives subsequent to convocation, whereas reciprocal labor is intertwined with perceptions of reciprocity, gift, or mutual aid. What distinguishes these forms of labor from capitalist work is that the "commons establishes its own autonomous measures of what, how, and when and how much labor, while for capital all these measures are prevalently defined from the outside condition of the markets, competitiveness and the particular needs of capitalist profitability."[20] The social labor of commoning is thereby valued by a plurality of measures that the community of commoners enacts. There are several examples wherein community is formed not simply because of a common characteristic (such as a belief system, geography, etc.), but rather through working together—including cooperating, collaborating, and communicating—on common goals and resources.[21] Unlike the rural commons, urban commoning often involves the gathering of strangers, and thereby there is always the potential for conflict.[22] This potential for conflict is a form of working-in-common and can be learned only by doing the work itself.[23] Through laboring together, commoners learn how to engage in democratic processes and are empowered to take action.

Common Space as a Site of Politics

The coexistence of a material "common space" and a collective community that maintains this space is a key requirement for an urban commons. Commoning is intimately tied to common space—"spaces produced by people in their effort to establish a common world that houses, supports and expresses the community they participate in."[24]

If both public and private spaces remain under the control of a particular authority, what makes common spaces distinct is that they are free of such control and managed through the negotiation of a plurality of views. Common spaces act as nodes where the city becomes the site of politics—where dominant forms of living and working are questioned and potentially transformed, challenging the very idea of ownership.[25]

25
Ibid., 261.

While issues such as gentrification and displacement cannot be solved by architecture alone, the following proposal asks how these concepts could be materialized on the specific geography of the Southeast Waterfront. Admittedly, the challenge of judging such proposals is rooted in the difficulty in gauging the self-sufficiency—economic and political—of the commons and commoners. Enclosed within neoliberal models of evaluation, we are starved for new notions of value that the commons can surely provide. Ultimately, it is the ability for commoners to labor together that will denote the success or failure of the commons. While these acts emerge directly from the commoners and are continually evolving, we can still speculate and strategize on what locations and spaces might offer emancipating potentials. This includes working both urbanistically—honing in on key moments of urban systems, examining ownership structures, in addition to flows and movement—as well as architecturally—creating the frame for a community of commoners that acts autonomously yet is integrated into surrounding systems. These physical interventions are not immune to the enclosing agendas of neoliberalism; they can, however, maintain their resistive potential through commoners acting together. Laboring together is in fact the "work" of action.

Our proposal begins by challenging the homogenizing and normalizing force of the Blue Greenway, which presents a limited view and experience of the waterfront. Our contention here is that if one does not see and experience the true diversity of spaces, unique fabric, and range of uses along the Southeast Waterfront, the consistent representation acts as an isolating force for those spaces, people, and practices that are underrepresented. Proposing an alternative circuit that presents a counternarrative enables one to witness the full range of living, working, and land-use conditions of the Southeast Waterfront. This circuit ties together mass-transit stations, catalytic neighborhood programs, open space, and the existing residential fabric with key moments of the waterfront and Blue Greenway. Stitching together new developments along the waterfront and the existing residential fabric, the circuit presents a plethora of conditions that more precisely reflect the complexity of the Southeast Waterfront. This new armature enables the autonomy and

Bird's-eye view of the counter-circuit, bringing the existing neighborhoods into conversation with new developments. Credit: Neeraj Bhatia & Blake Stevenson

integration of these distinct neighborhoods. Further, the circuit is primarily situated on "unaccepted streets"—city streets that are maintained not by the city but rather by the property owners who reside on the edge of the right-of-way. While this presents a dubious situation of civic responsibility, it also means that residents on these streets have more agency of over the right-of-way. If public space is space maintained through an authority and has implicit implications of power, unaccepted streets offer a space that is free of such constraints.

As this commons circuit weaves through the neighborhoods of the waterfront, it links together a series of urban commons that act as key moments of gathering. The commons are strategically placed along the circuit in areas of infrastructural interchange (such as mass-transit stops) or fragmentation in the path (such as broken stairs, topographic shifts, or places where infrastructure might segregate a neighborhood), in areas where existing community programs or open spaces are sited, and in areas that are embedded within neighborhoods and rhythmically sequence one's experience along the circuit. Most of these are placed in threshold spaces—passages of

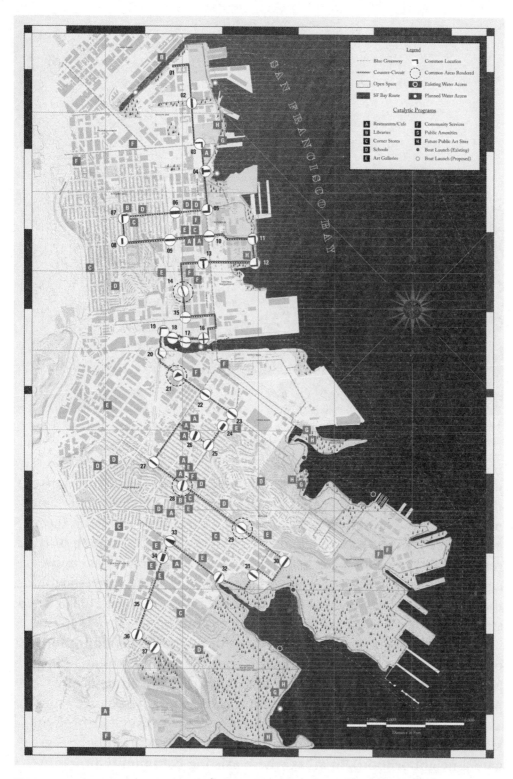

Masterplan drawing showing counter-circuit in relationship to catalytic programs, existing open space, the Blue Greenway, and moments of fragmentation.
Credit: Neeraj Bhatia & Blake Stevenson

connection and separation. These threshold spaces are often linked to catalyzing collective inventiveness—where space and subjects are in a parallel process of constant negotiation, making them communities and spaces in the making.[26]

26
Stavrides, *Common Space*, 5, and Aimee Felstead, Kevin Thwaites, and James Simpson, "A Conceptual Framework for Urban Commoning in Shared Residential Landscapes in the UK," *Sustainability* 6119, no. 11 (2019): 8–9.

View of the proposal from the northwest.
Credit: Neeraj Bhatia & Blake Stevenson

The industrial lineage of these waterfront neighborhoods centered on labor (both domestic and material) that connected a diverse group of immigrants. One resident, Ruth Eshow Upton, when describing the Bayview during the 1920s, proclaimed, "The young mothers bonded because of their common interests in keeping house and raising a family. There seemed to be no envy; everyone was more or less in the same financial level and they all shared the same goals: to make a good life for their children."[27] And while these workers were locked into a system of land ownership and wage labor, working together with collectively shared goals proved to be a key instrument in forming a pluralistic community. These cultures of communal and reciprocal labor act as a powerful weapon to resist neoliberal agendas, as De Angelis posits:

27
Ruth Eshow Upton, "1920s Melting Pot in Bayview: I was there," *FoundSF*, http://www.foundsf.org/index.php?title=1920s_Melting_Pot_in_Bayview.

In centers where there exist factories that concentrate workers and tie them into industrial rhythms of work, networks of labor reciprocity among worker's families—often maintained and reproduced along ethnic or national lines—are often the basis of broader labor union constitution and organization. All the same, there are neighborhoods in modern Western cities that for a variety of reasons have managed to keep up networks of reciprocity and communal labor, allowing them to maintain social cohesion which is very useful when the neighborhood is threatened by neoliberal urban "regeneration" processes.[28]

28
De Angelis, *Omnia Sunt Communia*, 219.

Our proposed urban commons contain a series of programs centered on working together through material cultures of making, harvesting, and repairing. San Francisco has been the hub of making culture for several years now, a culture that arguably emerged from neighborhoods like the Southeast Waterfront. From Burning Man to Maker Faires, as society is increasingly disconnected from physical objects, these spaces remind and empower us to use our hands. These forms of making often have the DIY ethos that emerged from the domestic realm but use tools and equipment that exceed the capacity of an individual household. Given the historic culture of the Southeast Waterfront, a series of urban commons centered on making can not only bring people together but, more importantly, remind us of what we hold in common.

Repair commons situated in the right-of-way in a currently vacant traffic island.
Credit: Neeraj Bhatia & Blake Stevenson

As a series of diffuse nodes, these urban commons present an iterative approach to urbanism that is low risk, with little capital investment. The commons can be phased in stages, funded in a distributed manner, maintained by the community and local groups, and used as

Ceramics commons situated as a connector between topographically separated neighborhoods.
Credit: Neeraj Bhatia & Blake Stevenson

tools to learn about and influence future nodes. The more urban commons that are built, the stronger the network becomes, yet its overall functioning is not contingent on all of the commons being deployed. Each node maintains its autonomy while being linked into a polynuclear network that allows for sharing at a larger scale and nested forms of governance. While individually modest in size, each of these nodes can have a critical impact that extends beyond its footprint. Perhaps most important, the urban commons act as an institution-in-the-making to empower people—individually and collectively—not just to use their hands but to remember that when we work together, a new collective realm can be formed. This collective realm produces a feeling of belonging, and this feeling is one of the most powerful weapons to prevent displacement and empower those who increasingly are silenced in the neoliberal city. Ultimately, through the practice of laboring together, the urban commons has the potential to once again make the city a site of politics.

The author would like to acknowledge the Piero N. Patri Fellowship in Urban Design and SPUR for commissioning this design-research. The project presented in this article is part of a thorough study on the Southeast Waterfront authored by Neeraj Bhatia and Blake Stevenson with Liz Lessig. The full project was published as a book, entitled, "Recommoning the Frontier", (SPUR, 2017).

The Internet of People Strikes Back:
Two Future Scenarios and a Proposition

Paolo Cardullo

Introduction/Background

As "smart cities" become more involved in data-driven processes of growth and governance, their advocates have been pushing for 5G technology to increase network and data capacity flows. To date, however, critical scholarship has focused less on the physical infrastructure of the internet and smart technologies in relation to urban commons, practices of commoning, and everyday materiality of social reproduction.

This paper advocates for a public data and internet infrastructure to be run by the city and its citizens, suggesting alternative ecologies for the development of the Internet of People rather than the Internet of Things currently promoted by the smart-city spinning discourse. This has become a more urgent matter during the pandemic crisis, which has forced most of the world population to stay at home, thus increasing their demands on the "network of networks."

While I was writing in confinement from my flat in Italy, the coronavirus crisis exploded in all its dramatic social, economic, and political violence. As entire nations decided to lock down their populations at home, the pandemic manifested mainly as an urban crisis, intertwining deeply with digital and smart technologies: an urban crisis is also a smart-city crisis. The smart city is a fairly recent formulation that has gained traction in the last few years: essentially, it implies the intertwining of urban processes and infrastructures with algorithm-led technologies for monitoring, tracking, and managing mobility, governance, consumption, policing, and service utilities.[1] Although smart cities are not just about broadband connectivity, access to unlimited, super fast, and possibly free internet has been symbolically crucial to their creation: the internet is thought to be the smart-city backbone, "the backbone of modern society, a platform for businesses, governments and citizens to exchange news and views, as well as to provide services, whether essential or trivial."[2]

On the one hand, the crisis has brought to the fore a series of issues that were long-standing with regard to digital society: for instance, teleworking, online courses, and digital classrooms have become, slowly and chaotically, the "new normal" of these troubled days. Many people, especially professionals, realized that working at distance can be enhanced only by widespread recourse to digital technologies and that much more should be done to guarantee that the internet becomes a public service accessible to "the many."

1
See, for example, R. Kitchin, "The Real-Time City? Big Data and Smart Urbanism," *GeoJournal* 79, no. 1 (2014): 1–14.

2
The Digital Agenda for Europe, https://ec.europa.eu/digital-single-market/en/news/broadband-big-pipes-potential-growth.

On the other hand, smart technologies have been heralded as the ultimate fix to the coronavirus emergency. Contact tracing and confinement apps, for example, have been unveiled as a series of (problematic and patchy) remedies that bring together many assumptions of the smart-city discourse, from technological determinism to surveillance capitalism: Bluetooth- or GPS-powered mobile apps and sensors that track, monitor, follow, alert, map, police, control, and chart population movement, social contacts, and medical condition via mostly automatic and autonomous algorithm-led processes.[3]

From this dense accumulation I want to propose two possible future scenarios around internet connectivity and digital society at large: the first one is the current techno-political landscape of smart-city adoption subsumed to the Internet of Things (IoT); the second future points to the Internet of People (IoP) as a gateway for a democratic and participatory civic infrastructure that builds and supports our disposition toward each other, our communities, and the social fabric. In the second part of the paper, I open to issues of data commons and *commoning*, proposing an alternative configuration to the prevalent neoliberal one, an "intelligent city."

3
For a comprehensive overview, see R. Kitchin, "Civil Liberties *or* Public Health, or Civil Liberties *and* Public Health? Using Surveillance Technologies to Tackle the Spread of COVID-19," *Space and Polity* 0, no. 0 (2020): 1–20.

Future 1: The New IP

As microprocessors become increasingly embedded components of devices and systems, a crucial change has happened in the everyday life of cities. The internet as we know it, initially built for people, has become the vector for the development of millions of other devices, objects, and machines. The current socio-technological landscape is dominated by different configurations we can group under the heading Internet of Things. These "things" are digital devices that typically have a communication interface, processing and storage units, and sensors for detection of environmental changes or for service provision to other clients. Thus smart technologies are always somehow linked to an algorithm-led response, even for a simple card payment or for an instance of communication. Ultimately, algorithmic functions represent the "smart" bit in smart technology. These functions *always* involve some production and transmission of information or data from one agent (machinic, human-operated, or human) to another. The combination of short-range mesh networks and the wider cellular network can provide wireless connectivity to these "things" in order to exchange data on the wider internet. Recording, storing, and transmitting data are

4
M. Fuller, ed., *How to Be a Geek: Essays on the Culture of Software* (Cambridge, UK, and Malden, MA: Polity Press, 2017).

5
Huawei Technologies, "NEW IP Framework and Protocol for Future Applications," 2020.

6
https://blog. dellemc.com/en-us/ distributed-analytics-meets-distributed-data-with-a-world-wide-herd/.

7
R. Li, A. Clemm, U. Chunduri, L. Dong, and K. Makhijani, "A New Framework and Protocol for Future Networking Applications," in *Proceedings of the 2018 Workshop on Networking for Emerging Applications and Technologies—NEAT '18* (Budapest, Hungary: ACM Press, 2018), 21–26, http://dl.acm.org/citation. cfm?doid=3229574. 3229576.

8
See, for example, I. Apostol and P. Antoniadis, "Central Urban Space as a Hybrid Common Infrastructure," *Journal of Peer Production* 14 (2020), http:// peerproduction.net/issues/ issue-14-infrastructuring-the-commons-today-when-sts-meets-ict/ peer-reviewed-papers/ central-urban-space-as-a-hybrid-common-infrastructure/.

9
P. Cardullo and R. Kitchin, "Being a 'Citizen' in the Smart City: Up and Down the Scaffold of Smart Citizen Participation in Dublin, Ireland," *GeoJournal* 84, no. 1 (2019): 1–13.

10
See Kitchin, "Civil Liberties or Public Health."

the *modus operandi* of smart technologies, their reasons to be, fetching and communicating data to remote servers somewhere in "the cloud." The novelty of smart devices is that they appear personal and portable but are also always interconnected with platforms, systems, and cloud spaces that are very centralized.[4]

In this regard, 5G giant Huawei suggests evolving connectivity via a new "extra dynamic IP addressing system,"[5] while Dell proposes the development of the "World Wide Herd"[6]: islands of hyperconnectivity permitting gadgets, devices, and nodes inside the mesh to communicate instantly with one another without having to ship data throughout the Web. For instance, driverless cars could roam through islands of data exchange within proximity of the "herd" of data-led devices. It is data, not communication between people, that really matters to high-tech industry today. Data powers the new horizons of connectivity and future imaginaries of technocracy, from the "Industry 4.0" to the smart city.

The upcoming configuration is moving away from the Internet of People (IoP) that animated the early deployment of mass connectivity, through VoIP (Voice over Internet Protocol), blogs, and personal webpages, toward the Internet of Things (IoT), which boosts much faster and uncompromised connectivity of sensors, devices, and personal consumer goods. The "Next Internet," such as 5G (or 6G) technology, promotes a different kind of experience—a user dealing with a personal home assistant like Alexa or possibly even a holographic communication system for a "tangible, immersive, and interactive communication experience"[7]: from a network of social relations (e.g., the Network Society) to islands of super-connectivity for "things" (e.g., the World Wide Herd). Although some insist on the hybrid convergence of users, space, and devices,[8] the roles and aims of such hybridity remain confined within a paternalistic framework of nudging users to become learners, testers, or players with very limited smart-citizen rights. In the future scenario dominated by the IoT, people too are framed as sensors, data points, and ultimately as products of this algorithm-led exchange.[9] Indeed, communication and exchange between algorithms that regulate many aspects of daily life happen in milliseconds, which tends to preempt human-oriented responses. For instance, contact tracing apps matter for very sensitive and personal situations (e.g., potential exposure to contagion), performing trust without trust. They become attached to unreliable monitoring systems—such as Bluetooth or GPS, alphanumeric handshakes, remote controlling algorithms—and sketchy data policy and procedures:[10] *both* trust *and* governance are to happen at distance, regardless of the gravity or sensitivity of the potentially life-changing situations they concern.

I would argue that the traumatic consequences of the coronavirus crisis have left little space for the futuristic narratives animated by caring robots, driverless cars, and holograms, since these are imbued in sci-fi imaginaries, STEM handbooks, and geeks' private-life issues with little relevance to real-life situations and people's needs. In a few words, the bullshit has come to the fore.

Future 2: The IoP Strikes Back

The coronavirus crisis has indeed marked the return of the Internet of People in the public discourse:[11] teleworking, digital classrooms, platform delivery services, VoIP-powered video calls across the globe, blogging and social networking, digital ethnographic methods, academic online forums, and home leisure are only some of the features of a popular and accessible network. As Manuel Castells has recently written in light of the pandemic, "Now we know what the Internet is for. To communicate, as always was obvious. It doesn't isolate, it relates. It doesn't alienate, it encourages. It does not eliminate emotion, but feeds it."[12] Digital society seems to endure, and it brings benefits, too.

In this guise, the Italian government launched the *solidarietà digitale* initiative,[13] through which hundreds of tech players have been offering services and discounts on their digital products: extra gigabytes of home entertainment, free online access to magazines and e-books, discounted server storage, free certified e-mails, and distance-learning tools for teleworking and schooling. In the US, the Federal Communications Commission has asked Big Cable "to relax their data cap policies" and telephone carriers "to waive long-distance and overage fees."[14] Free Press, too, calls for ISPs to play their part: "Especially during a crisis, Internet and phone access should be accessible public services like water and electricity."[15]

What does this mean in terms of the digitalization process of the everyday, the internet and data infrastructure, and the "right to the smart city"?[16]

First, digital infrastructures are a pressing need in many fields: online working or leisure and communication activities are in increasing demand nowadays. Although exceptional, the current crisis is creating a boom in the digital sector and online business, forcing digital practices and learning also onto people and institutions that have resisted

11 This is obviously not a new theme. Activists have been fighting almost since its inception for a free and universal internet: hence a "return." However, the new trajectories of development of smart technologies and the post-pandemic society are very new and upcoming issues.

12 https://www.lavanguardia.com/opinion/20200425/48700040274/manuel-castells-digital.html.

13 https://solidarietadigitale.agid.gov.it/.

14 https://www.techrepublic.com/article/dozens-of-companies-offering-free-wi-fi-and-other-services-to-those-working-or-studying-from-home/.

15 https://www.freepress.net/news/press-releases/free-press-calls-major-internet-providers-waive-broadband-bills-risk-people-and.

16 P. Cardullo, R. Kitchin, and C. Di Feliciantonio, eds., *The Right to the Smart City* (Bingley, UK: Emerald Publishing, 2019), https://books.emeraldinsight.com/page/detail/The-Right-to-the-Smart-City/?k=9781787691407.

this change thus far. In the present scenario of a growing demand for connectivity from people to "things," it is easy to believe that the capacity of the networks will be increased and expanded. We can move the above question to the supply side and ask: *how* and *on whose terms* is this infrastructural development going to happen? Universal access and local governance of the network ought to be priorities of modern digital society if we consider equality, fairness, and democratic participation as its driving principles.

Second, good corporate social responsibility has been slow to emerge: the "digital solidarity" campaign has shown that the market does not react automatically and accordingly, with Big and Medium Tech rather pursuing opportunistic marketing ventures. Unfortunately, in the prevalent neoliberal framework, public investments for the internet provision are admissible *only* for supporting areas and communities that have fallen through the net of private providers' profit, or "market failure." That is, public investment takes place only "where the market *is not* providing the desired connectivity,"[17] rather than being animated by strategic and social objectives founded on rights and the common good. But as Jamie Peck writes, "Markets themselves are not, never have been and cannot be spontaneously occurring and naturally self-regulating."[18] While acquiring monopolistic positions everywhere and being heavily subsidized by federal money, for example, Big Cable in the US has persistently lobbied politicians to dismiss municipally and community-owned infrastructures as a breach in free-market principles.[19]

It follows that, third, such a critical infrastructure cannot be left to private and unregulated providers, as it is at present almost everywhere. As distance learning and teleworking become the new normal for millions of people, we need instead to ensure that access to high-quality broadband is qualitative and not exploitative, and equitable and widely available rather than exclusive and selective. An intelligent city ("intelligent" is posed here as an oppositional term to "smart") can work only with regard to the increasing (digital and material) needs of people and things in the context of globalized economies and localized solutions. In other words, public discourse around the "digital society" needs to be shifted back toward the IoP: not smart vehicles without drivers, not caring robots, but connecting infrastructures and digital services for "the many"; utilities that become "useful" again for a whole series of purposes that matter for everyday practices of working and inhabitation. This is not going to challenge the many faces of digital capitalism, but it will provide one gateway for more local

17
https://ec.europa.eu/digital-single-market/en/state-aid.
18
J. Peck, "Geography and Public Policy: Constructions of Neoliberalism," *Progress in Human Geography* 28, no. 3 (2004): 394.
19
H. Trostle and C. Mitchell, "Report Dives Deep into Big Cable and Telecom Monopolies," Institute for Local Self-Reliance, 2018, https://muninetworks.org/content/report-dives-deep-big-cable-and-telecom-monopolies.

control and accountability in the life cycle of data. Going up on the connectivity stack, a whole set of services, platforms, data centers, clouds, and infrastructure governance would need to be brought into public hands and/or regulated by the state (for larger infrastructure build, such as the "backbone"), by municipalities and communities (for the last-mile delivery and local governance), to be organized and delivered by municipalities as a public service for the common good.

But what are *commons* and what is the value of *commoning* in a city increasingly regulated by processes of data acquisition and exchange?

Commons and Commoning in the Smart City

For Michael Hardt and Antonio Negri, advanced capitalist production expresses a form of "collective intelligence";[20] this is unlocked by the forced multiplicity and proximity that urban living implies. Production extends to society in its totality: it is the social factory 4.0, which creates value through the very practices of urban dwelling, social encounters, and social reproduction. Thus many activists and scholars advocate for digital commons, where ownership and control of data become a democratic practice of appropriation of everyday technologies; others, for data revenues to be socially shared or redistributed;[21] still others call for a "basic social income," which acknowledges digital labor as a producer of use-value, too.[22] At the least, citizens should have the right to understand what data are being generated about them, how these are compiled into information, and to what end.[23]

A common good, however, has no ontological substance in itself. It *becomes* a commons because of the qualitative relationship with one or more subjects; it is the use-value (of place or data) that makes it relevant to the commons: "You don't have a common good, you share in common good."[24] For Duncan McLaren and Julian Agyeman, "sharing and cooperation are universal values and behaviours" and, therefore, "sharing is an opportunity to release [people's cooperative] capacity, confined by competitive markets and bureaucratic states."[25] So if cities are shared creations with shared public services, streets, mass transit, and shared spaces, "truly smart cities must also be sharing cities."[26]

Therefore, scholars prefer to put the emphasis on *commoning*, a set of practices that "actively seek to integrate resources from the state and capital into commons circuits."[27] *Commoning* concerns the

20
M. Hardt and A. Negri, *Commonwealth* (Cambridge, MA: Belknap Press of Harvard University Press, 2009).
21
M. Mazzucato, *The Value of Everything: Makers and Takers in the Global Economy* (London: Allen Lane, 2018).
22
J.-M. Monnier and C. Vercellone, *Basic Income as Primary Income* (Université de Paris 1 Panthéon-Sorbonne [Post-Print and Working Papers, 2017]), HAL, https://econpapers.repec.org/paper/halcesptp/hal-01486202.htm.
23
R. Kitchin, "The Ethics of Smart Cities and Urban Science," *Philosophical Transactions of the Royal Society* A 374, no. 2083 (2016): p.20160115, https://doi.org/10.1098/rsta.2016.0115.
24
Mattei, cited in C. Iaione, "City as a Commons," in *Second Thematic Conference of the IASC on "Design and Dynamics of Institutions for Collective Action: A Tribute to Prof. Elinor Ostrom,"* 2012, http://papers.ssrn.com/sol3/papers.cfm?abstract_id=2589640.
25
D. McLaren and J. Agyeman, *Sharing Cities: A Case for Truly Smart and Sustainable Cities* (Cambridge, MA: MIT Press, 2015), 24.
26
Ibid.
27
B. J. Birkinbine, "Commons Praxis: Toward a Critical Political Economy of the Digital Commons," *tripleC: Communication, Capitalism & Critique. Open Access Journal for a Global Sustainable Information Society* 16, no. 1 (2018): 290–305.

28
An Architektur, "On the Commons: A Public Interview with Massimo De Angelis and Stavros Stavrides," *e-flux* 17 (2010), http://www.e-flux.com/journal/17/67351/on-the-commons-a-public-interview-with-massimo-de-angelis-and-stavros-stavrides/.

29
A. Huron, "Working with Strangers in Saturated Space: Reclaiming and Maintaining the Urban Commons: The Urban Commons," *Antipode* 47, no. 4 (2015): 973.

30
I. Susser, "For or Against Commoning?" *Focaal* 79 (2017): 1.

31
Hardt and Negri, *Commonwealth*.

32
See P. Cardullo, "Gentrification in the Mesh?" *City* 21, nos. 3–4 (2017): 405–419.

33
M. De Angelis, *Omnia Sunt Communia: On the Commons and the Transformation to Postcapitalism* (London: Zed Books, 2017).

34
N. Schneider, "Next, the Internet: Building a Cooperative Digital Space," *Cooperative Business Journal* (2018), https://ioo.coop/2018/02/next-the-internet-building-a-cooperative-digital-space/.

35
Cardullo, Kitchin, and Di Feliciantonio, eds., *The Right to the Smart City*.

reproduction of the *commons*, its long-term maintenance process, its contested, open-ended, and political character.[28] For Amanda Huron, commoning is "the true challenge of the commons";[29] this needs a "grassroots project to build a new form of consensus around a different set of values and ethical codes."[30] Forms of democratization of data and software instead risk fostering *commons* as a goal in itself. Hardt and Negri call the new digital commons "immaterial";[31] however, each commons presents a new set of social relations and spatial organizations. Thus, a materialist critique of digital commons (information, knowledge, data, software, etc.) ought to center on daily practices of inhabitation and social reproduction: for instance, the issue of "rent" through which the social reproduction of activists, digital enthusiasts, and ethical hackers is articulated, and "stewardship" through which these actors exert their technical knowledge and acquire status in the community of interest.[32]

Massimo De Angelis suggests a move away from the classic triad Private/Public/Commons to the emerging configuration of Capitalism/City/Commons.[33] Here, the struggle for appropriation of value moves iteratively through the two circuits for creation and circulation of wealth and well-being: the circuit of capital and that of the commons. At the same time, the city becomes a flexible scale of reference—that is, from the federal scale of the backbone and licence governance to the neighborhood scale of the last-mile provision. There is plenty of room for a municipalist policy to become the policy of the commons. Cities have a lot to learn and gain from nurturing urban commons—the spaces of solidarity, social reproduction, and mutual help—through ethical procurement and cooperatives and collectives of people pursuing goals other than the private profit in public service provision. Common-focused institutions would maintain "trust on trustless networks,"[34] fostering transparent governance, for instance. This has been exceptionally lacking in networked and digital societies after decades of neoliberal governance at distance, marketization of public services, individualization of social responsibility, exasperating nudging behavior, and overarching algorithmic control and surveillance.

In this guise, pursuing the "right to the smart city" means creating cities that are not rooted in and driven by technological capitalism and solutionism.[35]

Advocates of digital and data commons have a stake in the growing debate around both future scenarios, the IoP and the IoT. A commoning approach is, however, recommended here, through research and exploration into alternative ecologies of implementation and maintenance of the internet and its data infrastructure. Such ecologies would focus on municipalization and democratic governance of critical infrastructures and public-commons partnerships between the city, cooperatives, and social movements and organizations. The next IoP, as many imagine, has to maintain the following three characteristics.

State-Funded

The private sector and the dominant neoliberal discourse downplay massively the role of the public in driving innovation and growth via core infrastructures and investments in skills and literacy and in taking on board the political-economic risks of failure.[36] As Tung-Hui Hu points out, "The all-but-forgotten infrastructures that undergird the cloud's physical origins often originated in a state's military apparatus."[37] Broadband carriers always rely on a massive public subsidy, with the expectation that they will create and maintain a high-quality network.

In the US, fiber-to-home service is mostly in the hands of quasi-monopolist Big Cable, such as Comcast, Verizon, Time Warner Cable, and AT&T. These giant providers control the internet provision, acting as a gateway for people and things, metering and throttling connectivity at a high price and slowing down at will. As a consequence, line-sharing plans at the top level of network provision have been slowly scrapped,[38] with increased costs at the end of the pipeline for families and companies.[39] Capping the internet was never a reflection of technical reality: if AT&T can remove caps during the coronavirus lockdown, it is clear that such restrictions are not dictated by technical needs of efficiency. Rather, it is a question of the unfair accruing of profits by private digital companies. A major obstacle for the adoption of the IoP seems to be exactly this scarcity that capitalism is so good at fabricating via market imperatives of privatization and efficiency.

Municipalist

From the fiber-to-home service to the remote data farms, technology presents itself as a composite assemblage where issues of social justice and democratic governance are to be addressed at each step. Perhaps no city can control the overall process or gain complete "technological and

36
W. Lazonick and M. Mazzucato, "The Risk-Reward Nexus in the Innovation-Inequality Relationship: Who Takes the Risks? Who Gets the Rewards?" *Industrial and Corporate Change* 22, no. 4 (2013): 1093–1128.

37
T.-H. Hu, *A Prehistory of the Cloud* (Cambridge, MA: MIT Press, 2015), xvii.

38
https://www.vice.com/en_us/article/ev8n3e/big-telecom-lobby-says-theres-too-much-broadband-competition-pushes-fcc-to-harm-smaller-isps?mc_cid=4b685d0495&mc_eid=4c4b31ca2e.

39
https://www.newamerica.org/oti/policy-papers/the-cost-of-connectivity-2014/.

40
G. Charnock, H.
March, and R. Ribera-
Fumaz, "From Smart to
Rebel City? Worlding,
Provincialising and
the Barcelona Model,"
Urban Studies (2019),
p.0042098019872119.

41
https://tech.cityofnewyork.
us/internet-master-plan/.

digital sovereignty."[40] However, some cities, such as New York, are moving toward the goal of more favorable access to the internet;[41] others, like Amsterdam, have taken further steps by fostering data commons; or, like Barcelona, by pursuing a policy of "technological sovereignty." These and other cities have joined together in the Cities Coalition for Digital Rights, which centers on the respect of privacy and human rights in the use of the internet and related technologies.

A search through successful stories of municipal broadband service in the US reveals that most of these initiatives have built their own citywide telecommunications networks based on cabling already operated by a municipal electric utility. This is important because it shows how public services can become cumulative and build upon local strengths and skills while negotiating provision at a reduced price. Chattanooga, Tennessee, for instance, was the first city in the US to offer one gigabit per second (1 Gbps) high-speed internet (at the time, over 200 times faster than the national average) in 2010 and implemented the world's first community-wide 10 Gbps internet service in 2015. Chattanooga transformed its image of a polluted and failing metropolis into the thriving "Gig City." More important, this infrastructure was offered via the municipal and nonprofit Electric Power Board, making it the largest public investment in the US on the matter.[42] Another good example is NextLight in Longmont, Colorado.[43] The service is provided by LPC, the city's community-owned and not-for-profit electric and internet services provider, which began building the NextLight fiber network in 2014 and has provided Longmont's electric service since 1912.[44]

42
Electric Power Board
(EPB), "EPB to Offer
Discounted Internet for
Low-Income Families,"
2015, https://epb.com/
about-epb/news/articles/8.

43
https://www.
longmontcolorado.
gov/departments/
departments-e-m/longmont-
power-communications/
broadband-service/
in-the-news.

44
https://longmontobserver.
org/featured/
nextlight-longmont-wins-
2019-cornerstone-award-
for-excellence/.

But speed and reliability are not going to solve digital divides; they actually risk creating islands of fast connectivity. To counteract this risk, in 2017 New York City started installing a Wi-Fi network for the provision of a free 25 Mb broadband service (the current minimum speed for a legal definition of broadband in the US) to the largest public housing complex in the country: the 7,000 low-income residents spread in the 95 buildings of Queensbridge Houses, Long Island City. The city acted as an authoritative buyer for several thousand people, negotiating a reduced price for the piping of the cables (fiber to home) and the acquisition of Tier 1 broadband. Similarly, 14 rural communities in Colorado recently completed Project Thor, a 481-mile network that offers a reliable backbone for local internet service providers. They negotiated as a single large customer, putting together Northwest Colorado Broadband, a nonprofit cooperative that was soon joined by the local hospital, electric utility, community college, and others.[45]

45
https://coloradosun.
com/2020/04/16/
internet-service-western-
colorado-rural-broadband-
nwccog-sb152/.

Paolo Cardullo

While Chattanooga remains a good example of efficient public service delivery, but apparently with limited impact on marginalized population,[46] New York City's experiments in its public housing show how utilities can be delivered as public service with redistributive effects and even foster a more democratic model of urban governance.

There are solid grounds for reversing the privatization and the consequent centralization of the internet in the hands of very few and powerful companies, a situation that has been particularly acute in the US for a series of historical reasons. In January 2019, there operated over 800 small providers, 500 served by some form of municipal network and over 300 by a cooperative.[47] Beyond the neoliberal rhetoric of the "market failure," public resources and skills should be turned toward more equitable urban infrastructures, by facilitating and supporting *commoning* ground—the contested process of delivering, protecting, and maintaining infrastructures as a *commons*.

People-Focused

Discourses around data and digital commons run the risk of fostering a certain determinism, sometimes focusing more on the object (data sets or software being made available as common good) rather than the process that leads to and maintains it (commoning). Internet equality claims do not stand as an exception, since having more connected people does not translate automatically into fairer communities or more livable cities. This is because cities are messy and complex places and because infrastructures are socio-technological assemblages that depend for their functioning on the practices, uses, and therefore skills of those involved. With algorithm-led technologies, this assumption is often subsumed to the process of acquiring data, selecting optimal profiles and responses, and enabling feedback. Thus, there is room for a conclusive cautionary note around the implementation and maintenance of a public data and internet infrastructure, with two issues emerging in relation to community involvement and commoning.

The first issue concerns the differences between algorithm trust and social trust. The Internet of Things is powered by devices and mobile apps that turn citizens into sensors and data points: people and things are actuators of the data exchange through networks, continuously performing acts of trust at the margin of the mesh. We can see this happening with contact-tracing apps promoted by technocratic elites through the advocacy offered by Big Tech and academic coalitions and communities of geeks. But while algorithm trust happens in milliseconds between long alphanumeric keys that recognize each other and perform

EPB now counts more than half of the civil and commercial residents of Chattanooga as customers, which drops to about 20 percent in its poorer neighborhoods, according to J. Koebler (see "The City That Was Saved by the Internet," *Motherboard*, October 27, 2016, https://motherboard. vice.com/en_us/article/ ezpk77/chattanooga-gigabit-fiber-network). Despite EPB offering half-priced, subsidized internet for families with students enrolled in school lunch programs (Netbridge), it appears that poorer residents prefer signing up with Comcast, which offers a cheaper service, although much slower and capped.

47 Institute for Local Self-Reliance, https://muninetworks.org/communitymap.

a so-called handshake, social trust hinges on long-term relationships and slow exchanges, often performed face to face in the spaces of daily inhabitation and around social spaces shared in common. Without social trust, personalized medical support, and an army of trained testers, such experimentation risks being useless (despite whether these apps ensure privacy by design or data trusts).[48]

The second cautionary note draws a vector of possibilities along stewardship and socio-technical skills, both needed to maintain smart technologies as a working infrastructure. Stewardship becomes essential because the higher the involvement of laypeople, the harder it will become to include them: indeed, most of the technologies currently deployed in the smart city are beyond people's agentive interaction, with their computational processes enabling black-boxed, autonomous, and automated responses. Moreover, smart technologies demand cultural and social capitals from users because they are linked to forms of social exchange and their implementation is conditional to contextual arrangements in communities of interest and localities: there is nothing automatic and deterministic about platforms and sensors in making communities "operative." Here, there is room for ethical hackers and community organizers with strong technical skills to mobilize knowledge transfer and try to limit digital divides, and for people to get actively involved in the creation or maintenance of networking technologies, such as communitarian mesh and localized internet provision. However, communitarian initiatives like these have lagged behind in many places because ethical hackers abandon the projects: sometimes because their interest shifts toward other initiatives more fashionable or lucrative, such as blockchain and IoT,[49] or because urban space becomes divisive around the issue of rent,[50] or because academic funding runs out.[51]

As a consequence, I would suggest a mixed approach in the provision of the internet and the urban data infrastructure, involving city and the commons rather than the market: grass-root initiatives (in the forms of cooperatives, citizen groups, and social enterprises such as small and ethical ISPs); public engagement from the city (as an organization with social and political goals); the sharing of networks and licence spectrum (this is a commons too, rather than a commodity);[52] and an adequate level of public investments (not only in place of market failure). By developing, maintaining, or controlling their own internet grid, cities can negotiate more favorable and ethically binding last-mile access for their citizens—for instance, by leveraging their contractual weight toward digital providers and platforms. A public

48
See, for example, https://www.wired.com/story/health-officials-no-thanks-contact-tracing-tech/.

49
Global Information Society Watch, *Community Networks*, 2018, https://www.giswatch.org/community-networks.

50
Cardullo, "Gentrification in the Mesh?"

51
N. Bidwell, "Tragedies in Translation: Fostering Community Networks in the Global South," *Journal of Peer Production* (2018), http://peerproduction.net/issues/issue-14-infrastructuring-the-commons-today-when-sts-meets-ict/peer-reviewed-papers/tragedies-in-translation-fostering-community-networks-in-the-global-south/.

52
See APC, "What's New on the Spectrum? 'Let's Make Sure We Can Use It for What Is Needed': A Conversation with Peter Bloom from Rhizomatica," *Association for Progressive Communications*, 2018, https://www.apc.org/en/news/whats-new-spectrum-lets-make-sure-we-can-use-it-what-needed-conversation-peter-bloom.

internet grid and city-owned data trusts would allow municipalities or their alliances to have more negotiating power toward digital platforms—for instance, when setting new urban policies, standards, and regulations for companies such as Airbnb or Uber. Social movements and interest groups can set standards of data ownership and ethics of data extraction, treatment, and reuse—perhaps with their own manifesto, audits, and feedback loops.

In sum, the global pandemic offers a chance for ditching neoliberal urbanism and algorithm-led governance at distance, and instead for providing a useful infrastructure for "the many": a fair and empowering Internet of People rebuilt with cooperation among small-scale and community network operators, governed through low-cost and open-access network infrastructure, and operating for the public-community coproduction of urban policies. However, infrastructuring is an ongoing and contested process beyond designing or setting up participatory pilots: in an intelligent city, the governing bodies and social movements would own and deliver their data infrastructure for the common good, a rights-based and municipally owned internet service.

On the Idea of the Commons

An Interview with Massimo De Angelis
by Mojdeh Mahdavi and Liang Wang

New Geographies   The term "commons" entails a handful of definitions and meanings across different contexts in history. The most common definition has to do with the relationship between human collectives and natural resources, which also constitutes one of the central issues in the discussion of the commons. Building on this conception, you have proposed that we need to open up the concept of commons by bringing the social relation to its definition. How do you think new social relationships would inform our understanding of the concept? In your book *Omnia Sunt Communia*, the approach to the commons has been positioned clearly within a historical lineage. Can you share with us how recent sociopolitical events have renewed your understanding and definition of the commons?

Massimo De Angelis   The commons traditionally have been referred to as natural resources in the sense Ostrom refers to—that is, everybody has access to the natural resource system that the community can use for its own reproduction. Nowadays, in urban settings, the corner side squares and parks are often called commons. The traditional conception is still useful and is often used in daily conversations to refer to cyberspace, centers for the Occupy movement, urban fab labs, and so on. If we go back in history, we will find that the idea of commons has been mobilized by the labor movement in relation to a particular resource being pulled together. At the root of all these definitions is a community—a network of individuals who engage in a process of commoning and defining their own social relations around a set of resources. These are the three basic aspects that every commons share — some common resources, a community of people and a process of doing in common or commoning—and we could apply them pretty much everywhere. The commons is the life activity and a form of social labor in a general sense that is essentially rooted in the ethic of care and mutual recognition. Commoning is a different way of mobilizing social labor for social cooperation and is in contrast with the abstract labor that is rooted in capitalist exploitation and alienation within big corporations, factory floors, offices, and in many schools. Social labor classically defines us as human.

        However, commoning based on the ethic of care and mutual recognition is not sufficient for engendering social transformation. At the same time, social transformation—which goes back to the notion of social revolution—has to rest on the idea of the commons to create an alternative reality. To understand this contradiction, we need to think about the commons as systems within systems. Commons should create value not only for their members and commoners but also for a broader system. So it is really important to conceive not just the specificities of a given system and its own internal operations, but also its relation to its environment—the outside. A system, as I have learned from systems theory, is always in relation to an environment. The system-environment relation constitutes a greater system and opens the question of the need to have porous boundaries, as opposed to strictly defined boundaries. We need to establish virtuous connections with the outside, whether it is with other commons or the environment, and be alert so that the values produced by commons are not coopted by capital. Through these interactions, we start building larger-scale networks to get larger support to give rise to new institutions.

Value creation for the system—not only the individual commoners—is what distinguishes a transformational commons from one that closes in on itself. The notion of care here is quite important and is linked to the notion of biopolitics, which is broadly defined through the production activities of human beings and by the means of human beings. I think the biopolitical field is the most strategic field of action today that can form transformational commons. This is because the means and the ends in a production relationship have the potential to coincide, to be aligned to one another, and perhaps to be redefined based on new values.

One example is the case of a Dutch NGO called Buurtzorg in the Netherlands, which is composed of 10,000 nurses, self-organizing themselves in small groups of 10 to 12 people. They have empowered themselves to make decisions, manage themselves, make their own budget, and provide care without top-down orders. The entire workflow is organized in a completely different way than in care organizations, which are structured along hierarchical managerial top-down control. Here, the nurses decide what is best in terms of the purpose of their work and the way to do it. They also empower patients to speak up and be vocal about their needs. As such, they have constructed a different commoning relation. The new purpose for a nurse is not simply to visit the patient and tell them what to do, but to act as a facilitator of social care within the neighborhoods and as an agent for the empowerment of every single part of this new system. This is an example of how, through self-management and autonomy and the building of bridges, new systems can be created and supported at various scales. This is what I call boundary commoning, which extends outside the boundaries of a given commons system and in relation with other commons, forms new subjectivities and new commons systems at greater scale.

The pandemic has shown and confirmed once again how commoning is the activity that creates a lattice of support. In recent years, Hurricane Katrina and the Greek crisis have demonstrated how networks of mutual aid and support have emerged to respond in a bottom-up, horizontal, and diffused way to the challenges that various crises have provoked.

The pandemic has shown that there is an incredible energy in the society that comes out in times of emergency and crisis, triggered but not caused by them, as some people would think. Solidarity is constituted in the bones of society and has historical origin in that sense. The question posed to us is, how to sustain and scale up such spikes of solidarity and commoning to form common institutions and leave a more durable impact on social reproduction? How can this energy be mobilized to address bigger questions such as climate catastrophes? Social movements such as Black Lives Matter are particularly important because they seek to shift the constraints that have been socially constructed and consolidated by the hegemonic system of power. In this sense, social movements move away from particular layers of top-down control and try to reformulate and open up space.

Again, the question becomes how to create institutions of the common in the singular that promote the connection between the commons and social movements. Because we need to both create space and constantly shift its constraints upward to occupy that space. The idea of commons as a singular has been discussed as a mode of production—for instance, by Michael Hardt and Antonio Negri and various scholars within that tradition, to which I'm sympathetic in many ways. It has also been conceptualized as a political principle, by the French scholars Pierre Dardot and Christian Laval, for example. For me, the commons as singular should be regarded as a political principle and mode of production in conjunction with social production and grounded in social practices.

The other notion I have been struggling with is the notion of holons, that is, systems within systems. In this conception, systems are made of elements that are in themselves systems, and so they can scale up and down. This is a very powerful idea to mobilize both in theory and in practice in order to conceptualize the possibilities of movements in any civilization of the commons.

Boundaries are a selection principle, and in any given context, it is unavoidable to select. It's important to recognize that boundaries are unavoidable because this is fundamentally how we construct the world and make it intelligible for us. They give us the ability to make things distinct and to distinguish among them. Boundaries are problematic when they become the instrument of exclusion, domination, and exploitation. It is important to have boundaries and to continue to re-create them and deal with their related issues. This is boundary commoning—the continuous reformulation of boundaries and the search for new relations. Transformative commons need porous boundaries and continuous work on the strategic importance of that porosity.

NG   In discussions about commons, it is almost impossible not to contemplate the relationship between the capitalist mode of social reproduction and the idea of commons itself. In your book, you have laid out this fundamental question for us: "How can we find a collective path towards an exit from capitalist production and authoritarian and corrupted state systems through system change?" And you approached this question by proposing a system of the "commons, commoning, and commoners." How can we conceptualize social changes with them today? Are you envisioning this system as an alter-capitalist structure that operates entirely outside the existing modes of production? Or is it, rather, a network that works from within? You have also mentioned that commoning is the "smartest section of capital" at work and that commons have become the basis for new capitalist growth. How can we envision the formation of an anti-capitalist commons that transcends the relatively ephemeral social movements and results in the formation of counter-institutions?

MDA   The difference between the capitalist and anti-capitalist commons is their purpose. The purpose is crucial in defining the identity of systems, as learned from complexity theory and cybernetics. It is the *telos*, the fourth cause of Aristotle, which has been discredited by modern science because it wouldn't fit with its idea of objectivity. The purpose is what defines a living system's identity. Every system is engaged in an attempt to control itself for a purpose. The purpose for us is obviously changing the world we live in, a question that can be spelled out in different ways, at different scales, and in different contexts. We change the world we come in contact with and the context where we find ourselves, at the level of our households, our neighborhoods, or the broader community.

The capitalist system cannot prevent us from creating a tremendous ecological catastrophe, as accumulation propensity and growth are completely incompatible with ecological preservation. But we work with what we have, so the question of transformative commons is not an ideological issue. I would put it in terms of the scale and impact. In my previous book, *The Beginning of History*, I discussed and elaborated on the notion of "outside," and I claimed that the outside of capitalism is created by the commons in terms of new, alternative value practices and social relations. So, yes, the commons are outside the capitalist system, as they do not recognize the capitalist modality of creating value. Essentially, it is about distinguishing what is good and bad. However, it is a false conceptualization to assume that being outside the capitalist system structurally means that the commons do not need to interact with the capitalist system. Commons hold links of dependence on this system that can, of course, be politicized. As commons have their own value practices and internal relations, they are spheres of relative autonomy. Now, dealing with the degrees of dependencies is a question of scale. The expansion of the commons will necessarily deal with that dependency from capitalism, seeking to reducing it, while increasing their autonomy from it.

Different categories of relationship between commons and capital need to be conceptualized in terms of appropriate scale and in connection to different layers. Commons are made and remade by different subjects and, at the same time, belong to or participate actively or passively in different systems, including capitalist systems. So, essentially, it is important for each and every one of us to conceive subjects as a battlefield. A battlefield because we are the instruments for multiplication of different values that we encounter and practice. The values pass through our actions and shape our thinking, perceptions, mechanisms of filtering and selecting, and they are amplified in a certain way. Therefore, one important reason for the multiplication of transformational commons is to make them a force for creation of different types of subjectivities and activities.

NG   Garrett Hardin coined the term "commons" in his 1968 essay "The Tragedy of the Commons." David Harvey has pointed out that one of the fundamental conceptual failures in such a "tragedy" is the confusion between private and collective ownership in the logics of capitalistic development. How do you see the "tragedy" of the commons today? What are the most prominent challenges facing commoning practices today?

MDA   It is useful to recall what Garrett Hardin said about the tragedy of the commons. Hardin's idea was predicated on an imagined pasture where a group of herders took their cows to an open-access field. Each of the herders, in that narrative, intended to maximize their own self-interest by bringing more livestock to the field and feeding them as much as possible. When everybody was seeking to maximize their profits, sooner or later the pasture became depleted, and thus they all lost the source of their livelihoods. Hardin concluded that commons are not good and we need to enclose them—my own interpretation—either through assigning property rights to that field or by using the state's top-down control or competition.

Elinor Ostrom made a fantastic counter-argument by studying hundreds of cases where people in communities—herders or fishermen—come together, communicate with each other, and make rules together. For Ostrom, the root of the problem is not the commons but the open access. However, I think the dichotomic relation between open access and commons, as Ostrom conceptualized it, must be problematized. We have evidence of many social organizations and centers that practice an open access. Here, the open access is governed. A governed open access is an access that is taken care of within the constraints of the commons set by commoners: for example, we open this space for open access, but we reject racist discourse within it. Or we promote open access to this space, while at the same time encourage participation in the reproduction work necessary for its care. This connects to the idea of porous boundaries of commons systems, and to the need to politically problematize the principles of selection we use to construct those "pores" that filter the commons relations to its environment and context. To think about the most prominent challenges of commons today, we need to think about them not just as real existing systems but also as a way of looking at the world and framing it so as to expand the commons. This embeds a political principle.

The most important issues that we're facing today—from the climate catastrophe to the plural crises of public health, social precarity, access to income and resources at different levels—are the result of the tragedy of the open access. But tragedy of open access in the sense that these issue emerge because producers within the capitalist systems act like Hardin's self-interested herders. At the higher scale, the capitalist actors increase their self-interest by competing with one another and promoting accumulation while destroying what we would claim as resources in common. Think about the earth!

The first step in creating commons at every scale is to claim the resources, the natural wealth, as a common and a treasure for all. Seeing commons as a political principle, we start to recognize that it is the extractive activities that destroy communities and pollute the environment. Growing extractivism is the tragedy of capital open access on common resources. This tragedy can be addressed by the empowerment of different scales of communities of commoners who create institutions and conceive design. Through their interactions, commoners make new institutions emerge or transform the existing institutions into new ones in order to facilitate mechanisms of a diffused governance in which people decide together. We need a holacracy to be built from the bottom up.

NG   Trained as architects, we are curious about the potentials of conceptualizing space through the framework of the commons. As the commoning processes continuously change the substance of urban space—be it physical or virtual, material or cultural—some recent strands of scholarship have mobilized the concept of urban commons as a way of rethinking the production of space. In your opinion, how can spatial imaginaries deriving from the idea of the commons challenge the existing social and economic structures of the contemporary city? How should architects, planners, and designers in general reposition themselves in the commoning process as commoners? What kind of knowledge production would this insinuate?

MDA   The concept of transformational commons is important for design practices. As a political scientist, I have been mostly concerned about the question of time, but design goes hand in hand with the production of capitalist time. Design can facilitate boundary commoning. I wonder whether examples such as current strands in participatory design can be understood in terms of efforts for commoning.

Participatory design isn't the means, it's a tool. If used within the broader institution of commons, it can produce anti-capitalist commons. It has also been used in the mainstream capitalist production of space. Here, the distinction is fundamental, as it gives a system its identity. The purpose of these tools and approaches needs to be aligned to this question of reproduction of labor power, as the Marxist feminists would put it.

Design can question or reproduce existing systems of social reproduction, whether they create new conditions for reproducing human beings with dignity and social justice and reaching and maintaining ecological balance, or reinforce the extant capitalist social polarizing logic and ecological catastrophe. We must also keep in mind that the general problematic of reproduction can be defined as the production of human beings by the means of human beings. This also means both the question of articulating, in a socially just way, human means and human ends in reproductive relations, as well as redefining the relation between human beings and the environment. So the purpose, then, is targeting all the activities that enter the realm of reproduction to reduce our dependency on the capitalist system.

In European countries, there are discussions about universal, unconditional basic income as a fundamental political battle for the expansion of the commons. This would help to reduce our dependence on the capital system and allow us not only to have more time and more resources to work with others to create different systems, but also more power to refuse capitalist logics. That is a battle for inclusion but also a question of designing and redesigning our activities. We need to have both the imagery of space and the knowledge of specific aspects of the challenges that a community faces. Imagination and knowledge are best tapped when you have a diffuse coordination system, when you are able to have cognitive commoning with the greatest number of people. I don't know whether it is obvious or not, but design is fundamentally about setting up constraints that channel social cooperation in given forms, while leaving maximum autonomy to individual people and commons. The more people participate and get involved in the design process, the more diversity is pulled together and the more answers can be found.

Making Public Space More "Common"

Katherine Melcher

West 8's redesign of Rotterdam's Schouwburgplein was hailed as "an ingenious reinterpretation of the traditional town square" by the curator of the Museum of Modern Art's 2005 *Groundswell* exhibit.[1] Despite this critical success, three years later, the city and adjacent institutions stepped in to enliven the space. René Dutrieux, project manager for the plaza, observed, "Despite the many visitors to the institutions and the nearby shopping streets, the square has been a void in the city instead of a place for (cultural) gathering."[2] This story is not unique to Schouwburgplein; many cities contain award-winning public spaces that end up empty, unused, and neglected by the public.

1
Peter Reed, *Groundswell: Constructing the Contemporary Landscape* (New York: Museum of Modern Art, 2005), 17.

2
René Dutrieux, "Slippery Squares and Concrete Buildings," in *The City at Eye Level: Lessons for Street Plinths*, ed. Hans Karssenberg, Jeroen Laven, Meredith Glaser, and Mattijs van 't Hoff, 2nd ed. (Delft: Eburon, 2016), 181, https://thecityateyelevel.files.wordpress.com/2016/02/ebook_the-city-at-eye-level_english.pdf.

Schouwburgplein in Rotterdam, designed by West 8.

In this essay, I suggest that the underlying problem with these public spaces does not rest solely in the design; instead, it comes from poorly theorized ideas of "public." It comes from what philosopher Mark Kingwell observes as "the bankruptcy of our current notions of public space."[3] Inspired by philosopher Jean-Luc Nancy's "Of Being Singular Plural," I argue that contemporary discourse on public space tends to view the public as either political subjects or individual users. Public spaces, in turn, are caught between the abstract ideals of a democratic public sphere and a commodified spectacle. Schouwburgplein illustrates how design can get trapped between these two ideas of society.

Nancy suggests "being-with" as a different way of thinking about ourselves as public beings, one where the public is not subordinate to individual or collective needs, but where we become who we are—singular and plural, here and now. This alternative understanding of who we are as public beings suggests a new relationship to place and design, one

3
Mark Kingwell, "Masters of Chancery: The Gift of Public Space," in *Rites of Way: The Politics and Poetics of Public Space*, ed. Mark Kingwell and Patrick Turmel, Canadian Commentaries (Waterloo, Ont.: Wilfrid Laurier University Press, 2009), 19.

that can be illustrated by the contemporary urban commons movement in Europe, where places are collectively controlled and managed by local citizens. The Prinzessinnengärten, a community garden in Berlin, exemplifies how this alternative understanding of public can translate into alternative ways of making places.

Community garden Prinzessinnengärten in the Kreuzburg district of Berlin.
Source: Marco Clausen
License: Creative Commons NonCommercial-ShareAlike 2.0 Generic (CC BY-NC-SA 2.0)
Website: https://www.flickr.com/photos/39367406@N04/5340898112/in/album-72157717490034908/

Although professionally designed public spaces (such as Schouwburgplein) and vernacular commons (such as Prinzessinnengärten) are often placed against each other as opposites, it does not mean that a public space cannot be a common space. In this essay, I use designer Ezio Manzini's understanding of public spaces and commons. For Manzini, "not all public assets are commons, and not all commons are public. A neglected and abandoned piazza is a public asset but is not part of the commons because there is no community to look after it."[4] But a public space can be a commons if a community exists in relationship with the place. If we restate the primary purpose of public space design as creating a space where people can explore who they are in relation to one another, then public spaces can become more like the Prinzessinnengärten, where the physical material of place is an invitation, an opening, for people to engage with the place and with one another. Design that considers how the physical material of space can engage and support relationships between people and place will help make public spaces into commons.

4
Ezio Manzini, *Politics of the Everyday*, trans. Rachel Anne Coad, Designing in Dark Times series (London: Bloomsbury Visual Arts, 2019), 15.

Defining Public as Subjects or Users

What is the purpose of a public space? What is the "public" that one designs for? In "Of Being Singular Plural," Nancy identifies two meanings of "together": "the 'together' of gathering . . . a unified totality" and "the 'together' of a juxtaposition . . . , [of] isolated and unrelated parts."[5] Public spaces are often justified through these two meanings.

Nancy's first meaning of "together" as "a unified totality where the relation surpasses itself in being pure"[6] suggests that the role of public space is to develop a sense of commonality and connection between people. Often public space aims to achieve this cohesiveness by expressing a shared cultural meaning or through collective celebrations and events. As a place of collective identity, public space reflects what we have in common, who we are as a community. Landscape architect James Corner argues that expressing collective meaning is an important aim for the design of public space: "Public space in the city must surely be more than mere token compensation or vessels for this generic activity called 'recreation.' Public spaces are firstly the containers of collective memory and desire, and secondly they are the places for geographic and social imagination to extend new relationships and sets of possibility."[7] In a similar vein, architect Alberto Perez-Gomez calls the design of public space "a poetic proposition disclosing collective order."[8]

In the second meaning of together as an association of individuals, public space is justified, as a public service, through the benefits it provides for individual users. Historically, Italian squares provided potable water for the city's residents through wells and fountains; in colonial New England, the town commons provided a protected space for the grazing of animals. A current manifestation of public space as public service can be seen in Park Rx programs that "prescribe" park visits as ways to alleviate various mental and physical health issues.[9] Satisfying the needs of the public is a valuable function of public spaces, but designing solely for individual benefits can neglect other dimensions of public space design, such as meaning, connection, pleasure, and delight.[10] Public space as public service does not necessarily express the uniqueness of the place or the people connected with it.

Nancy argues that in each of these meanings of together—as a collective or an association of individuals—the simple act of being with one another becomes a means to another end. This critique could also be levied against our thinking of public space's purpose as a collective identity or public service. Public space for a collective identity is instrumentalized toward a common end, such as a sense of collective belonging. Alongside

5
Jean-Luc Nancy, "Of Being Singular Plural," in *Being Singular Plural*, trans. Robert D. Richardson and Anne E. O'Byrne, Meridian (Stanford, CA.: Stanford University Press, 2000), 60.

6
Nancy, "Of Being Singular Plural," 60.

7
James Corner, "Terra Fluxus," in *The Landscape Urbanism Reader*, ed. Charles Waldheim (New York: Princeton Architectural Press, 2006), 32.

8
Alberto Perez-Gomez, "Architecture and Public Space," in *Rites of Way: The Politics and Poetics of Public Space*, ed. Mark Kingwell and Patrick Turmel, Canadian Commentaries (Waterloo, Ont.: Wilfrid Laurier University Press, 2009), 47.

9
Park Rx, "Park Rx: About," https://www.parkrx.org/about.

10
In their classic text *Public Space*, Carr et al. divide the aims of public space into three dimensions: needs, rights, and meanings. Meanings and connections can be overlooked when designers focus solely on the needs and rights of people in a public space. See Stephen Carr, Mark Francis, Leanne G. Rivlin, and Andrew M. Stone, *Public Space*, Cambridge Series in Environment and Behavior (New York: Cambridge University Press, 1992).

11
Kurt Iveson, "Putting the Public Back into Public Space," *Urban Policy & Research* 16, no. 1 (1998): 25.

12
Setha M. Low, Dana Taplin, and Suzanne Scheld, *Rethinking Urban Parks: Public Space & Cultural Diversity* (Austin: University of Texas Press, 2005), 1.

13
Kingwell, "Masters of Chancery: The Gift of Public Space," 9.

14
Ibid., 19.
15
Ibid.
16
Mark Kingwell and Patrick Turmel, "Introduction: Rites of Way, Paths of Desire," in *Rites of Way*, xvii.

this collective purpose for public space remains a fear that becoming part of a community requires a commonality—and therefore a denial of differences or individuality. For example, urban design theorist Kurt Iveson points out that "successful public space as proposed in the community model is only achieved where diversity is denied, or fused together to form a common, harmonious whole."[11] On the extreme end of this public space for a collective identity, one can think of military parade grounds and other ceremonial spaces that enforce a collective belonging through dominating forms and symbols. Less obviously, design and management strategies based on middle- and upper-middle-class white values "can reduce the vitality and vibrancy of the space or reorganize it in such a way that only one kind of person—often a tourist or middle-class visitor—feels welcomed."[12] In these cases, group identity and individual identity become the means for a collective end of shared belonging.

Public space as a public service is instrumentalized toward individual needs. Kingwell criticizes this prioritization of private interests over public purpose as creating "the strange case of unpublic public space," where "space is, conceptually speaking, owned by the dominant rules of the game, which are hinged to the norm of private interest."[13]

Selecting one of these perspectives as the primary purpose of public space reduces people as public beings to either users (consumers of goods) or subjects (subjected to a collective power). In neither case are we being-with-one-another by itself and for itself. Kingwell ends his critique by suggesting that "public space is not a public good so much as an existential one."[14] While Kingwell suggests that this additional purpose is to serve "democratic politics,"[15] I wonder if public spaces could also be places that "allow us to reflect on all aspects of our embodied consciousness,"[16] where we explore and experience who we are as public beings in a larger sense of the word.

Public Space as Public Sphere or Spectacle

Public space, often conceptualized as a physical embodiment of community, is a space into which our ideas and ideals of community are projected. According to Nancy, in modern society, one finds only two realms where our collective values are projected: the realm of law and the realm of self-representation. These two realms—also known as the public sphere and the spectacle—are primary concepts from which theorists critique public space as well. In the realm of the law, being public means being a part of the public sphere, the arena governed by law and legitimized through the Habermasian ideals of a "general communicational arrangement, which presupposes a 'rational subject' of communication."[17] Inspired by the political theories of Hannah Arendt and Jürgen Habermas, urban design theorists often suggest that public space should be the physical setting for democratic processes.[18] The accepted understanding is that, as a public sphere, a public space should be open to all equally, creating a setting where rational debates can occur between political beings.[19]

The second form of being-together, based on Greek theater, "is defined by being-together-at-the-spectacle."[20] While the public sphere embraces the "intelligible reality"[21] of abstract thought and aims toward universal rights, the spectacle embraces sensible appearances and aims toward amusement and play. The spectacle does not define itself against a universal ideal, as the law does; instead, the spectacle reflects society toward itself. The spectacle is "defined by this game of mirrors, and losing itself in the scintillating play of light and images."[22] Because it plays with the world of representation and imagery, it is susceptible to becoming commodified and has been frequently criticized as being inauthentic.

While the public sphere is held up in design theory as an ideal aim, public space as a spectacle is typically characterized as a direction we should avoid at all costs. Perhaps the best known of these critiques is Michael Sorkin's *Variations on a Theme Park* (1992), subtitled *The End of Public Space*, in which the author laments the privatization and commodification of urban places. Sorkin observes that cities are becoming spectacles: "This new realm is a city of simulations, television city, the city as theme park. . . . The architecture of this city is almost purely semiotic, playing the game of grafted signification, theme-park building."[23] Similar to Nancy's characterization of the spectacle as a mirror reflecting society back at itself, Sorkin's primary concern is the loss of authenticity. Sorkin worries that the city is made up of "an architecture of deception which, in its happy-face familiarity, constantly distances itself from the most fundamental realities."[24] He argues, "The theme park presents its happy regulated vision of pleasure—all those artfully hoodwinking forms—as a substitute for the democratic public realm."[25] In other words, the sensible appearances of the spectacle (the physical material of our architecture) threaten to distract us from the intelligible reality (abstract democratic processes).

By envisioning public space as a moral choice between a democratic public sphere or a commodified spectacle, theorists trap design in what Nancy calls the "contrary double form of the '[illusory] spectacle' and '[rational] communication.'"[26] Although the public sphere is held up as the ideal for public space, its foundation on abstract relationships exists in tension with the sensible realm of appearances, which includes

17
Nancy, "Of Being Singular Plural," 57.
18
Urban design theorists who link democratic processes to the core purpose of public space include: Sennett, Harvey, Iveson, Hou, Kingwell, Iveson, and Carmona et al. See Richard Sennett, *The Fall of Public Man* (New York: W. W. Norton, 2017); David Harvey, *Rebel Cities: From the Right to the City to the Urban Revolution* (New York: Verso, 2012); Iveson, "Putting the Public Back into Public Space"; Jeffrey Hou, ed., *Insurgent Public Space: Guerrilla Urbanism and the Remaking of Contemporary Cities* (New York: Routledge, 2010); Kingwell, "Masters of Chancery: The Gift of Public Space"; Matthew Carmona, Tim Heath, Tanner Oc, and Steve Tiesdell, *Public Places, Urban Spaces: The Dimensions of Urban Design* (Boston: Architectural Press, 2010).
19
Although Habermas's concept of the public sphere is well critiqued within theory and philosophy, the concept remains central within public-space design discourse. For example, Kingwell cites the public sphere in his critique of the privatization of public space: "This larger notion of public space brings it closer to the very idea of *the public sphere*, that place where, in the minds of philosophers at least, citizens hammer out the common interests that underlie—and maybe underwrite—their private differences and desires. . . . Public space enables a political conversation that

favours the unforced force of the better argument, the basis of just social order." Kingwell, "Masters of Chancery: The Gift of Public Space," 7.

20
Nancy, "Of Being Singular Plural," 51.

21
Ibid., 53.

22
Ibid., 49.

23
Michael Sorkin, ed., *Variations on a Theme Park: The New American City and the End of Public Space* (New York: Hill and Wang, 1992), xiv.

24
Ibid.

25
Ibid., xv.

26
Nancy, "Of Being Singular Plural," 57.

27
Henri Lefebvre, *The Production of Space* (Oxford, UK, and Malden, MA: Blackwell, 1991); Harvey, *Rebel Cities*; Jacques Rancière, *Dissensus: On Politics and Aesthetics*, trans. Steve Corcoran (London and New York: Continuum, 2010).

28
Helena Gentili, "Moving Lights: Schouwburgplein in Rotterdam," *Gizmo: Architectural Review* (blog), February 16, 2014, paragraph 30, http://www.gizmoweb.org/2014/02/moving-lights-schouwburgplein-in-rotterdam/.

29
Adriaan Geuze, quoted in Alexandra Lange, "Play Ground," *New Yorker*, May 16, 2016, 72.

the materiality of our physical environment—the very medium of design. The rational communication that is the foundation of Habermas's public sphere requires an equal footing between participants. All voices must be heard and evaluated without prejudice. However, as theorists such as Henri Lefevbre, David Harvey, and Jacques Rancière point out, the sensible realm is shaped by forces of power, and therefore physical places reflect and reinforce existing power structures.[27] Through symbolism and what Rancière calls the "distribution of the sensible," the materiality of public spaces expresses forces of power of some form or another. Power expressed through physical place can control, exclude, or limit the equality required for rational communication. Therefore, to achieve the ideal of the public sphere, all aspects of a design that might express power or control would need to be removed, leaving little more than an empty lot.

Schouwburgplein as Public Sphere and Spectacle

The design of Schouwburgplein in Rotterdam illustrates how design can be trapped between the ideals of the public sphere and spectacle. Schouwburgplein was designed to be both. As a spectacle, it was designed to be a theatrical event space, "an active public stage, where the citizens of Rotterdam, surrounded by theatres, a concert hall and cinemas, could perform and be admired by spectators and customers of nearby cafes."[28] To give the place a unique identity, the design was intentionally "self-reflexive";[29] it mirrors the identity of Rotterdam's port—most notably through the overhead lights that mimic the form of shipping cranes.

Schouwburgplein and the adjacent theater, Rotterdam.

The shipping crane–inspired mast lights at Schouwburgplein.

But while critics laud the design for being "a compelling formal exercise in material and meaning,"[30] they also praise how it did not need "illusions or stopgaps"[31] in order to become "a place for public participation in unprogrammed activities rather than passive spectating."[32] According to Peter Reed, the designer Adriaan Geuze of West 8 "saw little need to impose a program on the design of this public stage, believing that people will use the space in unpredictable ways."[33] Landscape architect Thomas Rainer argues that the design represents a shift "from . . . a site of representation and power to a site of democracy and openness; from overprogrammed public space to an enabling territory,"[34] in other words, from an authoritarian spectacle to a democratic public sphere. The openness of the plaza, approximately three acres in size, was expected to allow for "roller bladers, kids playing in fountains, temporary markets, and people partaking of myriad other activities."[35]

Although the design discourse on public space often equates political openness with physical emptiness, Schouwburgplein demonstrates how emptiness is not necessarily enabling or empowering. Schouwburgplein, like many public squares, on an uneventful, normal day feels barren and sterile. In the open plaza, everything is transparent and understood at one glance; people appear small and unattached, equal but exposed. Without physical objects (Nancy's sensible realm) to interact with, there is nothing to do but keep on walking. The only raised element in the plaza is the triangular entrance

30
Reed, *Groundswell*, 17.
31
Bart Lootsma, quoted in Reed, *Groundswell*, 17.
32
Reed, *Groundswell*, 34.
33
Reed, *Groundswell*, 17.

34
Thomas Rainer, "The Most Important Urban Square You've Never Heard Of," *Grounded Design: Landscape + Culture* (blog), April 17, 2010, paragraph 8, http://landscapeofmeaning.blogspot.com/2010/04/most-important-urban-square-youve-never.html.
35
Reed, *Groundswell*, 17.

36
Dutrieux, "Slippery
Squares and Concrete
Buildings," 181.

to the underground parking garage. Children try to climb it, longing for something to be *with*. René Dutrieux, project manager for the plaza, observed, "Theatre-goers tend to arrive just before their show and depart quickly after, spending little time on or around the square."[36] Because of this lack of activity, in 2008, the city and adjacent institutions started programming more events and adding physical improvements such as mobile seating, a small outdoor stage, planter boxes, and a "carpet" of artificial turf.

The open space of Schouwburgplein.

People drawn to the garage entry at Schouwburgplein.

Although the design for Schouwburgplein was celebrated as one intended to promote active freedom and democracy, the motivation for the design was in some ways the opposite. The emptiness was not originally intended to encourage freedom but, instead, to satisfy the city's desire to create a place that can be easily surveilled, monitored, and maintained. Before the redesign, Schouwburgplein was known as a needle park.[37] The brief Geuze designed for "was for a defensible space, with no place to hide, and no complicated elements that would be hard to maintain or easy to damage."[38] The design of Schouwburgplein tried to be a public sphere by embracing physical emptiness as a sign of political openness. This not only failed to inspire active participation in the space, it also failed to create a space of joy or pleasure that one might associate with a spectacle. All it created was an exposed, easily surveilled space where people are not comfortable being who they are.

Defining Public as Being-With

What if we approach the design of a public space with the idea that the public is not only a political collective or just a means for serving individual needs, but is instead a way of developing our own understanding of who we are together? Nancy's elaboration of Heidegger's *Mitsein* (being-with) suggests a similar vision, where people are together in a way that is neither purely political nor purely functional; this relation does not require a sacrifice of self but is instead ourselves—who we are—at once singular and plural. But this shift in defining public requires a shift in how we think about the purpose of public space and the role that design and physical material play in that purpose.

For Nancy, "with" is "at the heart of Being."[39] "With" is proximity, yet it also implies a separation, a spacing between. Therefore, in being-with, we retain our singularity in "the almost-there of distanced proximity."[40] Other concepts of being-together fall into the trap of thinking that we are first singular beings who are then brought into relation with one another. Nancy points out that we are always already with other people. From the start, we become ourselves as individuals in relationship with other people. Kingwell suggests a similar understanding of the public when he says:

> We imagine that we enter public spaces with our identities intact, jealous of interest and suspicious of challenge, looking for stimulus and response. But in fact the reverse is true. We cannot enter the public because we have never left the public; it pervades everything, and our identities are never fixed or prefigured because they are themselves achievements of the public dimension in human life.[41]

37
Lange, "Play Ground," 71.
38
Ibid., 72.

39
Nancy, "Of Being Singular Plural," 30.
40
Ibid., 98.

41
Kingwell, "Masters of Chancery: The Gift of Public Space," 18.

In the together of the collective, we think our individuality is suppressed when we connect with others. But being-with is a fundamental part of how we define and understand our own individuality; we are singular *and* plural. Because "with" is a copresence of any kind, our relation to others is not predetermined. The relation is not necessarily one of love; nor is it necessarily one of competition. The "with" is instead a *praxis* and *ethos*; how we act with each other. It is never finalized, always "coming-*to*-be."[42]

42
Nancy, "Of Being Singular Plural," 95.

Public Space as the Staging of Co-Appearance

For Nancy, being-with is also a being-there, a location. But because being-with occurs in both space and time, it is an event or an experience as much as a physical object. Therefore, a public place is not a simple material cause or effect of society; it is instead a part of the experience of being (or, more accurately, becoming) a self and society. This suggests that public space designed for being-with would not be just a backdrop for the creation of a new sense of community nor a physical expression of existing culture. A place for being-with would be part of the act, "a *praxis* and an *ethos*,"[43] or what Nancy calls "the staging of co-appearance."[44]

43
Nancy, "Of Being Singular Plural," 71, 98–99.
44
Nancy, "Of Being Singular Plural," 71.
45
Nancy, "Of Being Singular Plural," 65.

This staging of co-appearance is not the neutral, political stage of the public sphere. The staging of co-appearance is "a stage [*scene*] on which several [people] can say 'I,' each on his own account, each in turn."[45] This saying "I" is not a question of identity where one is required to identify with the whole, but rather, a question of identification, where the individual is given the opportunity to define himself or herself through the praxis. Therefore, this staging differs from the public sphere because it does not reduce individuality in order to create equivalence within the social realm. It requires people to bring—or, more accurately, *develop*—their individuality in interaction with others. Applied to the design of public space, a staging of co-appearance is less a blank, open space waiting to be filled by individual expression and more an opening for interaction. It could be an opportunity to plant flowers, to leave a note, to climb a tower, or to sing a song while swinging on a swing.

The symbolic and sensible, the physical material of a place, are considered fundamental to this staging of co-appearance. Nancy claims that "the 'symbolic' does not imply an aspect of being-social: on the one hand, it is this Being itself."[46] This staging of public-being can be considered a spectacle because it embraces materiality and symbolic

46
Nancy, "Of Being Singular Plural," 58.

representation. But these representations are not illusory or inauthentic. Nancy explains that there is not one true version of society that these mirrors are distracting us from. Instead, this play is how we try to see ourselves as public beings. It is, as Nancy says, "society making its appearance by facing itself in order to be all that it is and all that it has to be."[47] Therefore, the stage of co-appearance "is not a stage in the sense of an artificial space of mimetic representation. It is a stage in the sense of the opening of a space-time for the distribution of singularities, each of whom singularly plays the unique and plural role of the 'self' or the 'being-self.'"[48] A designer need not create one symbolic element that all people relate to; a designer can allow people to bring their own materials and then combine them in new and interesting ways.

47
Ibid., 59.

48
Ibid., 66.

Following Nancy's thoughts, if we consider the public not as something forced upon an individual as he or she enters a public space, but as a fundamental part of who we are, public space can become more than a public service or collective identity, a public sphere or spectacle. Public space for being-with could be an opening, a place where people experience who they are in relationship to one another, in all the rich complexity that each of their singular experiences creates.

Prinzessinnengärten as a Staging of Co-Appearance

The Prinzessinnengärten, a community garden started in 2009 on a vacant lot in Berlin's Kreuzberg district, has become a model of the contemporary commons movement in Europe. It can also be considered a model of how Nancy's being-with could apply to physical space. As a place developed through a collective praxis, it has become more than a public sphere or spectacle. It allows for multiple ideas and voices to be incorporated into the creation of the place. As a result, the physical material of the place plays an important role in engaging people with the place; its materiality functions not just as a symbolic representation of ideas but also as tangible objects of engagement.

The Prinzessinnengärten is not just a political arena or a symbolic expression of a unified community, although it does contain elements of each. Its complex form reflects the different ways people have been involved in the making of the place. A combination of staff and volunteers maintain the garden, while visitors have many options: they can wander through the space, harvest vegetables, buy food at the outdoor food court, read books at the library, attend workshops, climb the observation deck, or sit on the swings.

The vegetable garden at Prinzessinnengärten, Berlin.

Food court at Prinzessinnengärten.
Source: Staffan Cederborg
License: Creative Commons Attribution-Share Alike 2.0 Generic

The observation deck at Prinzessinnengärten.

Prinzessinnengärten is a stage where people can "say 'I'" of their own accord and contribute to the space in their own way. Writer Ana Lisa observes that "Prinzessinnengarten is a platform for people who want to do something; anyone can pop in and help in the urban garden with whatever might be needed at the time."[49] This openness results in the diversity in the place: "Through the opportunity to contribute and to participate in open workshops, through the garden café and a variety of cultural events, the Prinzessinnengarten has become a lively meeting place with appeal far beyond the neighborhood."[50] Robert Shaw, who

49
Ana Lisa, "Mobile Urban Agriculture Blooms in Berlin's Prinzessinnengarten," *Inhabitat* (blog), December 18, 2011, paragraph 3, https://inhabitat.com/mobile-urban-agriculture-blooms-in-berlins-prinzessinnengarten/.
50
Marco Clausen, "Cultivating a Different City," Prinzessinnengarten, 2012, paragraph 3, https://prinzessinnengarten.net/about/.

cofounded the garden with Marco Clausen, explains that this praxis is the foundation for how the garden runs: "The garden basically functions like Wikipedia, and we are its editors."[51]

An openness to individual ideas and experiences has created a space of plurality that is specific and incommensurable. In Prinzessinnengärten, design is a praxis of building-with the physical world. Materials are an important part of the place—not as serious, symbolic expressions of who we are but as items to *make-with*, to try out and suggest. By engaging with materials in building the place, the people of Prinzessinnengärten create new expressions of being-public. These expressions are rich, diverse, and ever-changing.

51
Robert Shaw, quoted in Esra Erdem, "Reading Foucault with Gibson-Graham: The Political Economy of 'Other Spaces' in Berlin," *Rethinking Marxism* 26, no. 1 (2014): 71, https://doi.org/10.1080/08935696.2014.857845.

Sheds made out of recycled materials at the Prinzessinnengärten.

Conclusion

What do we desire to be as public beings? What kind of public spaces can inspire us to be that kind of public? Is it the vast openness of Schouwburgplein in Rotterdam with its larger-than-life lights looming overhead? Or is it the homely, homemade, gated Prinzessinnengärten in Berlin with its overgrown greenery beckoning passersby to enter and discover a jumble of garden beds, picnic tables, food carts, and handmade structures?

In the Prinzessinnengärten, I see the potential for a public space that is not just about being political or being served but something more: a simple being-with-one-another-in-place. The materiality of the place is not just about representation or symbolic identity but instead is a means of an open-ended engagement with place. Its openness does not come from physical emptiness, as at Schouwburgplein; its openness comes from how people are encouraged to interact with the place. Unlike Schouwburgplein, Prinzessinnengärten uses the physical material of the place as a central part of the ongoing making of the place, an ongoing making of the public realm.

Some may argue that professional designers, limited to design and separated from management, can do little to make public spaces more like urban commons. It is a question of management or ownership, not design, they say. However, designers can make public spaces more "common" in the sense that they can develop places that encourage community interaction. If designers take Nancy's conception of being-with as the primary inspiration and purpose for public spaces, they could create spaces where people engage with the world around them and with one another in an active exploration. This would require a rethinking of the role of physical material in creating a public space. It does not have to just be the material of representation, symbolizing what being-public means through the viewpoint of the designer. It can be an invitation for engagement, an opening, a way to encourage people to interact. If design can consider physical material as a means for engagement rather than only symbolic representation, perhaps professional designers will create rich, complex, tangible, and lively public spaces.

This vision of public space founded on being-with may seem idealistic and sentimental, but, as Nancy says, "To want to say 'we' is not at all sentimental, not at all familial or 'communitarian.' It is existence reclaiming its due or its condition: coexistence."[52]

[52] Nancy, "Of Being Singular Plural," 42.

How to Design, Defend, and Sustain Urban Commons and How to Demonstrate Their Value for Resilience?

Doina Petrescu and Constantin Petcou

With the question of *commons*, we are at the heart of current discussions on democracy. According to Antonio Negri and Michael Hardt, the contemporary revolutionary project is concerned with capturing, diverting, appropriating, and reclaiming the commons we produce as a key constituent process.[1] It is a reclaiming but also a reinvention requiring new processes, new institutions, and new agencies that could be the fundament of new forms of democracy.

1
A. Negri and M. Hardt,
Commonwealth
(Cambridge, MA: Harvard
University Press, 2009).

The question of commons is also directly related to other major challenges we face today. At the moment, our global society consumes the resources of two and a half planets. This accelerated overconsumption has many consequences: climate change, resources depletion, and related ecological, economic, and social crises. The ecological disaster is too big and complex to be solved by existing capitalist structures. It is also because these very capitalist structures are at the core of the disaster. Built on relations of collective care, regeneration, and resilience, commons can have an important role in contributing to the planetary ecological repair and providing an alternative to the extractive and exploitative relations of the capitalist economy.

Learning how to govern our planet as a commons is part of the imperative of becoming more resilient, but also more democratic. The ecological question should be asked not only in terms of environment but also, as suggested by Guattari, in terms of politico-economic and mental ecology. The mode of governance of the commons (based on care and responsibility) is the best approach for ecological repair and resilience at all these levels. This is because, as very well demonstrated by Elinor Ostrom, the commons governance involves an "agreement" and a "shared concern" to not destroy the resources on which all members of the community depend.[2]

2
E. Ostrom, *Governing
the Commons: The
Evolution of Institutions
for Collective Action*
(New York: Cambridge
University Press, 1990).

This governance needs to take place at all scales, and collective agreements and shared concerns need to materialize both at the planetary level and at the scale of the states, cities, and neighborhoods. Urban commons can be a key factor at these smaller scales, generating local synergies and involving citizens in resilience practices. However, this process needs actors and agencies, and architects can indeed play an important role by putting to work their capacity to design and build resilient spaces, programs, and actions.

Designing

Our example, R-Urban, is a project initiated by atelier d'architecture autogérée (AAA) as a commons-based network of civic resilience hubs in the Parisian suburbs. The *R* in R-Urban stands partly for resilience, a transformative condition that allows us not only to adapt but also to transform and reinvent our society toward more balanced, equitable ways of living. The *R* also stands for resourcefulness, situating resilience in a positive light and relating it to the empowerment and agency of citizens and emergent communities.[3] Although conceived and initiated by architectural designers and urban researchers, the R-Urban framework is designed to be enacted through coproduction with local residents and a wide range of actors, all of whom have a role to play in the process.

The R-Urban framework involves setting up interconnected, self-managed collective hubs that act as "niches" for socio-technical innovation.[4] The hubs boost the capacity for resilience within neighborhoods[5] by providing spaces where skills, knowledge, labor, and creativity around urban agriculture, recycling, eco-construction, and cooperative housing are shared. Essentially, these hubs are spaces where commoning can be learned, practiced, and valued.

Commoning is a key component of the commons. It is the process by which a pool of resources (material or immaterial) that is held, governed, and produced collectively is shared by a community of commoners.[6] R-Urban is indeed an urban intervention that provokes commoning—creating spaces that foster a resilient alternative to the current way of governing resources within a community and beyond.[7]

The first step in implementing the R-Urban strategy is to access urban space and install a physical infrastructure that creates assets for civic resilience hubs where commoning activities can take place. The second step involves identifying and enrolling stakeholders, including existing organizations, initiatives, and individuals throughout the locality who can use the space and infrastructure and share the resources and the training provided by the hubs. Accessing urban space can be achieved by using available private or public land, including spaces that can be temporarily and reversibly used. The third step is to create networks of stakeholders around these assets and allow them to function through local economic and ecological cycles. As such, energy is created locally, waste is recycled and transformed locally, food is produced locally, and so on.

At a moment when austerity measures have taken a disastrous toll on public infrastructures,[8] the model of the civic resilience hub

3
D. MacKinnon and K. D. Derickson, "From Resilience to Resourcefulness: A Critique of Resilience Policy and Activism," *Progress in Human Geography* 37, no. 2 (2013): 253–270.

4
J. W. Schot and F. W. Geels, "Strategic Niche Management and Sustainable Innovation Journeys: Theory, Findings, Research Agenda, and Policy in Technology," *Analysis & Strategic Management* 20, no. 5 (2008): 537–554.

5
F. Stevenson and D. Petrescu, "Co-Producing Neighbourhood Resilience," *Building Research & Information* 44, no. 7 (2016): 695–702, https://doi.org/10.1080/09613218.2016.1213865.

6
An Architektur, "On the Commons: A Public Interview with Massimo De Angelis and Stavros Stavrides," *e-flux* 17 (2010), http://www.e-flux.com/journal/view/150; P. Linebaugh, *The Magna Carta Manifesto: Liberties and Commons for All* (Berkeley: University of California Press, 2008).

7
Ostrom, *Governing the Commons*.

8
A. Fitz and E. Krasny, *Critical Care: Architecture and Urbanism for a Broken Planet* (Cambridge, MA: MIT Press, 2019).

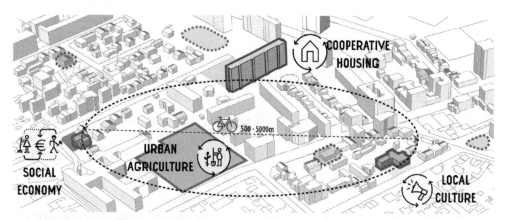

NETWORK OF CIVIC HUBS

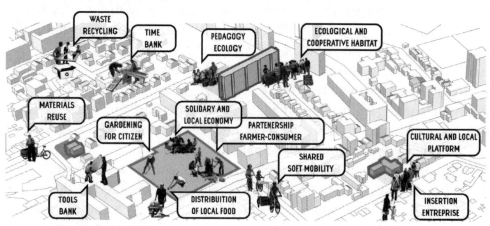

CIVIC PARTICIPATION

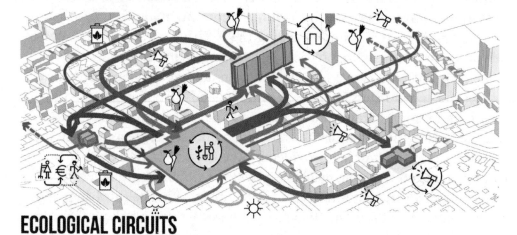

ECOLOGICAL CIRCUITS

R-Urban principles: networks of resilience hubs, civic participation, ecological circuits.

proposed by R-Urban offers a new type of urban equipment that is self-sustainable and citizen-run. The hubs are managed as commons, providing collective resources for the inhabitants of a neighborhood and enabling them to develop resilience practices. The R-Urban governance strategy is based on a multipolar network involving local and regional actors, formed around the various nuclei of activities that animate forms of exchange and collaboration.

The R-Urban framework was implemented in 2011 in Colombes, a suburban town near Paris, and in Hackney Wick, London. Three hubs were planned in Colombes: Agrocité, Recyclab, and Ecohab.[9] (Agrocité was located on a 2000 m^2 plot of vacant land near a large social housing complex, Recyclab was built on one lane of a disused road, and the Ecohab housing development was to be built on a vacant plot of land midway between the other two hubs.) Hubs were located within easy walking and biking distance of one another to enable the circulation of food, waste, recycled materials, repaired goods, people, knowledge, and cultural exchanges.

From 2011 to 2016 some 6,900 citizens participated in the Colombes R-Urban sites, and of them, 400 became active stakeholders. The majority participated in Agrocité's microfarming and community-garden plots. A building was constructed from recycled wood to house a café, a teaching space, a market, a greenhouse, a kitchen, and a workshop space. The site became a hub for ecological education and community learning. Some participants set up small businesses and generated income for themselves and for the R-Urban collective.

9
The initial implementation of this R-Urban framework was supported by an EC Life+ innovation grant.

Agrocité: An R-Urban hub for urban agriculture, Colombes, 2014.

The Recyclab was the community recycling and eco-construction center that was self-constructed using secondhand materials. Repurposed shipping containers served as the ground floor, with a first floor built out of wood. The structure housed workshops, materials storage space, a design studio and apartment, and garden deck. Agrocité and Recyclab established systems to reduce CO_2 emissions, harvest and use rainwater, compost organic waste, and collect and recycle other urban waste. Immaterial flows such as knowledge transmission, social exchanges, and green jobs creation were also generated by the network.

Recyclab: An R-Urban hub for recycling and eco-construction, Colombes, 2014.

RURBAN PILOT FACILITIES AND CYCLES

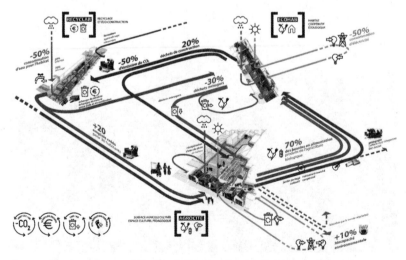

The resilience outcomes of the first R-Urban network in Colombes, 2011.

Both hubs were organized as civic organizations (i.e., associations loi 1901), with each type of activity (composting, recycling, cooking, gardening, bookkeeping, repairing, etc.) managed by a collective of active members who were passionate about these practices. These thematic collectives were represented in the governance structure of each hub, together with AAA and the city, with each having an equal say in the collegial decision structure of the hub. Decisions were made during general assemblies of all hub members, which took place four times a year. For a "constructed commons" such as R-Urban, conceiving an appropriate governance format was indeed part of the codesign process.

Unlike the marketized, technocentric approaches to resilience, which often involve externalized (and expensive) technological fixing of ecological failures, the R-Urban hubs are low-tech facilities run by citizens with the goal of improving resilience from within by maintaining an ecology of local practices in neighborhoods. Resilience in this case means maintaining the community capacity to overcome the climate change disaster and the related ecological and economic crises by enabling citizens to organize themselves to take action and produce what they consume (i.e., food, energy, water), reducing waste and carbon emissions locally. Resilience implies not only a more ecologically virtuous society but also a more cohesive, inclusive, and just society.

The democratic governance of the network of R-Urban commons promotes concrete, hands-on action and becomes a catalyst for urban transformation, innovation, and creativity, facilitating the emergence of new commons within a wider collective urban resilience movement.

Defending

There are also many challenges within these undertakings, however. The processes of setting up commons are long and do not conform to current administrative formats and ways of running politics in short electoral cycles. It is hard to sustain the agreements set with municipal teams and to support such initiatives beyond the electoral cycles, when local politics are usually substantially revised.

Following the change in municipal representation after the local elections in 2014, and before AAA and the R-Urban team could complete Ecohab (the planned cooperative housing units), the R-Urban hubs were threatened with eviction, generating a wave of protests. In June 2015, the new mayor decided to replace Agrocité with a temporary private car park and also expressed his intention to demolish Recyclab in order to clear the land for future city projects.

This incident confirms that setting up urban commons today is not only a social, economic, and ecological project, but also a political project. It subverts the capitalist order and its dominant modes of production. It reclaims and captures resources that are embedded in capitalist transactions and redirects them to commoning dynamics.

The mayor asked for the demolition of the two R-Urban hubs through a litigation procedure at the Tribunal Administratif. This was a challenging moment for the R-Urban community, and for us as designers and initiators. We had to quickly learn how to organize resistance through press campaigns and civic protests. We realized that creating urban commons means not only supporting them throughout their development but also overcoming their potential enclosures. We realized also how challenging it is to set up and sustain commons in a capitalist society that is specifically based on principles of commons enclosure, privatization, and unrestricted exploitation of the planet's resources.

Protest campaign against the eviction of Agrocité, Colombes, 2016.

Many contemporary urban commons around the world are haunted today by new forms of "enclosure,"[10] most of the time driven by capitalist political or economic motivation.[11] The enclosure forces could be private developers or property rights holders but also public governments, as in the case of Colombes. Although contested, these new enclosures are most often successful because the current capitalist laws support private or state ownership against the common use.

Currently, there is a lack of specific legislation to protect the commons in Europe,[12] and there is no political definition and legislation to

10
Linebaugh, *The Magna Carta Manifesto*.
11
L. Alden Wily, "The Global Land Grab: The New Enclosures," in D. Bollier and S. Helfrich, *The Wealth of the Commons: A World beyond Market and State* (Amherst, MA: Levellers Press, 2012), 132–140.
12
F. Capra and U. Mattei, *The Ecology of Law: Toward a Legal System in Tune with Nature and Community* (San Francisco: Berrett-Koehler Publishers, 2015).

How to Design, Defend, and Sustain Urban Commons and How to Demonstrate Their Value for Resilience?

260

13
C. Petcou and D. Petrescu, "R-URBAN or How to Coproduce a Resilient City," *Ephemera* 15, no. 1 (2015): 249–262.

14
S. Gutwirth and I. Stengers, "Le droit à l'épreuve de la résurgence des commons," *Revue juridique de l'environnement* 1 (2016).

15
M. Bawens, *Sauver le monde: vers une économie post-capitaliste avec le peer-to-peer* (Paris: Les liens qui libèrent, 2015).

16
B. H. Weston and D. Bollier, *Green Governance: Ecological Survival, Human Rights and the Law of the Commons* (Cambridge: Cambridge University Press, 2013), 199.

17
A. Méndez de Andés Aldama, "Becoming-Common of the Public Space," PhD confirmation report, University of Sheffield, 2020.

18
C. Iaione, "The Right to the Co-City," *Italian Journal of Public Law* 9, no. 1 (2017): 80–142.

19
L. Van Eeckhout, "A Colombes, la lutte d'une ferme urbaine contre un parking," *Le Monde*, https://www.lemonde.fr/planete/article/2016/02/07/a-colombes-la-lutte-d-uneferme-urbaine-contre-un-parking_4860995_3244.html; J. Tribillion, "Why Is a Paris Suburb Scrapping an Urban Farm to Build a Car Park?" *Guardian*, https://www.theguardian.com/cities/2015/sep/11/paris-un-climateconference-colombes-r-urban-urban-farm-car-park.

protect what could be called a "right to resilience" through commoning.[13] In the absence of such legislation, the commons depend on the good-will of local governments or other external administrations, which can refuse to recognize the legitimacy of self-organization,[14] as was the case in Colombes. In the absence of protective legislation, commoning communities need to collaborate with a "partner State"[15]—a State that "assists, enables and supports"[16] the institutionalization of commoning for resilience approaches and sustains the human rights that are part of this process. Among the very few positive examples of public policy supporting the commons is the experience of municipalist governments. In Spain, for example, governments in cities like Barcelona, Madrid, and Coruña sought to reorganize the social and political agreements region-ally through democratic participation and co-creation of institutional tools to support commons. Barcelona set up crowdsourced policies for a "commons collaborative economy." Coruña supported the creation of regional units that are managed in common at the scale of the city; called "Districts of Common," they cover areas such as the beach, the port, or protected green areas.[17] Another positive example was the experience in Bologna, Italy, where the municipality launched Bologna's Regulation on Collaboration between Citizens and the City for the Care and Regeneration of the Urban Commons, which provides a legal framework and administrative process by which citizens can directly care for urban commons such as parks, streets, cultural assets, schools, and much more.[18] The situation was very different with R-Urban in Colombes. After a court appeal and despite a civic protest campaign, the verdict went in favor of the right-wing municipality, and Agrocité was sentenced to eviction.[19]

Sustaining

We learned from this incident that, in the absence of protective laws, architects need skills not only for designing and building but also for defending the urban commons and making them resilient in adverse conditions. As an immediate takeaway, we found inspiration in the self-defense techniques in aikido. The act of "blending," for example, shows us that in order to stop an attack, one has to move around the punch! We negotiated to relocate the hub in a neighboring city that has a left-wing municipal team. We used the fact that Agrocité was designed for a reversible installation incorporating resilience principles such as the possibility for dissembly/reassembly. The building was conceived to be sustainable beyond the period of land availability. All the construction details were designed to make possible the intelligent demolition and reconstruction of the building: 90 percent of the building materials were recycled (wooden cladding elements, reused drying panels, and windows reclaimed from demolitions), and the wooden structure and the pile foundation were conceived to be easy to dismantle. This is a principle AAA had applied in previous projects in order to ensure sustainability and resilience beyond their temporary installation on land available for a limited time. The short-term land availability outside market transactions is indeed an important challenge in metropolitan contexts, one that can affect the sustainability of projects. Over the years, the AAA projects invented tactics to overcome this challenge, by proposing mobile and flexible building systems that can be easily transported and reinstalled in a different context, allowing for the continuation of the project and strengthening the community around it.[20] The reversibility of land use is also an important resilience principle valued in AAA's work.

20
D. Petrescu and C. Petcou, "Tactics for a Transgressive Practice," *Architectural Design* 83, no. 6 (2013): 58–65.

In February 2017 Agrocité was dismantled and rebuilt in Gennevilliers. Also, in the same year, Recyclab was dismantled and rebuilt in Nanterre. Ninety-five percent of the materials used in the initial construction were reused in a full cradle-to-cradle manner. The R-Urban members were proactive in maintaining and relocating the functions until the infrastructure was reestablished. The former users became the experts of the project, participating in the reinstallation process. They were motivated by this new opportunity, which brought new life to the project. Some of them continued to be active in the project in the new location, joining with new users living in that neighborhood.

Demolition of Agrocité in Colombes, 2017.

Doina Petrescu and Constantin Petcou

Reconstruction of Agrocité in Gennevilliers, 2017.

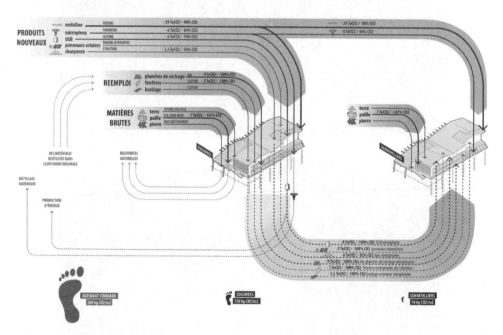

Rebuilding of Agrocite in Gennevilliers, a cradle-to-cradle approach, drawing by aaa, 2018.

21

D. Petrescu, C. Petcou, K. Gibson, M. Safri, "Calculating Commoning Value for Resilient Urban Futures," *Environmental Policy and Governance Journal* (2020): 1–16, http://dx.doi.org/10.1002/eet.1890.

In parallel with these events, we conducted research to demonstrate the value created by these kinds of urban commons, which are often neglected by politicians and developers, as was the case with R-Urban in Colombes. The precarity of urban commons, as we have seen in this case, is partly produced by the inability to assert their value in the face of the capitalist urban private-property market with its inflated financial returns on investment. In order to begin to address this legal and financial precarity, a much more robust understanding of value in social, ecological, and financial terms, as well as a more honest identification of full costs and benefits, is required. With feminist economists Katherine Gibson and Maliha Safri, we calculated the commoning value created by R-Urban during its functioning in Colombes.[21] For this, we combined estimates of the direct revenues generated by the hubs, the market value of voluntary labor, in addition to the value of training and education conducted on-site through formal and informal channels, and the new jobs and earnings generated by R-Urban activity. We also estimated the monetary value of the savings made by our environmentally conscious design, which focused on water recycling, soil and biodiversity improvement, and social and health benefits, breaking them down by savings to the organization, participants, and households involved in R-Urban itself, as well as savings to the state and the planet. The calculations demonstrated that the "value of commoning" (including the value of voluntary labor and the ecological and environmental repair) was around €2 million per annum for the first two hubs in Colombes. This represents a 180 percent community return on investment: 18 times greater than the 10–12 percent best-performance classical return on investment reported by the US stock market. This calculation method, which was built on the specific data of the R-Urban project, has wide applicability within urban commons of many types seeking to demonstrate the worth and value of all their many facets and activities. It is meant to provide evidence for commoners around the world in their fights and negotiations of assets with local governments.

22

D. Petrescu and C. Petcou, "Resilience Value in the Face of Climate Change" in "The Social Value of Architecture," ed. F. Samuel, special issue, *Architectural Design* (2020): 31–37.

23

J. K. Gibson-Graham, *The End of Capitalism (As We Knew It): A Feminist Critique of Political Economy* (Oxford: Blackwell Publishers, 1996).

In further work, we have also shown how this commoning value translates into value for resilience.[22] We have used the model of the diverse economy "iceberg" coined by Katherine Gibson and Julia Graham[23] to show the difference between the visible tip of the economy of the project, which represents the direct financial value created by the project, and the huge, invisible mass that represents the commoning value. We looked at how the iceberg evolved over the five-year period when R-Urban was functioning in Colombes and showed how the commoning value grew exponentially over time. We realized that the most significant value was created in the realm of increased capacities and saved costs in the field of well-being and ecology, and that the commoning value is also directly related to the value for resilience. This value, which is usually "invisible," became, in five years, ten times bigger than the visible part constituted by the direct financial revenue.

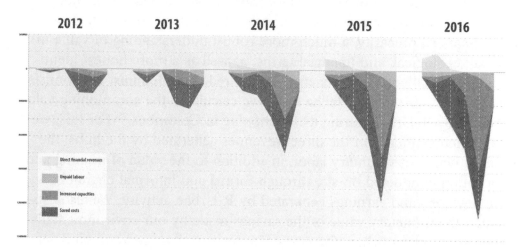

Diagram showing the evolution of the resilience value iceberg within the R-Urban project during its five-year installation in Colombes. Drawing by aaa, 2020.

The commoning value is in fact never considered in current transactions, and projects like R-Urban are usually dismissed because they do not generate direct financial revenue in the way a developer-run project does. This was the argument when the R-Urban hubs were threatened with eviction by the mayor of Colombes. However, this commoning value, which is also value for resilience, is something that should be considered an integral part of the diverse economy-ecology of any architectural or urban project. Its multiplication and expansion in time can contribute very directly and significantly to covering the costs involved in the ecological transition.

Other municipalities and stakeholders in the metropolitan region of Paris became interested in implementing resilience hubs and expanding the network. Two new hubs were built in Bagneux, while a few other municipalities expressed interest in building hubs in their regions. With the construction, slated for 2021, of the Wiki Village Factory in Paris, which is a cluster of social and ecological innovations and a sort of headquarters of R-Urban, we hope that the R-Urban network will have the centralized support needed to operate successfully at the

How to Design, Defend, and Sustain Urban Commons and How to
Demonstrate Their Value for Resilience?

266

A new R-Urban hub in Bagneux, 2019.

Wiki Village Factory, a cluster for social and ecological innovation, winning competition entry, Paris, 2017.

Doina Petrescu and Constantin Petcou

regional level in a few years' time. This will involve the construction of few more resilience hubs, the expansion of the network into a few other cities in the metropolitan region of Paris (such as Cesson and Cashan), and the increase in collaborations and flows at this scale via a R-Urban community trust.

In London, the R-Urban team led by Public Works is collaborating on a new development with the Poplar Housing and Regeneration Community Association. Instead of disappearing, the initial hubs have multiplied and networks have expanded.

Conclusion

R-Urban demonstrates that commons can be one important pathway for cities to become more resilient and offers insights into how architects can facilitate this process, whether by designing and managing or by sustaining and fighting. It also demonstrates that society has the means to act effectively against the climate crisis if opportunities are created for everyone to invest in and collectively reconsider the economic, social, and ecological values of their actions as part of connected and resilient commoning approaches.

At the same time, R-Urban shows once again that, despite the many advantages they offer, urban commons are continuously under threat. It is clear that a capitalist society based on private property does not "naturally" offer opportunities and conditions of support for commons, and conservative governments constantly undermine commons because they empower communities to promote postcapitalist agendas.[24] This is why commons at the neighborhood and city scale are particularly vulnerable to mainstream politics.

Protective policies, laws, and regulations are urgently needed to support existing urban commons and to encourage new commons to emerge. Currently, projects like R-Urban can develop only in contexts in which local governments provide funds, land, and assets for the initial installations.

R-Urban provides a model of networked urban commons that can be applied in suburban mass housing estates, where land and assets are still accessible. The network connects collectively managed hubs with other local assets and initiatives, enhancing community control over the metabolic system of the neighborhood. It specifically addresses ecology in political terms "not only preserving the commons but also struggling over the conditions of producing them."[25] This can

24
R. Cretney and S. Bond, "'Bouncing Back' to Capitalism? Grass-Roots Autonomous Activism in Shaping Discourses of Resilience and Transformation following Disaster," *Resilience* 2, no. 1 (2014): 18–31; C. O. Scharmer, "Seven Acupuncture Points for Shifting Capitalism to Create a Regenerative Ecosystem Economy," *Oxford Leadership Journal* 1, no. 3 (2010): 1–21.
25
Negri and Hardt, *Commonwealth*, 171.

How to Design, Defend, and Sustain Urban Commons and How to Demonstrate Their Value for Resilience?

268

26
Capra and Mattei,
The Ecology of Law.

be understood also as form of "generative institution"[26] at the neighborhood level and beyond, challenging existing public institutions to recognize communities' "responsibility *with* power." Indeed, the R-Urban commons carry a new political project and a new model of democracy, beyond traditional politics.

The hub is an important tool within the model, providing physical infrastructure, resources, and space where commoning and resilience can be learned, practiced, and valued. The hubs and their architecture make tangible all these processes. They also integrate a number of ecological devices that make visible and measurable the resilience activities: food and energy production, as well as water, waste, and carbon reduction. Compared with other networked models, the hub-based model draws on architects' skills and knowledge, and puts design and design thinking in the center of the commons–based resilience strategy. Affordable and technically easy to build and manage, the hubs can be easily reproduced by communities in almost any kind of neighborhood context, in Europe and beyond.

The R-Urban experience also suggests the need for new forms of design practice, based on engagement and alliances with citizens at local and translocal levels, shared knowledge, academic input, funding, and proactive support through policy developments on coproduced resilience. Design that is committed to resilient commons becomes itself a commoning activity, serving the collective efforts to move toward living and producing value differently in a more socially and ecologically just society.

Architects of the "Silent Revolution": Empowering Local Communities through Commons-Based Resilience Strategies

Nadia Bertolino

1

T. De Moor, "The Silent Revolution: A New Perspective on the Emergence of the Commons, Guilds and Other Forms of Corporate Collective Action in Western Europe," *International Review of Social History* 53, no. S16 (2008): 179–212, http://dx.doi.org/10.1017/S0020859008003660.

2

W. N. Adger, "Social and Ecological Resilience: Are They Related?" *Progress in Human Geography* 24, no. 3 (September 2000): 347–364, https://doi.org/10.1191/030913200701540465.

3

H. G. Bohle, B. Etzold, and M. Keck, "Resilience as Agency," *IHDP-Update* 2 (2009): 8.

4

D. A. Schön, *The Reflective Practitioner: How Professionals Think in Action* (New York: Routledge, 1992).

5

C. Baibarac and D. Petrescu, "Co-Design and Urban Resilience: Visioning Tools for Commoning Resilience Practices," *CoDesign* 15, no. 2 (2017): 91–109, https://doi.org/10.1080/15710882.2017.1399145.

6

L. Candy, *The Creative Reflective Practitioner: Research through Making and Practice* (London: Routledge, 2019).

Self-organized communities are more and more often actors of urban change. Through awareness of social, political, and economic dynamics, community-led initiatives of urban commoning are challenging market-driven modes of spatial production. These initiatives represent a contemporary "silent revolution"[1] aimed at producing socially sustainable and resilient ways of living by addressing the needs and aspirations of groups that would not currently sit at institutional negotiation tables. Drawing on the creative use of resources, a horizontal decisional structure, and the flexible use of space, urban commons can offer one possible and noncommodified response to today's environmental and social challenges.

Adger described social and environmental resilience as two sides of the same coin.[2] In fact, he defines resilience as the ability of communities to maintain themselves in the face of external disturbances as a result of social, political, and environmental change. From this perspective, urban commons enable forms of local resilience by strengthening "adaptive capacities, the ability for reorganisation and renewal, and the potential for self-organisation and learning"[3] through the agency of social actors leading the process of spatial production. Within this framework, the role of architects in the process of commoning urged a reflective way of practicing that draws on the critical understanding of specific contexts and situations, their uncertainty, and their unique potential.[4] Today spatial practitioners and local communities are experimenting with commons-based forms of local resilience to claim alternative, more sustainable ways of living in response to the challenges of an undefined future.[5] This newly established alliance urges practitioners to read places through the prism of community needs and aspirations, collective resources, and social dynamics, all of which become key design elements. This form of practice involves many interwoven activities as practitioners seek understanding through making works of different kinds.[6]

This speculative essay questions how architects can support and eventually empower grassroots groups to tackle social and environmental challenges through commoning practices. The four case studies discussed outline a wide range of scenarios and suggest four possible responses to this question. More broadly, this essay aims to intervene in the public debate around the role of architects in radically sustainable urban transformations, introducing and discussing architects' contributions to a selection of actual case studies that have been chosen for their agendas and radical approaches to sustainability issues. They demonstrate how at least part of today's architectural practice has indeed shifted toward new directions where communications, negotiation, and knowledge-sharing skills are the foundational principles of a new way to (co)design and (co)produce places.

Since David Harvey's *Spaces of Hope*,[7] there have been several attempts to interpret urban transformations through the lens of the commons.[8] Recently, some scholars have focused on the relationship between urban commons and the city,[9] demonstrating that the specific spatial setting of commons in urban environments is central to its definition.[10] As commoning practices reveal a relational attitude within urban spaces,[11] they may actively contribute to redefining spatial entities that feature internal thresholds[12] and an ever-changing use of spaces. Urban transformations interpreted through the lens of the commons reveal the role of social practices in modifying the spatial dimensions of the city. This connection reveals the potential for more deeply investigating the commons and the related practices of commoning through or in relationship with disciplines like architecture, urban design, and planning. Within the disciplinary debate, De Angelis's definition suggests potential interactions with the architectural discourse and offers an appropriate framework to introduce the four case studies. According to De Angelis, commons share a pool of material and immaterial resources, are created and sustained by a community that defines rules for accessing and using these resources, and lastly, the commoners establish and develop spatial practices consistent with the sociopolitical agenda of the common.[13] This definition allows for a certain degree of flexibility, necessary to critically analyze the commoning experiences below, in relation to their spatial unfolding and the role played by the architects within the process.

Urban commons, as I define them here, are typically intimately connected to specific contexts, usually at the neighborhood or citywide scales, but also regionally, with several implications in terms of national laws and regulations. Moreover, commons are in most cases invisible to planning processes, as they do not define any property rights[14] and actually challenge the regulatory system of urban laws. In fact, the four experiences introduced here reveal complex scenarios in which property and the management of collective resources imply a novel interdisciplinary framework that involves civil society actors, architects, policy makers, and legal experts. Moreover, urban commons give voice to the needs and aspirations of groups of citizens that are not addressed by traditional urban laws.

I have previously researched theories and practices of urban commons using case studies in European cities and recently cofounded the City as a Commons, a translocal network, which was launched in September 2019 with an international symposium and summer school.[15] The intention was to make advances in the way the disciplinary discourse about urban commons is interwoven with that of architectural design and to foster reflection on expanded meanings of practicing architecture.

7
D. Harvey, *Spaces of Hope* (Edinburgh: University of Edinburgh Press, 2000).

8
E. Ostrom, *Governing the Commons: The Evolution of Institutions for Collective Action* (Cambridge: Cambridge University Press, 1990).

9
See J. M. Ramos, ed., *The City as Commons: A Policy Reader* (Melbourne: Commons Transition Coalition, 2016); S. Stavrides, "Emerging Common Spaces as a Challenge to the City of Crisis," *City* 18, no. 4–5 (2014): 546–550; S. Stavrides, *Common Space: The City as Commons* (London: Zed Books, 2016).

10
A. K. Müller, "From Urban Commons to Urban Planning—or Vice Versa? 'Planning' the Contested Gleisdreieck Territory," in *Urban Commons: Moving beyond State and Market*, ed. M. Dellenbaugh, M. Kip, M. Biemok, A. K. Müller, and M. Schwegmann (Basel: Birkhäuser, 2015), 148–164.

11
P. Chatterton, "Seeking the Urban Common: Furthering the Debate on Spatial Justice," *City* 14, no. 6 (2010): 625–628, http://dx.doi.org/10.1080/13604813.2010.525304.

12
S. Stavrides, *Towards the City of Thresholds* (Trento: Professionaldreamers, 2010).

13
M. De Angelis and S. Stavrides, "On the Commons: A Public Interview with Massimo De Angelis and Stavros Stavrides," *e-flux* 17 (2010), https://www.e-flux.com/journal/17/67351/on-the-commons-a-public-interview-with-massimo-de-angelis-and-stavros-stavrides/.

14
L. Porter, M. Lombard, M. Huxley, A. K. Ingin, T. Islam, J. Briggs, D. Rukmana, R. Devlin, and V. Watson, "Informality, the Commons and the Paradoxes for Planning: Concepts and Debates for Informality and Planning," *Planning Theory & Practice* 12, no. 1 (2011): 115–153.

15
The summer school and research symposium were held at the University of Pavia, Italy, in September 2019. On that occasion, students from different background worked in interdisciplinary teams to design commons-based strategies to reactivate underused spaces in the city. The school brief and topics discussed during the symposium can be read at: http://cityascommons.unipv.it/.

16
C. Petcou and D. Petrescu, "Co-Produced Urban Resilience: A Framework for Bottom-Up Regeneration," *Architectural Design* 88, no. 5 (2018): 58–65.

17
L. Molinari, "Milano che cambia tra le pieghe," in *Milano: Le Nuove Architetture*, ed. M. V. Capitanucci (Milan: Skira, 2012), 9–14.

The present essay critically engages with the body of research published thus far and introduces more recent case studies that disclose the notion of the urban commons in four geographical contexts. In fact, following the invitation of the editors of *New Geographies*, I have selected a number of relevant case studies with the aim of adding new meanings to the idea of urban commons and reflecting on the roles that architects, urban designers, and planners can play within this framework. I begin my reflection analyzing R-Urban in London by Public Works. I then discuss the approach of three young collectives whose recent works reveal the breadth of this phenomenon: Kollektiv Plus X, which promoted the Nomadisches Kultur-Zentrum in Berlin, the transdisciplinary group that initiated the El Warcha collaborative design studio in Tunis, and the Lab for Open Design and Fabrication (LUDD), which very recently launched the Clouds for Commons project in Athens. These case studies have been chosen for their social agendas and radical approaches to environmental issues. The spatial practitioners whose works are discussed in this essay share a common understanding of the urban space as a dynamic, often unbalanced system of social changes, political negotiations, and architectural propositions. In particular, the investigation into these case studies aims to unveil how architects can act as both agents and actors in the horizontal processes of urban transformations[16] and how they can enable grassroots groups to tackle social and environmental challenges through commons-based resilience strategies.

Within this cultural framework, local communities and grassroots groups demonstrate an intimate awareness of the urban space and its complex relationships;[17] they can stand in opposition to globally oriented, market-driven political choices and act as symbols of communal values and local resistance. The case studies draw on this premise and translate into spatial propositions a discourse on tangible and intangible resources to tackle "locally" social and environmental challenges that are usually deemed "global." R-Urban, Nomadisches Kultur-Zentrum, El Warcha, and Clouds for Commons define a notion of spatial intervention that goes beyond the idea of "public space" as we traditionally understand it in the architectural culture. Instead, they propose the idea of a "common space" intended as a neglected space that becomes meaningful only after being activated and inhabited by a group of self-organized citizens who share needs, resources, and principles through practices of commoning. In fact, the experiences in London, Berlin, Tunis, and Athens are all based on an understanding of common spaces as "distinct from public as well as from private, open to public use in which, however, rules and forms of use do not depend upon and are not controlled by a prevailing authority."[18]

A Brief Premise:
Who Owns the Right to the City?

For the past few years, my research has focused on Macao, an artists' collective that occupied Milan's former slaughterhouse in 2012 to establish its creative headquarters. After an intensive effort to make the space livable, Macao slowly began setting up a complex cultural project of everyday activities. It is now using the space to host a lively cross-sector program of performing arts, cinema, visual arts, design, photography, literature, new media, hacking, and meetings of citizens' committees.[19] Through urban commoning practices, Macao reached its current form and organization and now represents a major right-to-the-city movement in Milan,[20] standing in contrast to neoliberal political attitudes and acting as a symbol of community empowerment and local resistance. Macao is a self-defined social group,[21] and a community whose members share these resources and define for themselves the rules through which they are accessed and used. However, a workshop I ran in 2017[22] highlighted the marginal role of Macao activists as mediators and incubators of inclusive practices within the local community and revealed that the relationship between the activists and the neighborhood is actually shot through with controversy.[23] In fact, an article I coauthored for the *Journal of Peer Production* in 2018 concludes that there was room for Macao to become inclusive of more locally rooted groups and aspirations and to ensure better accessibility to and governance of the common resources that are used, shared, and peer-produced.

A Research by Design studio I taught at the Sheffield School of Architecture in 2016 focused on this aspect of Macao's practices. One proposal, developed by Salma Modawi, a postgraduate student, drew on the hypothesis of including architects in the cycle of spatial reactivation led by the multicultural community in the Molise-Calvairate neighborhood. In this framework, architects act as mediators between activists and the local community, with the important responsibility of negotiating with the relevant institutions over land use and facilitating the codesign process for the reappropriation of the entire abandoned site on which Macao settled. Modawi's Agri-Common is based on the idea of building up a piece of urban agriculture that is run and managed by locals who can invest their time and skills, benefit from the harvested products, and eventually trade them. The activists would keep their space in one building on-site and continue the successful program of cultural activities. Moreover, those in the collective with skills like materials upcycling and techniques of self-construction would be proactively included in creating the Agri-Common, which is designed to be self-sufficient and able to function without any further external support.

18
S. Stavrides, "Common Space: The City as Commons," 2.

19
I. Delsante and N. Bertolino, "Urban Spaces' Commoning and Its Impact on Planning: A Case Study of the Former Slaughterhouse Exchange Building in Milan," *Der öffentliche Sektor—The Public Sector* 43, no. 1 (2017): 45–56, http://oes.tuwien.ac.at/periodical/titleinfo/1953109.

20
C. Valli, "When Cultural Workers Become an Urban Social Movement: Political Subjectification and Alternative Cultural Production in the Macao Movement, Milan," *Environment and Planning A* 47 (2015): 643 – 659, http://dx.doi:10.1068/a140096p]http://dx.doi:10.1068/a140096p.

21
According to the definition of "self defined social group" in D. Harvey, *Rebel Cities: From the Right to the City to the Urban Revolution* (London: Verso, 2012).

22
The workshop "Alternative Models of Urban Transformation" was co-organized with Dr. Ioanni Delsante (University of Huddersfield) and Professor Aldo Castellano (Polytechnic of Milan). Participants were recruited through Molise Calvairate Tenants Association, which hosted the participatory session.

23
N.Bertolino and I. Delsante, "Spatial Practices, Commoning and the Peer Production of Culture: Struggles and Aspirations of Grassroots Groups in Eastern Milan," *Journal of Peer Production* 11 (2018), http://peerproduction. net/issues/issue-11-city/ peer-reviewed-papers/social- practices-commoning- peer-production-of- culture/.

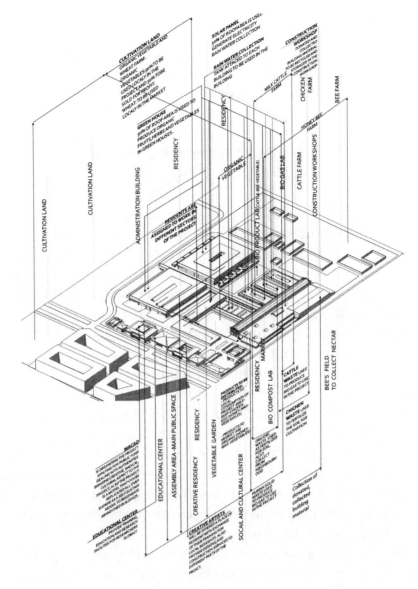

Research by Design studio. "Post Belonging: Stories of Transitional Spaces," MA Architectural Design, University of Sheffield, School of Architecture, 2016. Credit: Salma Modawi.

This work, combined with some recent literature and case studies, led me to examine the idea of urban commons from a different perspective, by looking for best practices of community-driven spatial interventions with a long-term social and environmental impact on hyper-local contexts and by questioning the role of the spatial practitioners within these processes. Of the four case studies that follow, R-Urban in London has an explicit environmental purpose that was explicit from its very first stages and developed through small local actions led by the community. A different approach underpins the Nomadisches Kultur-Zentrum, El Warcha, and Clouds projects, which aim to foster cultural change in the community, strengthen the feeling of belonging to a place, and take care of it as a collective resource.

Four Stories of Transitional Spaces:
London, Tunis, Berlin, Athens

The experience of R-Urban in Poplar is interesting in this regard. R-Urban is a bottom-up strategy initiated in Paris and "repeated" in London, one that aims to enhance the capacity of urban resilience by initiating a network of resident-run facilities. R-Urban sets up "locally closed ecological cycles that will support the emergence of alternative models of living, producing and consuming."[24] R-Urban Poplar is a two-phase pilot project with the aim of creating a collective and participatory process leading to the establishment of a new communal recycling facility centered on ecological and eco-construction principles while also exploring issues of mobile urbanism and the reversible use of vacant urban sites. In Hackney Wick, the project started engaging actors in civil society to reflect upon the potential reuse of wastes produced by capitalist circuits.[25] The agency of prototyping became a key means to produce peer-to-peer knowledge aimed at realizing resilient infrastructures that could be replicated at other sites. Nomadic in nature, R-Urban traveled from its first location in Hackney Wick across other urban sites and eventually settled in Poplar, East London.

There, shipping containers have been reimagined to house facilities to produce a circular urban ecology. The anaerobic digester transforms organic waste into gardening fertilizer or biogas, with the latter serving a community kitchen. The third container hosts a lending facility that promotes the cost-free sharing of building tools among locals. The fourth container is a peer learning space to support and disseminate the coproduced knowledge. With its educational focus, R-Urban in Poplar offers several workshops for the local community to promote a culture of environmental resilience. The role of public works has been crucial to initiating the entire process of commoning by identifying needs and finding common values that create a network through commoning practices and to designing a governance model that is shared and collaborative rather than hierarchical. However, as Colombo pointed out during the City as a Commons symposium

24
Atelier d'Architecture Autogérée and Public Works, "R-Urban ACT—A Participative Strategy of Urban Resilience," 2015.

25
C. Colombo, "R-URBAN POPLAR: Exploring the Sociospatial Permeability of Urban Commoning: The Possibility of Urban Commons as (Open) Social Systems," presentation at the City as a Commons research symposium, September 2–4, 2019, University of Pavia, Pavia, Italy.

Social dinner in R-Urban, Poplar, 2018. Credit: www.mypplr.com/blog/r-urban-poplar/.

R-Urban, Poplar, 2018. Credit: Public Works.

in Pavia, the process of building trust has been slow and not always smooth; much remains to be done for the designers to be identified by the local community as actual members of it.[26]

In fact, R-Urban in Poplar is located in an area of social and economic deprivation where people of different cultural and ethnic backgrounds scarcely integrate. This context challenged the designers, who faced distressed residents who felt victimized by a state-led displacement and social-cleansing effort aimed at attracting wealthier residents. In this scenario, as in the three case studies below, architects and planners identified sites for potential commons based on a preliminary socioeconomic analysis. Stavrides writes that "common spaces are the spatial nodes through which the metropolis becomes again the site of politics, if by 'politics' we may describe an open process through which the dominant

26
Ibid.

forms of living together are questioned and potentially transformed."[27]
In fact, it is not by chance that most commons-based projects are conceived locally but have the potential to be repeated, scaled up or down, and eventually adapted to different geographical contexts.

This is certainly true of the El Warcha collaborative design studio, a global project initially activated in Tunis by an interdisciplinary team including architects, anthropologists, artists, and product designers. The project has now traveled to Nefta, London, and most recently to Davis, California, where it aims to engage with economically marginalized and homeless communities. El Warcha relies on spatial practices through which neglected and underused urban spaces are reactivated. The agency of collectively "making" becomes the means to establish interactions among designers and members of the community. An informal conversation I had in May 2020 with some El Warcha members highlighted the vital relationship between the place and the project: "The spirit of El Warcha really belongs to this specific neighborhood; the way we built, the materials we used . . . all belong here."

The Tunis project is currently the most developed. Since its founding in 2016, it has moved across five different sites in the Hafsia neighborhood and has been able to engage a large number of participants of different ages: "It's been overwhelming to see connections and people involved spontaneously since the very first stages of the project." In September 2019, the group began experimenting with urban gardening, which led to the codesign and eventual coproduction with some residents of a hydroponic garden, a complex project requiring continuous care and management. This increased a sense of belonging for community members, who are now looking after the space and more actively contributing to the life of the workshop ("children often pop in when the workshop is open and see what happens"; "people always bring materials to up-cycle"). Although the project did not have an explicitly environmental agenda, it became clear to its initiators that the spatial practices put in place have contributed to sensitizing people to the importance of upcycling, reusing, and reinventing materials. This hands-on approach characterizes El Warcha's "sculptural processes" of spatial reactivation: as in many projects with a similar agenda, the practice of learning through making becomes crucial to guaranteeing a long-term impact on the community's everyday life. Moreover, the workshop activities—"even the very simple ones of everyday life: eating, drinking, playing cards—spill over into the street, onto the pavement." The workshop space acts as a diaphragm between the communal space of the street and the intimate space of the courtyard, blurring conventional definitions of public and private.

27
S. Stavrides, *Common Space: The City as Commons* (London: Zed Books, 2016), 55.

Assembly in the courtyard, Tunis, 2019. Credit: El Warcha.

The "nomadic objects" coproduced with the residents and made of upcycled materials contribute to overturning conventional ideas of in and out and make the presence of El Warcha recognizable and tangible within the community. A similar approach had been developed by postgraduate student Ruiting Liu in 2016 as one output of the Research by Design studio at the University of Sheffield's School of Architecture. Analyzing the conflicts emerging between Macao activists and the residents of Milan's Molise-Calvairate neighborhood, Liu developed the idea of "traveling devices" collectively produced by Macao and the local community that could be made indoors and moved freely around the neighborhood to reactivate underused public spaces.

Kollektiv Plus X dealt with similar challenges during the development of their Nomadisches Kultur-Zentrum (Nomadic Cultural Center) in Berlin. The designer group is heterogeneous and includes industrial designers, urban planners, and carpenters. They submitted their proposal in response to an open call for projects by the *Quartiersmanagement* (local community bureau), which has an annual budget for initiatives promoting cultural integration that could respond to the specific needs and aspirations of the Neukölln neighborhood. Kollektiv Plus X designed a structured

The hydroponic garden, Tunis. 2019.
Credit: El Warcha.

Seats and shelter, 2019.
Credit: El Warcha, Tunis.

Research by Design studio. "Post Belonging: Stories of Transitional Spaces," MA Architectural Design. University of Sheffield, School of Architecture. Concept traveling devices for the Molise neighborhood in Milan, 2016. Credit: Ruiting Liu.

engagement process: "We had quite a lot of different formats. We worked with schools, kindergartens, organized a street festival and backyard dinners. Most of the times we did recruit people to participate," Sascha wrote me in responding to my questions. The dinners among residents in the backyards of their houses have been the most successful part of the project in terms of social cohesion and community creation. In fact, the Neukölln area for which the project was intended has very few public spaces where people can meet and interact. As I learned from Sascha, the backyards of most Berlin houses are primarily used for functional purposes (storing bicycles, trash bins, etc.) and rarely host community activities. The lack of collective spaces and the potential of the backyards to be repurposed for community life inspired the designers to create a nomadic cultural center, a program of punctual initiatives to reactivate the neighborhood by multiplying the chances for human interaction, thus translating into practice the idea of contemporary architects as organizers of social relations.[28] In the backyard dinners, the bonds between designers and residents built up over time and were based on informal conversations. The team got in touch with some residents and proposed the idea of arranging a dinner: "If they liked the idea to do a backyard dinner, we asked them to invite their neighbors, and we provided a mobile kitchen and some tables and chairs. The neighbors brought some more chairs and the host cooked a dinner." On one occasion, the residents came together and met for the very first time. After the dinner, they self-constituted as a group and organized a collective protest against the sale of their houses.

28
S. Kwinter, *Requiem: For the City at the End of the Millennium* (London: Actar, 2010).

Nomadisches Kultur-Zentrum. Backyard dinner in Neukölln, 2019. Credit: Kollectiv Plus X.

Nomadisches Kultur-Zentrum. Backyard dinner in Neukölln, 2019. Credit: Kollectiv Plus X.

The designer team facilitated communication and established a long-lasting channel through an internal mailing list that allows residents themselves to organize future events without the need for further external inputs. In fact, the social agenda underpinning the project draws on the premise that self-organized citizens can proactively take a stand against the gentrification process in Neukölln: "We hope that by bringing people together we can help them organize and obtain information about how to get help."

It is interesting to note that the same aim—to enable encounters and nurture the community's awareness of its rights to use, activate, and inhabit spaces—underpins the Clouds for Commons project by LUDD in Athens. However, the tools to achieve this objective are different and rely on the potential of prototyped devices to be put in place, assembled, and eventually moved by the community to claim public spaces in several neighborhoods. In fact, Clouds is an open-design modular system used to build pop-up infrastructures that can facilitate social and cultural actions like community gatherings, exhibitions, workshops, performances, open-air libraries, festivals, and so on. The initiative began in September 2019 as the pilot project

START—Create Cultural Change, a capacity-building program. As LUDD's Emmanouil Levedianos explains, "We believe that by co-creating and providing the infrastructural tools for arranging temporary uses and holding events in the city around civil society issues and claims, Clouds has the potential to change the communities' perception on the social challenges in challenging neighbourhoods. By doing so, Clouds creates a space of collective action and challenges the conventional definition of public space."[29] The project has a two-phase process featuring a participatory design stage and a public space activation stage. During the first phase, the designers tapped civil society members to cover a wide range of unexpressed needs relating to the use of public spaces in deprived Athenian neighborhoods. Workshops were held not only at LUDD but also at crucial sites around the city, where assembling and exchanging ideas became the very first practices of commoning to reappropriate underused urban spaces.

29
Emmanouil Levedianos, personal communication with the author.

Clouds for Commons, participatory workshop, 2019. Credit: LUDD, Athens.

Like Kollectiv Plus X's "mobile kitchen," Clouds are prototyped devices that are free for assembly and use; however, their design conception does not belong to the specific spatial needs of a predetermined community. Instead, they are intended to be flexible enough to address a range of uses and spatial set-ups, which suggests a further reflection on the potential of such interventions to enable local collective responses to wider challenges. In fact, commoning practices are usually led by homogenous groups of people who do not appreciate their potential for expansion through networks and multiplication. The claim to act autonomously

Clouds for Commons, working groups, 2019. Credit: LUDD, Athens.

30
J. Pickerill and P. Chatterton, "Notes Towards Autonomous Geographies: Creation, Resistance and Self-Management as Survival Tactics," *Progress in Human Geography* 30, no. 6 (2006): 730–746.

31
R. Hollender, "A Politics of the Commons or Commoning the Political? Distinct Possibilities for Post-Capitalist Transformation," *Spectra* 5, no. 1 (2016), http://doi.org/10.21061/spectra.v5i1.351.

32
S. Stavrides, "On the Commons," *An Architektur* 23 (2010): 3–27.

often neglects the possibility of strengthening their agency by interacting with the wider social context, making the experience of commoning isolated and intrinsically ephemeral.[30] By contrast, initiatives like Clouds draw on long-term strategies to drive cultural change and the collective attitude toward the urban environment. Its first variant is a "politics of the commons," which includes initiatives that bring people together to build collective forms to share resources, spaces, and knowledge, in response to situational threats to survival or well-being. This non-transformational variant faces temporal and geographical limitations and is vulnerable to co-opting because it does not confront the structural, long-term, and systemic causes of enclosure and expropriation. By contrast, in the second variant of "commoning the political," anti-capitalist political processes themselves are held in common. This second approach goes beyond traditional state-based, Eurocentric, or universalistic leftist models to allow for a pluriversal and long-term transformation by combining radical political practices with antagonistic strategies for confronting capitalist domination and is therefore "transformational."[31] In fact, Stavrides, analyzing urban commons in relation to the spaces they "occupy" in the city and the thresholds they generate, makes clear that commoning practices can either be organized as a closed system or may take the form of an open network.[32] These two spatial systems correspond to closed and open communities of commoners, respectively, with the second characterized by broader actions to communicate and exchange goods and ideas beyond the geographical boundaries of a single community.

Participation Is Dead:
Long Live Participation!

"In reality, architecture has become too important to be left to architects," De Carlo wrote in 1968.[33] A few decades ago, De Carlo urged a concrete, radical change to develop new features in the practice of architecture and new behaviors among spatial practitioners: "All barriers between builders and users must be abolished, so that building and using become two different parts of the same planning process." Very recently, the Architecture Education Declares campaign in the United Kingdom launched a call for changes in architectural curricula,[34] based on the concern that "at present our education does not give sufficient weight to the inherently ecological and political basis of architecture, nor to our responsibility to meet our uncertain future with socially and environmentally informed practice." De Carlo's thoughts and today's concerns are clearly linked, as if architecture has not been able—in all the years that have elapsed—to chart clear courses among the new challenges in society and the environment. It is as if the digital obsession characterizing most of today's architectural practice has precluded any actual steps toward a more socially and environmentally sustainable future.

The four projects discussed here suggest that an alternative future for architectural practice is possible if the architect's role covers a radically expanded field that includes skills that do not belong to the conventional practice of architecture.[35] In this scenario, we have seen that interdisciplinarity is central: the Public Works, El Warcha, Kollectiv Plus X, and LUDD teams all include a wide range of spatial practitioners like architects, activists, industrial designers, planners, visual artists, carpenters, and anthropologists. This is because genuine participation is an extremely challenging business that requires communication skills at different levels. As Malachowski, one of the El Warcha initiators, writes, "The process is slow, full of setbacks, and emotionally challenging. . . . You have to build interest and partnerships, find allies, navigate bureaucratic hurdles, build trust with the local community, find support and funding, get material, encourage collaboration and creativity, and repeat it all over and over again each day for weeks or months before you even start to get somewhere."[36] Moreover, the projects discussed operate on different scales of intervention and enable different types of relations between the agents and actors involved in the process. Here, the designers act as knowledge-transfer "devices," as catalysts of experimental forms of cultural coproduction. They can drive negotiations with public authorities, seek support in securing funding, and lead campaigns when the commons are under threat.

33
G. De Carlo, "Architecture's Public," in *Architecture and Participation*, ed. P. B. Jones, D. Petrescu, and J. Till (Abingdon: Routledge, 2007), 3–22.

34
Architecture Education Declares, "Open Letter to the Architectural Community: A Call for Curriculum Change," 2019, https://www.architecture educationdeclares.com/.

35
Some reflections about the need to expand the field of what is commonly intended as "architectural practice" were made a few years ago by the pioneer project Spatial Agency, a research that moves "away from architecture's traditional focus on the look and making of buildings, and proposes a much more expansive field of opportunities in which architects and non-architects can operate. It suggests other ways of doing architecture." Read more here: J. Till, and T. Schneider, "Invisible Agency," in *Architectural Design* 82, no. 4 (2012): 38–43.

36
This is quoted from a personal communication with Justin Malachowski and other members of El Warcha, in May 2020.

37

D. Petrescu, "How to Design, Sustain and Struggle for the Commons," keynote talk at The City as a Commons research symposium, September 2–4, 2019, University of Pavia, Pavia, Italy.

As Doina Petrescu, one of the R-Urban initiators, noted during her keynote address at the City as a Commons symposium in Pavia,[37] the role of architects in relation to urban commons goes well beyond the conventional duties related to design; it must include actions to "sustain and struggle for" such initiatives. In this view, architects are proactively involved in the governance and maintenance of the commons and act within the group in ways consistent with its political, social, and environmental agenda.

In this new, radicalized form of participation, the distinction between designers and users collapses, leaving space for a comprehensive concept of "commoner" as an active citizen who is at once actor and agent of change. However, it is important not to underestimate the spatial and architectural dimensions of the commons. As Petrescu et al. write about R-Urban, "without designated spaces for convivial exchange during winter, when it rains or is windy, or places to hang out and make food together, the connections and trust building necessary to developing commoner subjectivity are harder to make and sustain."[38] In fact, there is room for further reflection on the spatiality of the commons, especially considering the space that results from transversal processes of codesign and coproduction, which can potentially conflict with the conventional modes of spatial production.

38

D. Petrescu, C. Petcou, M. Safri, and K. Gibson, "Calculating the Value of the Commons: Generating Resilient Urban Futures," *Environmental Policy and Governance* Special Issue (2020) 14, https://doi.org/10.1002/eet.1890.

Being architects of the "silent revolution" is not straightforward, and the cultural change that is needed for this process to take place brings with it limitations and new challenges. At the moment, our architecture curricula are not designed to educate "active citizens" before practitioners, although a substantial step forward has been made by students themselves, who have asked for a deep curricular review through the Architecture Education Declares campaign. In fact, architect-commoners, like those whose works have been discussed here, take upon themselves the responsibility to design for an uncertain future, where a technology-led approach can help but will not be the only or even the primary answer to address current social and environmental challenges. The four case studies discussed have demonstrated the diverse nature of practicing architecture within the cultural framework of the urban commons. Although the experiences in London, Tunis, Berlin, and Athens respond to their specific contexts by putting in place ad hoc spatial practices, there is a common thread that connects the skills these designers have demonstrated, which is the ability to build trust in the community by developing a genuinely inclusive environment where needs, values, and aspirations can be discussed and ultimately addressed.

Life as a Common:
Space for a New Biopolitical Project

Paola Viganò

This text addresses the concept of "life as a common" and posits that the occasion and the necessity of a new biopolitical space dealing with life as a common are now taking form. This space not only relates to public and institutional responsibilities (crossing scales, spaces, and modes of space production; a transversal understanding to species, both human and nonhuman) but also overcomes the traditional agenda of architecture, landscape, or urban design. The hypothesis is that, in the actual reconsideration of life and space relations, the biopolitical space will leave behind the modern project, codified by modern architecture and urbanism; it will also leave behind the actual confusing and con-tradictory moves toward the ecological, demographic, and economic transition. The text proposes a few possible lines of thought about how urban and landscape design can help to shape a new, more substantial biopolitical action about life as a common, consistent with current and future challenges. This concept opens to the radical alteration of design perspective, to the value of heterogeneity and coexistences, and to the importance of developing alternative eco-socio-spatial prototypes—three conditions inside which we can begin to rethink the biopolitical nature of the transition and grasp the importance of life as a common.

The text is structured in three parts: the first situates the concept of life as a common within wider debates about biopolitics and proposes a conceptual frame to orient the reading of the second and third parts as well as an autonomous reflexive device (*I. Urbanism and the Biopolitical Project*). The second part delves into the relation between life as a common and the concrete transformation of space through design. Here, soil is at the foundation of spatial design and one of the crucial agents connecting urbanism and life as a common (*II. Our Common Soil: Toward an Urbanism of the Living Soil*). The third part moves to a long-term ter-ritorial vision whose goal is not only to challenge the actual biopolitical structure but to read the territory as a subject through the lens of soil and labor; to embed its vision into alternative modes of space production—a specific space for exploring the ecological and socioeconomic shift and life as a common (*III. The Transition Project*).

I. Urbanism and the Biopolitical Project

In his last text on European urbanism and its tradition, Bernardo Secchi reframed Foucault's hypothesis of biopolitics, extending it to modern urbanism.[1] The entire European architectural and planning tradition is integrated in his last article as part of a "vaster biopolitical action" whose pillars have been modeling the disciplined modern body[2] and secured its continuation.[3] From the perspective of the construction and transformation of urban space, both architecture and urbanism were consequently engaged in sustaining, protecting, educating, and emancipating a population. Modern architecture and urbanism have been defined in relation to such a commitment, developing a deep and consistent reflection on space and life.

The modern project has received criticism from all possible sides; however, the modesty of today's contemporary urban project cannot be referred to the limits and abstract ambitions of modern architecture and urbanism. If space and time have been a medium to think through modernity and its architecture,[4] space, time and life as a common can be today's medium to reorganize design by delving into new ways of cohabitation, the redefinition of borders and porosities, heterogeneous and conflictual proximities. Porosity has to do with movements of bodies into space, their tolerable friction, and encounters that can displace borders or reinforce them.[5] This shift involves our perception of life, of the living,[6] and vulnerability of individuals, groups, society, species, activities, and practices, reopening the debate on the role of design and spatial policies concerning living bodies in a living space and life as a common value and responsibility. The biopolitical space, particularly the space designers intentionally work on, is considered not only as a coercive instrument of a disciplinary society, an apparatus of control exerted over a population, nor a mere tool to secure it, but as a powerful reservoir of possibilities for the subjects to emancipate themselves and to develop new relations among humans as well as among humans and nonhumans, revising their commonalities and the idea of a life *in* common and life *as* a common.

Three distinct fields of thought intermingle. The first is the emergence, in the 18th century, of what Foucault described as biopower, that is, society's power to manage life: health and life are maintained through a series of regulatory and control devices. The organization of space is part of this biopolitical project because it explicitly intends to keep human life productive. The second is the deep ecology approach, which recognizes living and nonliving subjects

1
Bernardo Secchi, "A tradição europeia do planejamento: culturas e políticas," in *XIII SHCU: Tempos e escalas da cidade e do urbanismo: quatro palestras*, ed. E. Ribeiro Peixoto, M. F. Derntl, P. P. Palazzo, R. Trevisan (Brasilia: Architecture and Urbanism, University of Brasilia, 2014).
2
Michel Foucault, *Surveiller et punir* (Paris: Gallimard, 1975); Foucault, *Il faut défendre la société* (Paris: Gallimard-Le Seuil, 1997); Foucault, *Sécurité, Territoire, Population: Cours au collège de France, 1977–1978* (Paris: Gallimard-Le Seuil, 2004); Foucault, "Naissance de la biopolitique: Cours au collège de France, 1978–1979" (Paris: Gallimard-Le Seuil, 2004).
3
Andrea Cavalletti, *La città biopolitica. Mitologie della sicurezza* (Milan: Bruno Mondadori, 2005); Sven-Olov Wallenstein, *Biopolitics and the Emergence of Modern Architecture* (New York: Princeton Architectural Press, 2009).
4
Sigfried Giedion, *Space, Time and Architecture: The Growth of a New Tradition* (Cambridge: Harvard University Press, 1941); Roger Friedland and Deirdre Boden, eds. *NowHere: Space, Time and Modernity* (Chicago: University of Chicago Press, 1994).

5
Walter Benjamin and Lacis Asia, *Neapel, Frankfurter Zeitung*, August 19, 1925; Paola Viganò, "On Porosity," in *Permacity*, ed. Jurgen Rosemann (Delft: TU Delft Press, 2007); Paola Viganò, "Porosity: Why This Figure Is Still Useful," in *Porous City: From Metaphor to Urban Agenda*, ed. Sophie Wolfrum (Basel: Birkhauser, 2018); Cristina Bianchetti, *Bodies: Between Space and Design* (Berlin: Jovis, 2021).

6
Baptiste Morizot, *Manières d'être vivant: Enquêtes sur la vie à travers nous* (Arles: Actes Sud, 2020); Corine Pelluchon, *Réparons le monde* (Paris: Rivages, 2020).

7
Arne Naess, *The Ecology of Wisdom: Writings by Arne Naess*, ed. A. Drengson and B. Devall (Berkeley: Counterpoint, 2008).

8
The emancipatory quality of modern rationalization, following Habermas, was underevaluated by Foucault and highlighted by Habermas's critique of Foucault's power analysis. See Michael Kelly, *Critique and Power: Recasting the Foucault/Habermas Debate* (Cambridge and London: Mit Press, 1994).

9
William Bryant Logan, *Dirt: The Ecstatic Skin of the Earth* (New York: Riverhead Books, 1995).

10
Paola Viganò, "Riciclare città," in *Re-cycle*, ed. P. Ciorra and S. Marini (Milan: Mondadori-Electa, 2011); Viganò, "Elements for a Theory of the City as Renewable Resource," in *Recycling City: Lifecycles, Embodied Energy, Inclusion*, ed. L. Fabian, E. Giannotti, and P. Viganò (Pordenone: Giavedoni Editore, 2012).

and their interaction with humans as an interaction among peers.[7] The awareness of environmental degradation and biodiversity loss are at the foundation of the deep ecology perspective. Life, in its multiple forms, has an intrinsic value that is not based on human goals. The third is the emancipation of the subject, which needs to be reframed and extended, and not lost, if the modern project, its emancipatory qualities,[8] and the traditional human perspective are to be overcome.

As fundamental theoretical interrogations and lenses, the three fields of thought are rarely considered together or used as a tripod in the exploration of the modern project legacy and its fundamental biopolitical scopes. The tripod synthetizes a design approach we have explored in the last decades; the tight relations among the three fields have been fed by our own design activity, which has progressively made explicit its aspiration to overcome the traditional biopolitical frame and to explore the spatial potential of life as a common.

II. Our Common Soil: Toward an Urbanism of the Living Soil

The soil has to do with life and with urban design, starting with its role as the "ecstatic skin" of the planet.[9] This skin is formed and degenerates, it is constructed and reconstructed, and it is the outcome of the incessant work of living and nonliving beings. Condemnation of the consumption of the soil cannot be the only outcome of a reflection on the soil from a design perspective. The rhetorical line that proposes considering the impoverished, eroded, and urbanized soil as a nonrenewable resource incapable of regenerating itself, unable to enrich itself or become alive again, is not entirely convincing. This hasty condemnation loses sight of the potential, also biological, of the huge surfaces left behind by urbanization and industrial activities that we can consider to be, at least partially, renewable resources.[10] It risks overshadowing a long reflection that cuts across modern urbanism, from the radical positions of a geographer like Kropotkin to the project of the green Functional city. In this research, nature—reconstructed through the regeneration of the soil—once again becomes alive and a support for new forms of life and production, in addition to the public space of the city.

Kropotkin dedicated a part of his classic *Fields, Factories, and Workshops* to the concrete methods of regenerating and enriching the soil, noting, "In the hands of man there are no unfertile soils."[11] It is worth remembering that manipulation of the soil is central in the formulation of these ideas: only the possibility of its transformation allows us to leave behind a geographical determinism that ends up specializing the entire planet (in Kropotkin's time, based on British imperialism, great manufacture of the world, or industrial concentration in a few hubs). The problems and dependence that this order of the world creates are now plain to see.

But the design of the modern open space is more significant than the green surfaces in Le Corbusier's *Ville Radieuse*. Having as a goal nature's return to the city, the Stockholm School[12] greatly influenced the modern European city design and was carefully studied for the Courrouze project in Rennes. The School follows two fundamental approaches. The first concerns the places—the identification of their possibilities and the magnification of their potential. The internal and specific conditions of each site are exploited "with emphasis and simplification." The second approach pertains to comfort, recreation, and pleasure: in this sense, the park is utilitarian, an asset for the greatest number of people considered as equals. For Erik Glemme, the designer in charge of the Stockholm Parks Department from 1936 to 1956, or Holger Blom, urban planner and director of Stockholm Parks from 1938 to 1971, the social program of the park and its naturalness were equally important. Returning to emphasis and simplification, the Swedish functionalist park re-created the characteristics of the regional landscape within the city in marginal places and in enhanced ways. It reconstructed nature where it no longer existed and rebuilt it through its archetypes: the rocky terrain of the archipelago and the pine forest, simple but highly symbolic landscapes, were reproposed within the city.

11
Peter Kropotkin, *Fields, Factories, and Workshops*, 2d ed. (New York: G. P. Putnam's Sons, 1901), 48.

12
Thorbjörn Andersson, "To Erase the Garden: Modernity in the Swedish Garden and Landscape," in *The Architecture of Landscape 1940–1960*, ed. M. Treib (Philadelphia: University of Pennsylvania, 2002).

La Courrouze—Grande Prairie.

Rennes, La Courrouze at the western side of the city center.

13
The commission was the result of a competition held between 2002 and 2003 for the reuse of a large area inside the city of Rennes. The masterplan and the realization of all the public space were assigned to Studio Secchi-Viganò and, since 2015, to StudioPaolaViganò, with Charles Dard, AMCO, and Pierre Bazin (Aubépine) after a competition, regular meetings with the client and a few citizens' associations. The project is currently more than halfway to completion and received the Nature en ville du palmarès Ecoquartier 2011 prize from the Ministry of Ecology in France.

The project to create a new part of the city in a formerly polluted and stratified military and industrial site of over 100 ha. in Rennes, Brittany (France), started in 2003, has been a design experiment on how to regenerate a city starting from its soil.[13] What type of space could be designed today, providing homes for around 12,000 inhabitants, jobs for at least 3,000 people, schools, shops, art galleries, and alternative uses, all for the enjoyment of the city residents, visitors, walkers, and others? The question is significant. Projects on this scale, in which urban designers can go beyond outlining a simplified idea of spaces for social and community life, are rare. The use of the masterplan as an abstract canvas superimposed on diversified situations, applying nonverified and generic principles, is all too frequent and avoids the basic question of how we want to live together, what are we sharing and why. This, however, is not a plea for the integral project, although we could develop the initial plan down to the details of the urban morphology, designing and realizing all the public spaces and infrastructures. On the contrary, it resumes a procedural hypothesis of the production of space, within a shared framework of reference that evolves over time.

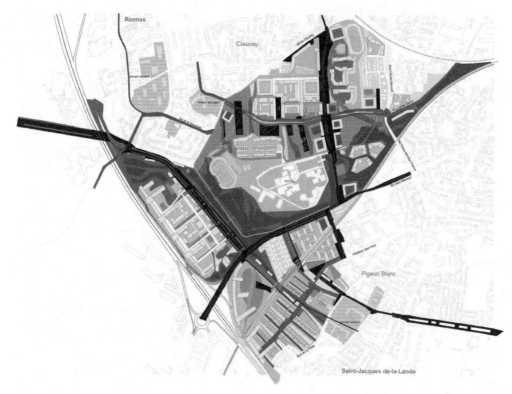

ZAC de la Courrouze masterplan.

The design of La Courrouze does not represent a "new town" but rather a part of the city. Its design is based on the idea that generous public space is what connects heterogeneous languages (of architecture and society) and a variety of practices (from intergenerational to mixed use). The extent of the public space, fully connected to the rest of the metropolitan green system (from the city center to the wet areas along La Vilaine River), the strong accessibility guaranteed by the creation of a new underground system with two stations opening in the area, and the presence of important regional headquarters make it not merely a neighborhood but, rather, an integrated part of the city. The spatial outcomes express the social and political goals, which were set high in this project and included prioritizing affordable housing (half of the residential production, with 20 percent allocated to social housing), while no major urban programs were proposed. La Courrouze is an everyday place, but its open spaces can play a metropolitan role.

An understanding of the site's complexity (polluted, not yet fully owned by the public authorities, rich in biodiversity and historical, military, and industrial traces) transformed the reading of the site into a continuous and parallel activity, while at the same time testing the main concepts

La Courrouze, Vallon Jules Verne.

La Courrouze, Vallon Jules Verne.

proposed in the competition, such as the "landscape as infrastructure," which clarified the importance of the preexisting vegetation and ecologies as a structural element of the new urban area. Leaving aside studies and efforts to depollute the area, we soon realized the need for specific expertise on the ecological conditions. The design hypothesis then evolved together with increasing knowledge of the soil characteristics. This meant that the inevitable functional organization was and is constantly reframed from the perspective of the soil, and in particular, of the *living* soil as a common resource. We did not impose an abstract general pattern on the existing configuration, but rather a topological reading within an ecological framework (compact vs. less compact soils, lower vs. higher land) that guides the design approach and the open-air water management.

The artifice of the archetype recomposes nature in the modern city and measures the distance between nature and human history. In the Courrouze project, the on-site reuse of the unpolluted area's soil, the goal of zero ground balance, the choice of open-air water management, and the link between the scarcity of fertile soil and the archetypes of the Breton landscape have created a rich, living landscape, not always inspired by maximum comfort (as in the traditional green lawn) but by highlighting the differences between ecologies and histories of different soils, within which housing types, landscapes, and public space define specific qualities and situations of living, regenerating, and maintaining life.

Paola Viganò

If the first conceptual frame, related to power relations, was not explicitly challenged in this case (given the great sociopolitical ambitions already present and the periodic questioning of its overall meaning, in particular by reinforcing the functional mix and the reuse/reconditioning of part of the spatial capital present), the second and third conceptual frames, related to deep ecology and emancipation, are strongly present in the revision of the past positions about soils, landscapes, and society. Soil and landscapes have been considered part of the common heritage, together with the history of this place, to be transmitted through the new project. The existing forms of life have been enhanced and the collective belonging reinforced. "Our common soil"[14] has lately become an academic topic centered on the dignity of all soils.

14
"Our common soil" is research funded by the SNF (Swiss National Fund), to be completed in 2021 at the lab-U, EPFL.

III. The Transition Project

The second hypothesis takes into consideration not only the modern biopolitical project and all that remains implicit in space organization practices, but also the contemporary biopolitical project that has lost its ambition to achieve the universality of the right to a better life and does not increase awareness of the new ecological regime. The idea of a new biopolitical project has been the focus of an interdisciplinary design study on the Great Geneva agglomeration (as part of the initiative launched by the Braillard Foundation in 2018, and now nearing completion).[15] This hypothesis highlights the ineffectiveness of current urban, social, and economic transformations and their now proven inadequacy in generating the transition: the inability to achieve radicalism. The emphasis has been placed on space and its potential role in social and environmental emancipation. "Soil and Labor" were the lens through which to observe a contrasting and highly polarized cross-border metropolis, where the border still represents heavy divarication between Switzerland and France and influences their future interactions. The vision we proposed explicitly refers to the possibility of a new biopolitical project oriented by the centrality of life as a common.

15
A vision for the Geneva metropolitan area has been developed by the new Habitat Research Centre at the EPFL.

At the start of the 20th century, soil and work were the main indications of a new urban condition, around which the profound transformation of the economy and society occurred.[16] Similarly, today and in the context of Greater Geneva, soil and work are guiding a new interpretation of the urban and metropolitan condition in which to tackle the ecological, socio-demographic, and economic transition. This was the initial idea behind the proposed work.

16
B. S. Rowntree, *Land and Labour: Lessons from Belgium* (London: MacMillan, 1910).

Having placed the emphasis on these themes, the vision proposes, in addition to scenarios concerning soil and work, a series of eco-socio-spatial prototypes that explore and bring together landscapes, economies, and social practices. All of these are studied, starting with drastic hypotheses on the evolution of mobility (toward a "no car scenario," which had already been envisaged in our previous research, putting the city-territory to the test)[17] but also rediscovering the "weak structure" of the territory that reveals its utility and reason for being within the scope of a new biopolitical project and life as a common.

The term "weak structure" belongs to the vast rethinking of the notions at the basis of Western modernization and its truth claims. Vattimo's "weak thought,"[18] a soft nihilism that leaves space for a *pietas*

17
Paola Viganò, Bernardo Secchi, and Lorenzo Fabian, *Water and Asphalt: The Project of Isotropy* (Zurich: Park Books, 2016).

18
Gianni Vattimo, *La fine della modernità* (Milan: Garzanti, 1985; published in English as *The End of Modernity: Nihilism and Hermeneutics in Post-Modern Culture*, trans. John R. Snyder [Cambridge: Polity Press, 1991]).

Collage realized by P. Andelic, N. Lecoanet; Design Studio Viganò, MA1_2018; Prof. P. Viganò, T. Pietropolli, Q. Zhang, S. Nguyen, EPFL.

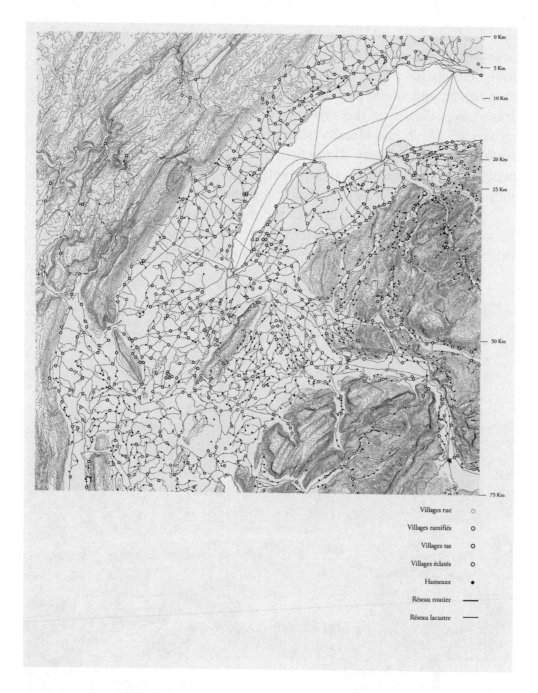

Villages rue ○
Villages ramifiés ○
Villages tas ○
Villages éclatés ○
Hameaux ●
Réseau routier ──
Réseau lacustre ──

0 Km
5 Km
10 Km
20 Km
25 Km
50 Km
75 Km

A metropolis made of villages.

Soil and Labour. The transition, a new biopolitical project 2018–2020.
Habitat Research Center (EPFL) : Prof. Paola Viganò (HRC director, LAB-U), Prof. Vincent Kaufmann (HRC-LASUR),
Prof. Alexandre Buttler (HRC-ECOS), MER. Luca Pattaroni (HRC-LASUR), Ass. Prof. Corentin Fivet (HRC-SXL);
Dr. Roberto Sega (HRC, LAB-U, team coordinator), Tommaso Pietropolli (LAB-U, team co-coordinator),
Dr. Martina Barcelloni Corte (HRC executive board coordinator), Dr. Qinyi Zhang (HRC e.b., LAB-U)

External experts :
Prof. Pascal Boivin (inTNE-HEPIA, HES-SO Genève), Prof. Olivier Crevoisier (Université de Neuchâtel),
Prof. Walter R. Stahel (Product-Life Institute), Jonathan Normand (B Lab Switzerland), Isabel Claus, Marie Velardi.

toward the past and opens to the new experience of truth as an aesthetic experience, is still fertile ground for design thought. It reconsiders the human and natural fields that have been destroyed, hidden, fragmented, or marginalized by the modern totalizing gaze, as in Foucault's genealogical work. In this perspective, design reveals, rediscovers, reconnects, repairs. However, weak structures are here intended also as *emancipatory devices* in a more subversive way, all the while tackling space as part of an emancipatory project. In this sense, the Transition project expands the previous conceptual frame where power relations, ecological concerns, and emancipation are all challenged and tied together by the investigation of the "weak structure," as an essential spatial configuration for a new biopolitical project (a life in common and life as a common) and its eco-socio-spatial prototypes.

The design of the weak structure took a multidimensional approach. The first aspect concerns the performance and functionality of a prototypical space, experimenting with the transition and its multiple dimensions, not only ecological but also economic and social. The weak structure is considered a privileged place for the various strategies relating to water, air, soil, and vegetation. The soils of the weak structure—along with the watercourses at risk of flooding, the reduced and fragmented green filaments, the minor dirty roads and paths, including patches of agricultural land, asphalt surfaces, mineral and impermeable urban spaces to be reconceived—are the prototypes for a regeneration project that should be expanded to the whole territory. The shift to "conservation agriculture," which in this space would find the conditions for experimentation, is essential to the whole of Greater Geneva. To start with, it is a question of envisaging the weak structure as a space for experimenting with ecosystem services to adapt the entire region to climate change.

Along with these functions, we consider a different type of mobility in a territory that is still seen as divided in two by the border and that continues to invest in large, car-based infrastructures. Reconsidering the space of the car allows us not only to regain urban land, demineralize the compact surfaces, and reduce CO_2 emissions but also to rethink the city-territory as a whole, starting with a new public space that can help to give meaning to and provide opportunities for urban intensification, today taking the place of traditional expansions. High levels of social and ecological conflicts are to be expected on the "urban densification" issue in the near future; the first signals are already visible in the harsh reception of such new projects by the public.

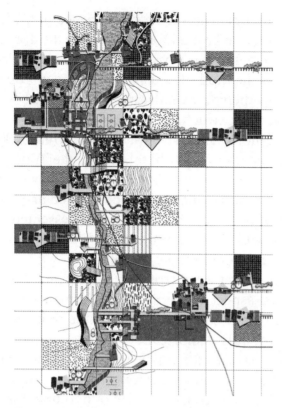

The weak structure, support for the transition.

But the radicalism of the prototype becomes comprehensible only if we add a further idea that has its roots in the status of *surface publique* (public surface), assigned to a significant part of the Canton of Geneva (roughly one-third of its surface) in previous visions for Geneva by urbanists Braillard and Bodmer about one century ago.[19] An isotropic mesh, indifferent to density, degree of urbanity, to urban and rural conditions, for the sake of continuity; an acute instrument of reading and valorization of landscape and cultural features.

    The design of the transition requires changes that we are not politically or economically capable of making and legislating: this is the current biopolitical project implemented despite the signals coming from the scientific world and a significant section of society. The "weak structure" is therefore configured as an opportunity for ecological, sociopolitical, and economic testing. Due to its collective nature, it is a space that represents the general interest: the commons. In the now century-old vision of Bodmer and Braillard, the *surface publique* was justified by the necessary preservation of the territory. This theme touched on the awareness, in the early 20th century, of the aggressive nature of the modernity of the *tabula rasa* and the generalized cultural and ecological destruction. The selection

19
Alain Léveillé, "1935: il piano direttore di Ginevra. Un piano decisamente moderno," *Urbanistica* 89 (1987); Elena Cogato Lanza, *Maurice Braillard et ses urbanistes* (Geneva: Editions Slatkine, 2003).

20
Guillaume Fatio,
*La campagne genevoise
d'après nature*, illustrated
by Fred Boissonnas'
photographic work
(Geneva: Editions
Slatkine, 1981).

of certain places, to be entrusted with the task of maintaining the memory and preservation of preindustrial local identities, went against this trend. The safeguarding of the natural and cultural landscape has not been entirely resolved, yet it remains a priority that extends to new concerns: today, as in the early 20th century, it is a question of safeguarding, protecting, regenerating soils, culture, work, and landscapes. But while in the *plan des zones* of 1936 and in the pages of *La campagne genevoise d'après nature*, published in 1899,[20] selecting what needed to be safeguarded served to carve out the minimum core to be protected from the backdrop of generalized modernization, in our vision the relationship between the weak structure and the territory is something else entirely. The weak structure experiments with a different territorial project that could be extended to the whole cross-border territory. It is not a scenario but a concrete proposal to engage in the realization of "prototypes of coexistence," valorizing spaces and economies of diffuse reconditioning, mitigation, and adaptation in the cross-border space of Great Geneva. Thus the weak structure is a "special zone" within which to experiment and give shape to different forms of managing the existing spatial and natural capital: cultivated areas, public services, maintenance of the territory, forms of social and solidarity-based economies, and different forms of living. In the past, free zones or special zones have made it possible to transgress the order of things, transform marginal places into attractive places, compensate for absences (the lack of territory in the case of the small Republic of Geneva, for example, with its long tradition of agricultural "free zones" that provided for its subsistence outside its perimeter). In the vision we propose, the weak structure represents a starting point for envisaging a radical reconstruction of practices, tools, and positions.

The weak structure proves to be a sophisticated instrument of territorial reading, but it needs to be represented, and this is the third approach, which accentuates and gives value to the heterogeneity and expression of the differences, beyond the strengths of the diagram. In addition to the structural aspect, the fieldwork reveals the descriptive strength of the weak structure, which not only seeks to organize the territory in open and flexible ways but is also, and above all, a concrete device for building sequences, aesthetic enjoyment, and a deeper relationship with the territory: I am here, not elsewhere. Iconic representations are based on images that are well rooted in the collective imaginary, a common heritage revolving around Geneva, such as the profile of the Alps sculpted against the purple and yellow sky with the thick black strokes of Ferdinand Hodler's paintings. The strength of these representations can be read as a foretaste of the iconic power that the weak structure might develop: an icon of the "city-landscape" of the 21st century.

Paola Viganò

Conclusion

The two design experiences (the first a concrete, ongoing urban project, the second an open vision for the future of a cross-border region) explore the reconstruction of commons, putting "life" as the first and fundamental feature. From a spatial perspective, it is the condition of inhabitability that matters, enlarged to the multiple lives that coexist with ours in the contemporary extended urban condition. Starting with "our common soil," which infuses urban design with the idea and challenge of an "urbanism of the living soil," to the Transition project, whose more explicit political and economic consequences involve the entire conceptual frame of biopolitics of space/deep ecology/emancipation tackled above. Together with our previous projects in Paris (Porous City) and Venice (Isotropic Territory), the experiences presented here are splinters of a new biopolitical project, open to deep ecology and maintaining the ambition of supporting emancipation in the redefinition of space/life and power relations. They have provided a forward drive to explore what could be the output of placing life—a life *in* common and life *as* a common—at the center of the design activity.

The Architectural Common

Peggy Deamer

We share bodies with two eyes, ten fingers, ten toes; we share life on this earth; we share capitalist regimes of production and exploitation; we share common dreams of a better future. Our communication, collaboration, and cooperation, furthermore, not only are based on the common that exists but also in turn produce the common. We make the common we share every day.
—Michael Hardt and Antonio Negri[1]

The failure of our studio-based architectural system to produce an effective architectural citizen—studio is too narrowly defined, too formally focused, too individualistic, too painful—is beginning to be discussed in many areas and on many platforms, but change at a more fundamental level is required.[2] The combined crises of climate change, COVID-19, racial injustice, and income inequality, all of which have huge implications for the built environment, require that our universities become think tanks. These crises need our intelligence, our spatial awareness, and our organizational skills; this is not a time for business as usual or the weak, Western-program-driven programs that guide our curriculum. In this, theory is central. The days when studio alone claimed our academic attention or when "history/theory/criticism" folded politely into (only) history are over. But a university's ability to function as a research institute taking on contemporary issues is increasingly uncertain, given its aversion to risk and anything that threatens its endowment; the manner in which we architects pursue and produce relevant knowledge is wandering away from academia proper.

I am an architect and ex-academic theorist, which is to say, I'm retired from teaching theory (and studio) at the Yale School of Architecture, but I still pay attention, in my own research and that of the Architecture Lobby, to theoretical ideas relevant to our current, crisis-driven moment. These ideas build on intellectual thoughts formulated when I was teaching, so previously imprinted biases direct my current attention—critical theory, post-structuralism, neo-Marxism. Still, biased or not, I am struck by two conflated thoughts: Why are architecture's expensive academic programs not serving our intellectual and societal needs? And why is it that ideas most relevant to our current moment, ideas that rightfully would fuel a think tank, come from places external to the academy? And beyond this, what is at stake in this change? To start with the latter, as a vantage point to address the other two queries, I believe we are witnessing the construction of a new "classroom," a new student, and a new education. I also hold that this is not a bad thing and that it revolves around the construction of a new "architectural common."

1
Michael Hardt and Antonio Negri, *Multitude: War and Democracy in the Age of Empire* (London: Penguin, 2005), 128.
2
See Jeremy Till, *Architecture Depends* (Cambridge, MA: MIT Press, 2009), especially "Contingency"; Jeremy Till, presentation at the symposium "Rebuilding Architecture," Yale School of Architecture, https://www.architecture.yale.edu/calendar/73-rebuilding-architecture; Peggy Deamer and Tsz Ng Yan, introduction to *Work*, a special issue of *Journal of Architectural Education* 73, no. 2 (2019): 138–140; Daniel Jacobs and Brittany Utting, "New Tactics for Architecture Pedagogy," in *Work*, 267–269; Reinier de Graaf, "I Will Learn You Architecture!," *Volume* 45 (October 16, 2015): 84–91; Murray Fraser, "Is Studio Culture Dead?," *Architect Journal* (July 25, 2014); Peggy Deamer, "Design Pedagogy: The New Architectural Studio and Its Consequences," in Lohren Deeg, Taylor Metz, and Richard Tursky, eds., *AMPS SIP*, vol. 18 (London: UCL Press, forthcoming).

The Common

The common, unlike the commons, is not a product, not a type of place, and not a thing external to us. As put forward by Michael Hardt and Antonio Negri in their *Empire* trilogy—*Empire* (2000), *The Multitude* (2004), and *Commonwealth* (2009)—it is more specific and more pervasive than the commons. It is more specific because it is distinctly located in post-Fordist, neoliberal production and functions in a world of social media, intellectual labor, technological production, and unscheduled and unsituated labor. It is more pervasive because it is immanent in contemporary being: we all experience the pull of capitalism as it invades our needs and aspirations;[3] we all struggle to identify which thoughts are ours alone versus which are force-fed to be everybody's; we all share our daily lives. The commons implies the places where democratic struggles find a home; the common is the living of that struggle.

The concept of the common is linked to the 1970s-era Italian movements Operaism and Autonomia. Operaism came into being in 1973 when the first large emigration of Italian unskilled workers from the impoverished south moved to the industrial north and—instead of submitting to the new system of mass production, which they believed privileged skilled workers—resisted the assembly line altogether. In the wake of mass unemployment, workers rethought the traditional Marxist analysis of capitalist exploitation. Marx assumes that what makes work alienating is capitalist exploitation; Operaists proposed instead that it is the reduction of life to work. "Workerists," agitating against work and the valorization of the proletariat, didn't want to "take over the means of production" but, rather, to leave behind traditional production altogether. The refusal to work inherently stood for three things: that the "working class" controls the movement of capital, not the other way around; that those in the working class are human before being capitalist-defined "workers"; and that true worker representation no longer resided in (top-down and centralized) unions or political parties, but with the individuals themselves.

After Operaism's dissolution in 1975 as a result of ideological infighting and lack of political success, the movement reemerged as Autonomia, an expanded demographic that included women, students, young workers, and the unemployed; it was rhizomatic, libertarian, anarchistic, ideologically open, and increasingly focused on post-factory modes of production.[4] Negri, involved in the workerist movement from the start and now reflecting on its failure, focused on the disappearance of the archetypal factory worker as, seemingly, predicted in Marx's *Grundrisse* (1939) "Fragment." This enigmatic text argues that

3
"Lohren Deeg, Taylor Metz, Richard Tursky, eds., *SIP* Volume 18: *AMPS* - Special issue: *Re-Design Teaching Design* (London: UCL Press).

4
Feminist thinkers such as Leopoldina Fortunati and Silvia Federici were influential in expanding the post-factory definition of work to include domestic/affective labor. They identified women's role in primitive accumulation—the foundation of capitalism—and demanded that, as long as the division between home and work supported capitalist production, domestic labor be paid.

the introduction of machines into the production process constitutes more than a development of tools of production and instead moves the laborer to the side of the production process. Under a system of automatic machinery, "Labour no longer appears so much to be included within the production process; rather, the human being comes to relate more as watchman and regulator to the production process itself."[5] An individual worker's labor-power in this context is in touch with "his understanding of nature and his mastery over it by virtue of his presence as a social body—it is, in a word, the development of the social individual which appears as the great foundation-stone of production and of wealth."[6] Many Marxists have ruminated over what its writer was implying, but for Negri, it offered a space of hope—or, rather, a new territory for struggle in which workers can and must pull the techno-informational opportunities in their direction even as capitalism is pulling in the other. This is the early formation of the common: a shared existential experience inherently tying together optimism with struggle and technology with social actualization. In this, sharing and struggle are foregrounded and intertwined.[7]

When Negri and other Autonomists were arrested for the kidnapping and murder of the Christian Democratic politician Aldo Morro in 1978, Negri exiled himself to France.[8] It was a natural home. The French Marxists had come to his defense during his trial and imprisonment, and they, too, were evaluating the failure of the intellectual left (particularly its responses to the student protest of 1968) and addressing the shift from factory workers to "social workers." Working with Félix Guattari, Negri argued that instead of "an eight hour wage slave, the worker now produced and consumed continuously for capital. Capital in the process became more socialized, advancing social cooperation, integrating the collective forces of labor even as it turned society into a giant factory."[9] Absorbing Michel Foucault's biopolitics, Negri saw that real, everyday life was subsumed into capital, and in this, power becomes focused on the technologies of the self and the production of subjectivity. And under the influence of Gilles Deleuze, Negri discovered the work of Spinoza, who believed that "the continuous production of collective being unites communication and liberation."[10] The French education allowed Negri to see that "the desolated territories of being subsumed by capital in the latest and most terrible phase of its destructive development are opened anew to the ethical hope and adventure of intelligence."[11]

On Negri's return to Italy from exile and the completion of his reduced prison sentence, the co-authorship of the *Empire* trilogy with

5
Karl Marx, *Grundrisse: Foundations of the Critique of Political Economy* (London: Penguin, 1973), 705.
6
Ibid.
7
I owe my knowledge of Negri's time in France, and many of these observations about his intellectual development there, to Kevin Charles's doctoral thesis, "The Common in Hardt and Negri: Substantiating the Concept through Its Urban, Digital and Political Moments," submitted to the University of Manchester, 2017, https://www.research.manchester.ac.uk/portal/files/77567118/FULL_TEXT.PDF.
8
Negri, facing lengthy imprisonment without trial, ran for election, knowing that election would mean immunity; he won, but later fled to France. He would not return to Italy until 1997, after negotiating a reduced sentence, which kept him incarcerated until 2003.
9
Antonio Negri and Félix Guattari, *New Lines of Alliance, New Spaces of Liberty; or Communists Like Us* (London: Minor Compositions, 1990), 34.
10
Antonio Negri, *Subversive Spinoza: (Un)Contemporary Variations* (Manchester: Manchester University Press, 2004), 96.
11
Ibid.

Hardt began. Each volume makes a different specific argument, but "the common" increasingly emerges as a foundational theme, especially as it intertwines with the more well-known ones of immaterial labor—labor that doesn't produce goods but instead produces knowledge—and the multitude—a plethora of individuals/singularities that are too multiple and rhizomatic for capitalism to control.[12]

12
See Chapter 5, "Architectural Work: Immaterial Labor," in my book *Architecture and Labor* (London: Routledge, 2020), 63–70.

Architectural Academia/Theory

The common, embedded in the individualities of the multitude and shaped by immaterial labor, is then a state of being, intrinsically linked with the shared struggle to find opportunities for a free future. The link to architecture may not be immediately clear, especially when it is decoupled from "the commons," but it should be seen as multiple, rhizomatic, untethered, uncentered, and de-institutionalized queries that all architectural citizens confront when grappling with the power structures that currently marginalize our role in society.

In the past, theorists like me used to get information from known and mutually agreed upon resources: history and theory texts and serious journals. Way back when, for me, this was *Oppositions, Assemblage, Domus, Lotus International*; then *ANY, Grey Room*, and *Log*. These journals were not produced in the academy per se, but they were "academic" inasmuch as all their editors were (and are still) full-time faculty members at prestigious universities. They gathered together theorists of equal academic stature whose writings appeared on the syllabi of the architecture schools where they all taught and from there to the ones where they did not. Some of us moved outside architecture to assess the larger cultural apparatus in which architecture operates—*Critical Inquiry, October*, Dia/Bay Press (Hal Foster) publications—but these, too, were part of an academic center of gravity.

What happened? Print journals became financially risky; social media empowered its own unaccredited spokespeople; disciplinary boundaries loosened; open access and the sharing economy expanded; globalization allowed/demanded that non-Western voices be heard. Whatever the (shared) cause, my own introduction to displaced information-gathering came through AAAAG (now AAAAAG), the acronym of Artists, Architects, and Activists Reading Group.[13] An online text repository, it is "a framework supporting autodidact activities" for contemporary art, critical theory, and philosophy. Set up in 2005 by the artist Sean Dockray, it seemingly holds every possible

13
https://aaaaarg.fail/.

critical theory article one will ever want to access, some badly scanned and marked up by enthusiastic readers, some pristine and offered by the original authors. Some are whole books; some are short articles. Anyone can add a text they like or find an article indexed alphabetically according to author. Gathering a community of enthusiasts from related fields who maintain, catalog, annotate, and run discussions relevant to their research interests, it was not developed to contest intellectual property rights but, rather, to be the foundation of what Dockray called The Public School—a school with no curriculum other than classes proposed by the public and teachers found on an as-needed basis.[14] For me, AAARG began as a super easy way to find the articles for my syllabi, but it quickly formed my bucket reading list.[15]

Soon after, I became aware of *Volume* when I was asked in 2005 to write a review of its first two issues for *Architects' Newspaper*. *Volume* was a revelation—it gathered smart people discussing culturally relevant topics via quick, unlabored texts that bristled with provocations both profound and irreverent. Not online per se, it was nevertheless a precursor of the kind of socially mobilized journal that mixes authorial types and disparate, often messy topics. Initially published jointly by *Archis* (the Dutch magazine of architecture media and culture), AMO of OMA research fame, and C-lab, the then new (with new dean Mark Wigley) research-publication wing of Columbia University's Graduate School of Architecture, Planning and Preservation (GSAPP), it challenged traditional publication practices: it cross-pollinated academic institutions (Wigley's GSAPP and Koolhaas's Harvard University Graduate School of Design) and gave equal voice to the journal publisher. Even before GSAPP bowed out (or was dismissed?), somewhere between issues 13 and 14, it was anti-institutional (as per Wigley's institutional agenda) and since has remained relatively true to the *Archis* agenda: to be "an experimental think tank devoted to the process of real-time spatial and cultural reflexivity and action," creating "a global idea platform to voice architecture any way, anywhere, anytime."[16]

After this, when I was invited to participate in an *e-flux* online publication, I began to see that its intellectual reach went way beyond the existing landscape of my private Northeastern university.[17] In 1992, when it was founded, *e-flux* used a new communication technology—e-mail—to disseminate a press release for a New York City event. E-mail became the engine of its financial success; because it is funded by set fees paid by museums and other institutions of art for disseminating their press releases, it is free to the public. The editors have taken advantage of this by making a website that, besides the

14
As the AAAARG website indicates, this has not dissuaded publishers—most notably OMA and Verso Books—from submitting cease-and-desist letters to AAAARG. The irony of these actions by "radical" organizations is clear. See also https://conversations.e-flux.com/t/the-lawsuits-against-and-global-reach-of-aaaaarg-org/3141.

15
In addition to the AAAAAG library and The Public School, in fall 2010, Fillip, a Vancouver-based publishing company, commissioned the *AAAARG Library* to be a site-specific installation in conjunction with the fifth annual NY Art Book Fair, held at MoMA PS1, Long Island City, New York. During the course of the fair, members of the Fillip staff served as librarians, fulfilling book requests from library "patrons" accessing the physical catalog files. Links to these files (typically OCRed PDFs created by scanning printed books) were then sent to patrons' respective email addresses.

16
A recent issue of *Volume* (no. 56, entitled *Playbor*) addresses an issue dear to my heart and pertinent to the theme of this paper. It is divided in two sections: POWERPLAY, in which we explore the renewed relations between work(ers) and leisure(rers) (burnout, identity, hierarchy, unionism, commoning), and PLAYGROUND, on the spatial implications of the focus on gaming (workspaces, data centers, dark kitchens, urban simulators, city games, citizen apps), http://archis.org/publications/volume-56-playbor/.

17
Around this same time, my Yale colleague Eeva-Liisa Pelkonen expressed something I also increasingly felt: she got much more intellectual satisfaction at the international conferences she attended than she did at Yale School of Architecture. This is less a critique of our particular institution than an expression of appreciation for the more expansive, generous, and open nature of more global forums.

18
See their website, https://www.e-flux.com/architecture/curriculum/262997/editorial/. The seven model new syllabi are "Mediating Theory" by Antonio Furgiuele and Matthew Allen; "Representation, Rhetoric, and Research" by Ginger Nolan; "Sites of Entanglement" by Ivonne Santoyo-Orozco, Jeremy Lecomte, and Jake Matatyaou; "From the Particular to the Universal" by Joseph Bedford; "Architecture Unbound" by Bryan E. Norwood, Ginger Nolan, and Elisa Dainese; "Global Disciplinary Knowledge" by Joseph Godlewski; and "Canonical vs Non-Canonical" by Marrikka Trotter, Gabriel Fuentes, and Joseph Bedford.

announcements, offers journals, reviews, education, programs, books, podcasts, videos and film, projects, and "architecture." I have become an *e-flux* student. Indeed, the recent attack (in its Architecture section) on the paucity of meaningful architectural theory in today's academies makes me want to return to teaching. In "Theory's Curriculum," *e-flux*'s Nick Axel, Nikolaus Hirsch, and Joseph Bedford offer seven examples of new theory syllabi, necessary, as they say, because since the 1970s and 1980s, when "scholars forged new links with ground-breaking theoretical movements of the time, from feminism and postcolonialism to semiotics, phenomenology, and deconstructivism," the new syllabi have not developed at all.[18]

These examples inspire me, but they also make me reflect on the real differences between the past architectural theory/knowledge collection and the current ones that continue to make the "architectural common." It isn't merely their presence online, although that is part of it. And it isn't merely that the information is freely had, although that is important. And it isn't that they are produced by and for architects outside the academic context, although that, too, matters. I guess the phenomenon I'm interested in exists in varying degrees of outsideness. As Sean Dockray of AAAAARG explains, besides "being on the outside," other critical information platforms are "stepping outside," "in the window," or "outside on the inside." So, following Dockray's categories, here are various extra-academic sources offering varying degrees of democratic access, topicality, and access to minds not warped by disciplinary autonomy.

"Being on the outside"
Platform and *Places Journal* come immediately to mind. *Platform* is a new (as of early 2019) digital platform organized around various degrees of elaboration/provocation: Opinion, Reading/Listening/Watching, Finding, Working, Teaching, Specifying, and Newsflash. Interested in expanding beyond traditional architectural historical/theoretical writing by experimenting with these various formats, the editors say their goal is to "move beyond academic writing and experiment with new formats and ideas and methods of presentation." Recent Teaching/Working pieces, for example, are "Rethinking Design Education through the History of Materials" and "City Smarts: An App for Civic Engagement." *Places Journal*, founded at MIT and Berkeley in 1983 but now not affiliated with any university (although, in addition to grants, it is largely supported by donations from schools of architecture), is, in contrast to *Platform*, one of the first journals to go entirely online,

doing so in 2009. Aiming to bridge the gap between the academy and the profession, it quickly broke the insularity of academics speaking to academics. Its goal was always more "practical" and timely—to "harness the power of public scholarship to promote equitable cities and resilient landscapes." Its "harnessing" has increasingly turned to advocacy for housing, climate change, and now COVID-19.

"Stepping outside"

Both Columbia University's Temple Hoyne Buell Center for the Study of American Architecture and the Ian L. McHarg Center for Urbanism and Ecology, at the University of Pennsylvania, are examples of centers housed in larger design schools but operating independently so that research can be issue-focused and of the independent board's choosing. Neither are online platforms per se, but both livestream their events and make their prodigious, often empirical research available online. The aim for both is public, not proprietary, intelligence. The Buell Center, founded in 1982, sits within the Graduate School of Architecture, Planning and Preservation and says it promotes "the interdisciplinary study of American architecture, urbanism, and landscape." In reality, it uses its research projects, workshops, public programs, publications, and awards more pointedly than this implies, making spatial and climate justice a priority. The current project, "Power: Infrastructure in America," follows "House Housing: An Untimely History of Architecture and Real Estate," "Foreclosed: Rehousing the American Dream," and "Public Matters: New York Architecture after 9/11." Most public of all was its symposium "The Green New Deal: A Public Assembly," held in November 2019 at the Queens Museum. It gathered advocates, organizers, and elected officials to explore the Green New Deal's (GND) relationship to society, policy, and the built environment.[19] The newly launched McHarg Center, created by the department of landscape architecture at the Weitzman School of Design at the University of Pennsylvania and supported by a $1.25 million gift, aims to be "a global leader in urban ecological design by bringing environmental and social scientists together with planners, designers, policy-makers, and communities." Available online is the center's important empirical research "The 2100 Project: An Atlas for the Green New Deal," which combines research from the teaching staff, doctoral candidates, and students in landscape and architecture master's programs—thoroughly academic on the one hand, but not possible within either the landscape or architecture departments. Indeed, the work of all involved is not to educate the PennDesign students but, rather,

19
The Buell Center is financially autonomous from GSAPP but works under the dean of GSAPP and the provost of Columbia University.

the public and the policy makers. The McHarg Center's one-day inaugural symposium, "Designing a Green New Deal," streamed in September 2019, was the most comprehensive gathering of policy makers, social activists, and scholars addressing the Green New Deal. The center's ongoing virtual symposia and discussion groups keep those interested in the GND connected to policy planners and financial analysts.

"In the window"

These journals are housed in schools of architecture but, with independent boards, they connect traditional architecture theory to specific and under-addressed practicalities. *Very Vary Veri (VVV)* and *New Geographies* (*this* journal), both out of Harvard Graduate School of Design (GSD), connect architecture to realms outside its own disciplinarity—*VVV* to other professional schools to consider design in relationship to law, finance, governance, real estate, and public health; and *New Geographies* to urban globalization. Neither are online journals, nor are they free, but they gather authors from outside the academic discipline and clearly see themselves as filling a void in the Harvard GSD.[20] The *Avery Review*, a project of the Office of Publications at Columbia's GSAPP, is, on the other hand, both online and free. The stated goal of the *Review* is "to explore the broader implications of a given object of discourse (whether text, film, exhibition, building, project, or urban environment), to expand the terrain of what we imagine architectural discourse to be, and to broaden the diversity of voices that our field typically hears from." Yes, the construction of the "common."

"Outside on the inside"

Student journals and podcasts are increasingly forums for students to gather real-world information missing in their course material—generally, facts, discussions, and analyses of how architecture as a profession and discipline fares in our current economy. *Pidgin*, out of Princeton University School of Architecture; *Room 1000*, from Berkeley's College of Environmental Design; *PLAT Journal*, from Rice; *Telesis*, out of Gibbs College of Architecture, University of Oklahoma; *Inflection Journal*, from Melbourne School of Design; the podcast series by the women's group WIASO at the architecture school at the University of Minnesota—these are all forums that begin as void fillers but develop an "other" within the schools, linking editors and contributors not only to each other but to like-minded student groups in other schools. But I know of only one student publication, Yale School of Architecture's *Paprika!*, that is free and online.[21] Coming out almost weekly, and thus

20
Update: *This* issue of *New Geographies* is online, a first for this publication. That it and *VVV* are not free is clearly tied to the fact that de-institutionalized projects struggle for funding, and it has to be acknowledged that much unpaid labor goes into these journals, many of which must rely on crowdsourcing and donations. Again, the fact that the institutions that have the money (the academies) are not supporting this essential work is the source of this new condition, at once inspiring (it produces the common) and problematic.

21
It also sells hard copies.

responding to the speed with which the world is changing, *Paprika!*, as it says, "celebrates the student voice—the critical, the raw, and the radical. *Paprika!* masters the ground, so that we all might stand on it."[22] In recent issues, such as "Out of Work//Out of Control" and "The Covid-19 Journals," contributors have brought to task the administration of the Yale School of Architecture for not addressing their precarious position both as students and as future professionals. Protesting begins. A new common forms.

This catalog leaves untouched the issue of who is writing the content for these forums, a not-insignificant concern. If these various and rhizomatic outlets publish the same old voices, nothing much of substance changes. But these platforms are filled with essays by authors not normally given an opportunity to speak—intellectuals of color; theorists outside both architecture and the academy; non-Western voices who speak of decolonization not from the perspective of a historian, but from life experience; organizations like the Architecture Lobby, which produces essays from the perspective of emerging and precarious professionals. Indeed, groups like ArchiteXX, the Beverly Willis Architecture Foundation (BWAF), *Failed Architecture*, and the Architecture Lobby don't even *want* to do research but are driven to it by the lack of analyses about our own discipline and how it links up with contemporary struggles. ArchiteXX, the feminist organization for women in architecture, produced the exhibition *Now What?! Advocacy Activism & Alliances in American Architecture since 1968* (2019) and an accompanying catalog of the history of activism in architecture because this documentation didn't exist in the architectural academy; they also knew they had to write women designers into Wikipedia. BWAF has commissioned women historians to write the biographies of women architects for its 50 Pioneering Women of Architecture website because these were not catalogued or written elsewhere. *Failed Architecture* goes after an architectural media that "reduces the design of society to a spectacular image that leaves a shallow understanding of what architecture is and what it can be," and provides inclusive platforms for critical urban discourse, unconventional narratives from an international network of contributors, and critiques of our neoliberal economy. The Architecture Lobby is needed to produce research on the state of funding supporting architecture research, on the nature of architectural contracts, on the history of the American Institute of Architects and other national professional architectural associations, on the consequences of the requests for proposals for the southern border

22
Paprika! should not be confused with *Perspecta*, the other student journal produced at Yale School of Architecture. *Perspecta* is produced each year with intense oversight by a board made up of past and present faculty members.

wall, and on the history and possibility of architectural cooperatives, because these are ignored in the academy.

The publications catalogued and the authors they allow to speak take advantage of the fact that they do not and cannot play within the constraints of academia, which insists that articles must be peer-reviewed in order to merit credit for institutional promotion. Once unleashed from institutional and careerist paradigms—which have been happy to produce PhD candidates examining colonized countries' architectural history but are loath to support critical evaluations of our discipline's lack of diversity and equity—both authors and journals can get to "common" work.

Conclusion

What does it mean for architectural education to function as a common and not as a factory? What does it mean for architectural education to operate as a think tank and not as the production of formally driven workhorses? Inevitably, academic institutions will struggle with a rhizomatic approach to knowledge gathering. Traditional scheduling, hiring, and course-load distribution go out the window, as do easy criteria for assessing student progress and competency or faculty promotion and "success." Studying and teaching become more and more alike. Information will be more easily gathered outside the classroom or the academic home, and online learning will increasingly flourish, not because of social distancing but because it makes practical sense: less time wasted, more time investigating, a larger catchment of knowledge. The bigger question, however, is how each school covers the vast array of material that a think tank must address in a crisis-driven era. My thinking is: we spread the work. We identify schools not according to what style of architecture they produce and/or what stars they have on staff, but by what area of expertise each is capable of taking on given its location and its larger university context. For example, Yale has access to its famous law school; Georgia Institute of Technology has access to extraordinary technological facilities; Berkeley has access to IT heaven. The goal is not silo-making but rather organizing areas of intelligence to complement each other in lieu of competing with each other for the same generic student with the same unspecific we-innovate-for-relevance rhetoric.[23]

How does this work in our current accreditation and licensing system? It doesn't. If we can't ween ourselves from traditional

23
Attending the conference "Intelligent Environments and Entrepreneurship" at Georgia Tech's School of Architecture, October 25–26, 2018, made me acutely aware of the fact that, as a school, Georgia Tech could test technology in a way that Yale School of Architecture, for example, never could. On the other hand, technology there was absent from any discourse of social or human relevance, something we were teaching at Yale. These concerns clearly needed to be thought together, but not in equal measures in both places.

accreditation procedures, the National Architectural Accrediting Board (NAAB) would need to adjust. Its new role could ensure that each individual school's advertised knowledge threads are properly populated and, across schools, appropriately shared. But if NAAB could so accredit, the National Council of Architectural Registration Boards (NCARB)—unable to properly categorize, evaluate, and standardize requirements leading to licensure—would baulk. This would be ironic since it is the role of state licensing boards to ensure public welfare even as its limited understanding of architecture-as-*building* and not architecture-as-*spatial justice* actually prevents architects from serving the public. But if it resists, forget licensure.

Since the completion of the first draft of this article, there is much, much more thought production to which we architects have access. The Black Lives Matter protests have stimulated statements and reading lists from nearly every architectural organization out there. The recognition that these will be shared, read, and (it is hoped) under-stood via social media, independent of journal outlets, indicates the spread of the "common" beyond those described above. One might be anxious about the diminished distinction between scholarship, journalism, and opinion, but as Negri made clear, the production of knowledge allowed by the free exchange of information is not primarily about scholarship but, rather, about struggle. To access and share infor-mation is to resist capitalism's desire for owning the same.

Contributor Biographies

Amy Balkin's work involves land and the geopolitical relationships that produce it. Her projects and collaborations include *Smog Index*, *A People's Archive of Sinking and Melting* (Balkin, et al.), *The Atmosphere, A Guide* and *This Is the Public Domain*. Forthcoming and recent exhibitions include *The Vienna Biennale for Change 2021* at MAK, *Overview Effect* at the Museum of Contemporary Art, Belgrade, *The Normal* at Talbot Rice Gallery, Edinburgh, and *Beyond the World's End* at the Santa Cruz Museum of Art & History. She is currently remote artist-in-residence with the Penn Program in the Environmental Humanities (PPEH).

Nadia Bertolino is an architectural theorist and researcher in urban commons and inclusive spatial practices. Standing in opposition to reductionist positions, her work focuses on the redefinition of the role of architects within non-commodified processes of spatial production. She holds a PhD in Architecture from the University of Pavia, Italy. She is Senior Lecturer in the Department of Architecture at Northumbria University, Newcastle (UK), where she is Architectural Humanities Lead. Prior to that, she worked at Sheffield School of Architecture as Director of the MA in Architectural Design. She has presented keynote talks at many institutions including Tongji University, University of Seville, Polytechnic University of Catalonia, Harbin Institute of Technology and the Indian Education Society. In 2019, Nadia was among the initiators of the popular Summer School 'The City as a Commons', and curator of 'The City of Commons' exhibition.

Neeraj Bhatia is an architect, urban designer, and educator whose work resides at the intersection of politics, infrastructure, and urbanism. He is an Associate Professor at the California College of the Arts where he also directs the urbanism research lab the Urban Works Agency. Neeraj is founder of The Open Workshop, a transcalar design-research office examining the negotiation between architecture and its territorial environment. He is editor / author of books *Bracket [Takes Action]* (2020), *The Petropolis of Tomorrow* (2013), *Bracket [Goes Soft]* (2013), *Arium: Weather + Architecture* (2010), *Pamphlet Architecture 30: Coupling* (2010) and *New Investigations in Collective Form* (2019). Among other distinctions he is the recipient of the Canadian Prix de Rome and Architectural League Prize.

David Bollier is an American activist, scholar, and blogger who studies the commons as a paradigm of social transformation, economics, and politics. He is Director of the Reinventing the Commons Program at the Schumacher Center for a New Economics [www.centerforneweconomics.org] (Massachusetts, US) and cofounder of the Commons Strategies Group, [www.commonsstrategies.org], an international advocacy project. Bollier is an author or editor of eight books on the commons, including *Think Like a Commoner* [www.thinklikeacommoner.com] (2014) and (with coauthor Silke Helfrich) *Free, Fair and Alive: The Insurgent Power of the Commons* (2019), and blogs at www.Bollier.org.

Paola Cardullo is senior postdoctoral researcher at IN3, Universitat Oberta de Catalunya in Barcelona (Beatriu de Pinòs, Marie-Curie 2018). Previously, postdoc at the Technology Adoption Group, Maynooth University School of Business, and on The Programmable City at NIRSA, Maynooth University. She was Associate Lecturer at Goldsmiths, University of London. See her projects on Open Science Framework and her profile on the Zotero Community.

Rachel Cobb is a New York City-based photographer who covers current affairs, social issues, and the natural world in the U.S. and abroad. Her work has been widely published in magazines and newspapers such as *The New York Times*, *The New Yorker,* and international publications. Cobb's critically acclaimed monograph *Mistral: The Legendary Wind of Provence* was published by Damiani in 2018. Her work has been recognized with a number of awards and exhibited in one-man and group shows in museums and galleries across the U.S. and in France.

William Conroy is a second-year PhD student in urban planning at Harvard University. His research engages broadly with the history of capitalist urbanization in the United States, the relationship between race and capitalism, and socio-spatial theory. His contribution to this volume builds on research undertaken while he was a master's student at Oxford's School of Geography and the Environment. You can reach him at williamconroy@g.harvard.edu or @WilliamWConroy on Twitter.

Peggy Deamer is Professor Emerita of Yale University's School of Architecture and principal in the firm of Deamer, Studio. She is the founding member of the Architecture Lobby, a group advocating for the value of architectural design and labor. She is the editor of *Architecture and Capitalism: 1845 to the Present* and *The Architect as Worker: Immaterial Labor, the Creative Class, and the Politics of Design* and the author of *Architecture and Labor*. Her theory work

explores the relationship between subjectivity, design, and labor. She received the Architectural Record 2018 Women in Architecture Activist Award.

Massimo De Angelis has been researching and writing around themes of commons, capitalism and social change for several years. His latest book is entitled *Omnia Sunt Communia. On the commons and post-capitalist transformation* (ZED Book, 2017). He is Emeritus Professor of political economy at the University of East London.

Rosetta S. Elkin is a landscape architect, educator, and practitioner known for her close reading of plant life, through a range of media from site-specific installations, international exhibits, and field-based research. Among her awards, Rosetta is the recipient of the American Academy of Rome Prize, and the Harvard University Climate Change Award. She is author and co-author of articles, book chapters, and monographs, including *Tiny Taxonomy* (Actar, 2017) and *Dryland: Afforestation and the Politics of Plant Life* (Minnesota, 2021). Rosetta is currently Research Associate at Harvard's Arnold Arboretum and Professor at McGill University, where she teaches design students to appreciate and value landscape.

Stefan Gruber is an Associate Professor at Carnegie Mellon's School of Architecture, where he chairs the Master of Urban Design. His design, research, and curatorial work explores the intersection between architecture and urbanism with a particular focus on practices of commoning and the political as articulated in the negotiation between top-down planning and citizen-led transformation of cities. Gruber co-authored *Spaces of Commoning* (Sternberg, 2016), guest-edited *ARCH+* journal 232: *An Atlas of Commoning*, as well as co-curated the eponymous travelling exhibition by ifa (Institute for Foreign Cultural Relations). His work has been recognized and supported by the Graham Foundation, ULI, ACSA, Akademie Schloss Solitude, Viennese Technology and Science Fund, and a Margarete Schütte-Lihotzky Prize, amongst others.

Fanny Lopez is Associate Professor of History of Architecture and Technology at the School of Architecture Paris-Est, University Gustave Eiffel. Her research and teaching activities focus on spatial, territorial, and environmental impact of energy and digital infrastructures. Her books include: *The Dream of Disconnection. From the Autonomous House to Self-sufficient territories* (Editions La Villette 2014 for the french édition), published by Manchester University Press in 2021; *The Electrical Order, Energy Infrastructures and Territories* (MētisPresses, 2019), awarded by the AARHSE Prize 2021 (French Academic Association for Research, History and Sociology of Energy).

Mojdeh Mahdavi is a Doctor of Design candidate, teaching fellow, and research associate at the Harvard University Graduate School of Design. Mojdeh's doctoral research focuses on digital transformation of urban governance and space. Her broader research engages with the evolving relationships between planetary urbanization, governance through space, infrastructure, and sociotechnical imaginaries. Mojdeh has practiced urban and architectural design in France, Iran, and Kazakhstan in well-established and experimental design firms. Her work has been presented at conferences in Paris, Zurich, Lausanne, Hong Kong, Singapore, and Montreal. She is currently a Performance and Innovation Fellow at the city of Syracuse, New York.

Katherine Melcher is an associate professor at the University of Georgia's College of Environment and Design, where she teaches courses in community-based design, urban design, and design as social action. Her research interests span two areas: landscape architecture theory and the social aspects of design, with a special focus on participatory design and community-built places. She co-edited the book *Community-Built: Art, Construction, Preservation, and Place*, published by Routledge in 2017. Her piece in *Landscape Research Record*, "Three Moments in Aesthetic Discourse," received the Outstanding Paper Award from the Council of Educators of Landscape Architecture in 2018.

Taraneh Meshkani is Assistant Professor of architecture and urban design at Kent State University, where she teaches courses on urban theory and systems. Meshkani's research examines the linkage of new information and communication technologies and their spatialities to the social and political processes of contemporary cities. Her work focuses on the divergence of physical and digital spaces in times of unrest. Meshkani served on the editorial board of *New Geographies* from 2013 to 2018. She is the co-editor of *New Geographies 7: Geographies of Information* (2015), and the editor of *River, Nahr, Río: A Riverscape Analysis of Cleveland, Beirut, and Medellín* (2020).

Marina Otero Verzier is an architect based in Rotterdam. She is Head of MA Social Design at the Design Academy Eindhoven and the director of research at Het NieuweInstituut, where she leads research initiatives such as *Automated Landscapes* and *BURN-OUT. Exhaustion on a Planetary Scale*.

Constantin Petcou is an architect and semiotician. Since 1996 he has taught in various schools and universities including ENSA Malaquais Paris, University of Paris 8, Harvard GSD and has lectured in Europe, Australia, and North America. He is co-founder with Doina Petrescu of the Atelier d'Architecture Autogérée (AAA), a collective platform that conducts explorations, actions, and research concerning participative archi-tecture, resilience, and cities' co-produced transformation. He has conducted research projects and initiated together with AAA the Rhyzom network (www.rhyzom.eu) and the R-Urban strategy (www.r-urban.net). He has collaborated on numerous publications and co-edited *Urban/ACT: a manual for alternative practice* (2007), *Trans-local-ACT: Cultural Politics Within and Beyond* (2010) and *R-Urban ACT: A Participative Strategy of Urban Resilience* (2015). AAA's work has received international recognition and numerous awards over the years including the Building4Humanity Resilient Design Competition (2018), The Innovation in Politics Award for Ecology (2017), 100 projects for the Climate/ COP21 (2016). Zumtobel Award (2012), Curry Stone Prize (2011), and the European Public Space Prize (2010).

Doina Petrescu is an architect and feminist activist. She is Professor of Architecture and Design Activism at the University of Sheffield and has been Visiting Professor at Harvard GSD, Architectural Association, Iowa State University, ENSA Malaquais Paris, and University Ion Mincu Bucharest. She is also co-founder with Constantin Petcou of

the collective platform Atelier d'Architecture Autogérée (AAA). Her research concerns issues of urban resilience in relation with urban commons, co-production, feminism, and politics of space. Her publications include *Architecture and Resilience* (2018), *The Social (re)Production of Architecture* (2017), *Learn to Act* (2017), *R-Urban Act: A Participative Strategy of Urban Resilience* (2015), *Agency: Working with Uncertain Architectures* (2009), *Trans-Local Act: Cultural Politics Within and Beyond* (2009), *Altering Practices: Feminist Politics and Poetics of Space* (2007), *Urban/ACT: A Handbook for Alternative Practice* (2007), and *Architecture and Participation* (2005).

Niklas Plaetzer is a doctoral student at the University of Chicago's Department of Political Science and Sciences Po Paris. His work is informed by the politics of social movements and explores languages of solidarity through radical-democratic and decolonial traditions of critical theorizing. Niklas' current research traces an alterna-tive genealogy of the notion of "institution" in Francophone thought, connecting the group *Socialisme ou Barbarie* with thinkers such as Grace Lee Boggs, Miguel Abensour, and Édouard Glissant. His most recent publication is "Decolonizing the 'Universal Republic': The Paris Commune and French Empire," *Nineteenth-Century French Studies* 49, 3-4, 2021, 585-603.

Ivonne Santoyo-Orozco is an architect, historian, and theorist. She is an Assistant Professor at Bard College where she also serves as Co-Director of the Architecture Program. She is currently at work on an architectural genealogy of property regimes in Mexico. She has held teaching positions at the Architectural Association, Central

Saint Martins, University of Creative Arts, and Iowa State University. Ivonne completed her Ph.D. in Architecture History and Theory at the Architectural Association, her master's degree was awarded by the Berlage Institute in Rotterdam and she graduated magna cum laude from the UDLA-Puebla in Mexico.

Stavros Stavrides, architect, is Professor at the School of Architecture, National Technical University of Athens, Greece, where he teaches graduate courses on housing design (social housing design included), as well as a postgraduate course on the meaning of metropolitan experience. He has done research fieldwork in Brazil, Uruguay, Argentina and Mexico focused on housing-as-commons and urban struggles for self-management. His recent publications include *Common Spaces of Urban Emancipation* (Manchester, 2019), *Common Space. The City as Commons* (London, 2016) and *Towards the City of Thresholds* (New York, 2019). He has lectured extensively in European and North and South American Universities on urban struggles and practices of urban commoning.

Paola Viganò, architect and urbanist, is Professor in Urban Design at the EPFL (Lausanne) and at IUAV Venice. *Doctor Honoris Causa* at UCL in 2016, *Grand Prix de l'Urbanisme* in 2013, she received the Flemish Culture Award for Architecture in 2017 and the Golden Medal of Milan Triennale in 2018. From 1990 to 2014, she founded Studio with Bernardo Secchi, working on projects and visions in Europe. Since 2015 StudioPaolaViganò has won several international competitions and works on urban and landscape projects and on public spaces. Recent publications: *The Horizontal Metropolis. A Radical Project*, with C. Cavalieri, eds., 2019.

Liang Wang is an architect, urban designer, and educator. He currently teaches at Syracuse University School of Architecture as the Harry der Boghosian Fellow. He is also a doctoral candidate and previously a teaching fellow at the Harvard Graduate School of Design. His scholarship and teaching concern history and theory of urban form, space and politics of the superblock, architecture and the idea of the city in East Asia, as well as the idea of the commons and collective living. Wang holds a MAUD with distinction from Harvard GSD and a MArch from Rice University.

Alan Wiig is an Assistant Professor of Urban Planning and Community Development at the University of Massachusetts, Boston. An urban geographer, he researches global infrastructure, smart urbanization, and the form, function, and politics of urban and economic development agendas across the North Atlantic.

Yan Zhang is British Academy Research Fellow and Affiliated Lecturer at the Centre of Development Studies at the University of Cambridge, where she is leading a research project on sustainability and transformation in China (2018-2023). Zhang serves as the Director of Studies in Economics Tripos and Bye-Fellow and Tutor at Newnham College; Research Associate at China Centre of Jesus College; Visiting Fellow at Cambridge Bennett Institute for Public Policy. Zhang received her MPhil and doctorate from Cambridge. As a highly motivated economist with a strong background in public policy, political economy, and sustainability studies, she has also obtained six years' first-hand work experience in public policy and practice in the Chinese government.

New Geographies 13 examines the territorialization and fragmentation of movement and circulation through the framework of corridor-spaces of empire, logistics, and migration. *NG13* offers a spatial frame for the unevenly covered patchwork of routes, channels, nodes, and zones of (dis)connection, designed—while constantly contested and appropriated from below—for the strategic movements and distribution of resources, energetics, labor, commodities, and cargo.